Essays on Indian Renaissance

History and Culture Series

ESSAYS ON INDIAN RENAISSANCE

Edited by
Dr. Raj Kumar

2003

DISCOVERY PUBLISHING HOUSE
NEW DELHI-110002

First Published-2003

ISBN 81-7141-689-6

Published by

DISCOVERY PUBLISHING HOUSE
4831/24, Ansari Road, Prahlad Street,
Darya Ganj, New Delhi-110002 (India)
Phone: 23279245 • Fax: 91-11-23253475
E-mail:dphtemp@indiatimes.com

Printed at :
ARORA OFFSET PRESS
Laxmi Nagar, Delhi-92.

Preface

Indian Poets, Saints, religious leaders and freedom fighters through the ages, sacrificed their yesterday to enliven our present and brighter our past. Have we lived up to their expectations?

Aim of this volume is to provide a brief account of the various aspects of Indian renaissance so as to enable the reader to understand the main currents of the movement and develop a vision of future, peaceful and prosperous India.

Raj Kumar

Acknowledgements

Indian renaissance has been an important subject. Renowned scholars like R.C. Mazumdar, R.C. Dutt, J.N. Sarkar, N.R. Roy, K.N. Pannikar, S. Kadhirvel, Sudhir Chandra, C.F. Andrews and Annie Besant have written extensitvely on the subject. In preparing this volume I have been influenced by their writings. I am deeply indebted to them.

Some of the universities and institutions, their librarians and staff members have been kind and helpful, we are thankful to them.

Last but not least my publisher Sri Tilak Wasan has been working very hard on the project. He deserves readers patronage.

Raj Kumar

Contents

1. Introduction

It is difficult to fix a date for the rise and development of the ideological cultural phenomenon know as Indian renaissance. In different periods of the history of Indian one witnesses such ideological-cultural uprisings. Here in this volume we mainly concentrated on the essay pertaining to 19th century onwards.

The pre-renaissance popular resistance against British rule, pointed out its strong and weak points and explained how the movement sought to and did remove the weakness in the earlier popular resistance to imperialism. The evaluation of these revolts would show that the ideology which gave rise to the renaissance was preceded by-infect based on-the earlier spontaneous revolt of the Indian people against British imperialism. The origin of the 19th century renaissance ideology can therefore be traced to the spontaneous anti-imperialist revolts that broke out almost for a century, since the British established their rule in India.

However, the renaissance movement was not aimed at the revival of the pre-British Indian society. Its aim was a renewal of Indian society. The ideology of modern nationalism and parliamentary democracy together with social equality, secularism and the scientific outlook was disseminated by Ram Mohan Roy and other leaders of this renaissance movement at that point of time. They took up the task of uprooting the old society weakened by the British rules. They were not pro-British in the sense of being blind to the oppression and exploitation of the British rulers. They in fact exposed the oppression and exploitation which was inherent in British rule.

While the renaissance was continuation and further development of the earlier spontaneous anti-British revolts, the subsequent growth of the freedom movement led by the Indian National Congress was a further development of the renaissance itself.

Let me conclude this introduction on the basis of my annual lecture to Banaras Hindu University.

"Your Indian and mine are probably very divergent... You know her, many of you, by taking part in the foreign government by which she is subjugated, and therefore you are very largely shut out from the real thought and the real life of the people. Whereas to me she is in very truth the Holy Land, the land whose great religion has been the origin of all religions, the mother of spirituality, the cradle of civilization. When I think of India, I think of her in the greatnesses of her past, not in the degradation of her present... That is the India I know... the India whose polity was built by King-Initiates, whose religion was moulded by divine men... For those who, though born for this life in a Western land and clad in a Western body, can yet look back to earlier incarnations in which they drank the milk of spiritual wisdom from the breast of their true Mother, they must feel ever the magic of her immemorial past, much dwell ever under the spell of her deathless fascination; for they are bound to India by all the sacred memories of their past; and with her, too, are bound up all the radiant hopes of their future, a future which they know they will share with her who is their true Mother in the soul-life."

Annie Besant

Renaissance

When Annie Besant came to India, in common with many other nations, Asia and otherwise, India was faced with the problem of adapting and adjusting her ancient cultural heritage to a set of new rapidly altering conditions brought about by the immense technological changes of recent decades. Jawaharlal Nehru then described himself as a queer mixture of East and West, out of place everywhere, at home nowhere. A terrible soul-sickness, remarked Coomarasway. This was the India to which karma brought Annie Besant in 1993. She counted no endeavour too difficult, no sacrifice too high, to restore India to her ancient glory. With her knowledge and experience she toured the country waking up slumbering people of India. She learnt Sanskrit and with the help of Bawa Bhagwan Das translated some of the Indian classical works. Her books like "Hints on the Study of the Bhagvad Gita", "The Wisdom of the Upanishads," "Introduction to Yoga", "The Ancient Wisdom", "A Study of Consciousness", The self and its Sheaths", "Life after Death", Reincarnation, Karma and Avataras brought the essential teachings of Hinduism to the attention of educated Indians ignorant of Sanskrit, who marvelled at the treasures of their own religion which they had never known.

Annie Besant delivered a series of lectures at the International Conventions of the Theosophical Society which were entitled "Seven Great Religions" covering Hinduism, Jainism, Zoroastrianism, Buddhism, Christianity, Islam and Sikhism, bringing out the beauties of each faith and the essential identity of the basic teachings of all of them. She declared that "The Indian nations of the future is not to be a nation of one single religion only, but to embody the essence of all religions; it will have in it the philosophy of Hinduism; the valour and learning of Islam; the purity of Zoroastrianism; the love and tenderness of Buddhism; the self-sacrifice of Christianity.... Every view of God is added to the views already held, and so, however infinite the perfection of God Himself, more and more knowledge of that perfect Being will come to India through the many religions born on its soil and nourished by itself."

Annie Besant passionately worked for Indian renaissance. Her Kamla Memorial Lectures dealing separately with Education, Philosophy, Religion, Art and Architecture deserve our best attention for reconstructing a happy, health prosperous India, nay the world. She believed that Indian awakening should be based upon Indian ideals. She illustrated from *Onhandogya Upanishad:*

Man is created by thought, and what a man thinks upon that he becomes; therefore think upon Brahman.

Annie Besant explained how India regenerated into an unrattled civilization. In her considered opinion:

(a) There was no creative thought other than that of Brahman in manifestation.

(b) There were so many in India who ever thought of that Supreme, therefore did India:

> Flower out into a civilization unrivalled in the depth of its Philosophy, in the spirituality of its Religion, and in the perfection of its Dharma of orderly and graded individual and, National life, expressing as none other has ever done that balance, that equilibrium, which is yoga, that which saved her, when all the contemporaries of her splendid nationality have been carried away by times tremendous rapids, and scattered as wrecks over the far horizon of the boundless ocean of the past. She shared their past, but they do not share her future, for not theirs the secret of her immortal youth.

That secret Annie Besant understood, lay hidden in India's Education and Culture.

As in England, mark of gentleman was his knowledge of the classics, Greek and Latin, so she advocated for Indians knowledge of Sanskrit. She emphasized the importance of Vernaculars and also Sanskrit the mother of all the Vernaculars of India in the regeneration of the people of India in training of the powers of men; in the cultivations of the higher mental culture, in creating a common language which will bind heart to heart, mind to mind, so that national conscious of common descent should feel a desire for common work, for common cooperation which will make men feel as brothers instead of men of different races. She advocated opening of Sanskrit colleges throughout India, which should be endowed for the support of the teachers attached to the colleges, who would not be dependent for their support upon the payments made by the pupils:

You should not introduce modern method of fees, which is being protested even in the West. The teaching to students must be free. The instruction should not be withheld because the boy is unable to pay a fee for being taught and if some pay and some do not you introduce vulgar money distinction between the pupils. Every son of India who desires to know the ancient tongue should find teaching open to him without the necessity for payment, as it was in the ancient days; and not only so, but there ought to be provision made for the maintenance of the students, so that they may be able to pursue their studies without any anxiety, and may be able to learn in order to be fitted to teach afterwards what they have learnt.

How Malaviyaji dedicated his whole life to its execution is well known to all of us. In order that C.V Ramans do not die with unfulfilled wishes; in order that India finds its own personality we must do some research on this subject of vital importance for the future progress of our country. Not that Independent India has not thought about it, but the whole thing has been followed in letters and not in spirit.

For this, Annie Besant wanted public opinion to be created and funds to be collected for the wealthy people and Rajahs and Maharajas. Another point for national resurgence was production of books written by Indian for Indians so that the young minds do not carry the impressions of alien's Vision on various subjects of their studies. Thus India could challenge the judgment of the educated world. For this, Annie Besant having revived Indian religions and started Muslim and Hindu colleges and schools and having studied Indian history and assimilated its lessons, said:

> We have resolved to revive the ancient ideals of Indian Education and Indian culture, to teach our children in their mother-tongue, to make Indian ideals the basis of Indian civilization, renouncing the hybrid and sterile ideals of anglicized Indianism and to adapt them to a new form, instinct with the ancient life, and moulding it into a glorious new body for the Ancient Spirit. India will then lead the world into a new era of literature and Beauty, Brotherhood and Peace.

Annie Besant had realized the importance of the concept of Dharma. It was B.C. Pal's "Soul of India", and during another seminar in BHU, which made me think only of this ancient concept. Annie Besant compared the Western idea of Right with this concept of Dharma and found this Western idea miserably wanting in her scheme of creating brotherhood of man. Her arguments in favour of Dharma are far more sound than the idea of world government later propounded by Bertrand Russel and Radhakrishnan. This needs to be examined in great details if the world is to be saved from total destruction. For her, like a true Hindu, the whole earth was her mother and she was its daughter.

Thus for her, crusade for Indian renaissance became the pivot for the salvage of the whole world.

—Raj Kumar

2. Hindu Renaissance in Middle Ages

The downfall of Hindu political power in the Gangetic valley and following it in most areas of Aryavarta was a stunning blow to Hinduism, the more calamitous as it was totally unexpected and took place with lightening rapidity. For over one hundred years Hinduism lay prostrate before the invader, deprived of political, social and intellectual leadership. But the surprising fact that emerges from the first hundred and fifty years of Islam's conquest of north India is the strength of the Hindu religion and the preservation of the independence of the Hindu mind. Every door was open to the Hindu who changed his religion and accepted the creed of Islam. Khusrau, and outcaste-slave from Kathiawad, even ascended the Delhi throne for a short time under the title of Nasir-ur-din. With the short cut to prosperity and power so clearly marked out to them the Hindu people preferred political subjection and the indignity of being a conquered race to the surrender of their mind and their faith to the invader.

Slowly Hinduism recovered from the shock of foreign conquest and everywhere in Hindustan, even in areas directly ruled by Muslim Sultans, an intellectual and moral revival of Hinduism became visible, affecting every aspect of thought and generating new moral forces which helped to revitalize Hindu life and give it the dynamism which enabled it to reassert itself in due course. In the sphere of religion and moral thinking, in law, in literature and even in political ideals, a new life came into being in India by the middle of the 16th century, which many justly be termed the first Indian Renaissance. Politically, it is the undying glory of the Rajputs and their main claim to India's gratitude that a determined and unbending resistance to foreign invasion was organized by them and kept up with continued heroism for a period of four hundred years. The great Hammira whose glory is sung in *Hammira Vijaya* was able to stand up for a long time to the might of Ala-ud-din. Kheta his son even occupied Ajmer, and by the end of the 14th century the Mewar Rulers had risen to the position of a major power in North India. Rana Kumbha of this dynasty (15th century) may well be considered the representative figure of Hindu Renaissance. A mighty warrior, he was also an accomplished musician, a scholar and poet, great builder, and a staunch upholder of the *dharma*. The author of *Sangita Raja,* a classical work on music, he was also the commentator of *Gita-Govinda*. As a builder, he was pre-eminent as the Tower of Victory in Chitor described by Fergusson as "in infinitely better taste as an architectural object than" the Victory Pillar of Trojan n Rome, would testify. He built no less than thirty-two fortresses, truly magnificent specimens of military architecture, especially Kumbhalgarh which even Akbar failed to take by assault.

The resistance of the South to the Muslim conquest is well known. An important factor in this resistance were the Lingayats or the Vira Shaivas and an allied seet known as Aradhya Shaivas. According to Prof. K.A. Nilakanta Sastri, "in its single-minded devotion to Shiva… and in its ideal of perfect equality among the *bhaktas,* the new Shaivism was a worthy rival of Islam, and the impetus it gave to politics had not a little to do with the failure of Tughluq rule to take root in many parts of Deccan."*

These movements probably paved the way for the foundation of the mighty Empire of Vijayanagara which for nearly three hundred years upheld the causes of Hinduism in Peninsular India. Here also it was the spiritual and religious renaissance that is of

**A History of South India* (1955), pp. 226, 417.

special significance. The most outstanding achievement of the first years of Vijayanagara was the standard commentary on the Vedas which was prepared under the direction of Sayana, leading to a great revival of religious studies. If Rana Kumbha is the representative figure of northern renaissance, Krishna Deva Raya is his counterpart in the Sough. A scholar, poet and author of no mean merit he was also a great warrior and builder, a restorer of temples and a patron of learning. In his court flourished the *Ashta-diggajas,* the eight immortals of Telugu literature, while the Raya himself, as the author of the classic *Amuktamalyada* ranks among the shining lights of Telugu literature.

This great political revival both in the north and in the south was rendered possible only by a spiritual and literary renaissance which begins to take shape in the fourteenth century. The continuous strengthening of the Hindu social body, as a result of the recognition of the crisis arising from the impact of Islam, becomes evident during this period. Kulluka, the most famous commentator of *Manu-smriti,* lived in the early fourteenth century in Bengal. Chandeshvara, who belonged to Bihar and wrote a number of digests to the Smritis, claims that he was a minister and had himself weighed in gold n 1314. In fact from the time of Devala and Medhatithi to Todarmal in the time of Akbar, Hindu law was being continuously re-interpreted with the object of strengthening the social bonds and of providing Hinduism with a defensive armour. But side by side with this process of defensive equipment Hinduism was demonstrating its inherent strength by assimilating new principles and creating new vehicles of religious experience. The revival of Hinduism during this period—1300-1500—may be claimed as the central feature of the renaissance. The Vaishnava movement with its great devotional figures, from Jayadeva to Chaintanya, Ramananda and Kabir in the North, Namadeva. Vallabhacharya, and Narasimha Mehta in the West, arose at this period and transformed the Hindu mind Ramananda's great movement, which is related to the earlier religious doctrines of the Tamil country, had its center in Banaras, and to its influence can be traced the eclectic teachings of Kabir, the poetic mysticism of Nanak and the devotional ecstasies of Chaitanya.

The importance of this religious revival, supported and upheld by temporal authority in the South, but essentially a popular movement in the rest of India, cannot be over-estimated. Every part of India shared in it equally. In view of the political divisions in Hindu India itself and of the authority of Islam over areas which were traditionally considered sacred, the universality of the religious movements, so far as the Indian world is concerned, is in itself a factor of supreme importance. Hinduism seems suddenly to have cast off her lethargy, called forth from the depth of her soul vast inherent powers of readjustment and set herself deliberately to a process of reorganisation. The great refashioning of Hindu doctrines which Shankara had successfully achieved prior to the Muslim invasion and which the great Acharyas, Ramanuja, Madhva and others had further supplemented, provided Hinduism within fundamental unity in her philosophic thought. It is undoubtedly on this basis that the new reforming movements erected their structures, thereby enabling Hinduism to keep the new sects and cults within her comprehensive frame-work. But generally speaking, the religious movements of the period were non-ritualistic, based on *Bhakti,* and emphasizing a theism, which while genuinely Hindu reflects also the vigorous monotheism of Islam. It is the one supreme God that is the object of the *Bhakta's* adoration; it is His grace and compassion that the devotee is asked to seek for salvation. All *Bhakti* cults are therefore essentially monotheistie, not in the exclusive sense that devotees cannot worship the same Supreme Being under other names, but in the affirmative belief that whether known as Shiva, Krishna or Devi they all symbolize the One and the Eternal.

The universality of the religious revival, *i.e.* its prevalence at the same time from Cape Comorin to the Himalayas is undoubtedly due to the pre-eminent influence that Sanskrit continued to exercise on the Hindu mind. In Rajasthan, in Gujarat, in the Vijayanagar Empire and after the 15th century in the Gangetic Valley itself,

Sanskrit maintained unchallenged its supremacy as the vehicle of all-India expression. The literature produced in these three centuries is extensive. In Rajputana, in the southern courts of Vijayanagar, Tanjore and Calicut Sanskrit literature was cultivated with an enthusiasm which finds few parallels in the earlier periods. It is not however the quality of the literary works of the period which gives importance to it; it is its character as a vehicle of expression for the whole of India making it possible for movements in one area to have influence and authority elsewhere that gives to Sanskrit a supreme importance at this juncture. Sayana's commentary written in the Court of Bukka influences Vedic studies everywhere. Kulluka Bhatta's commentary on *Manusmriti* written in Bengal is studied all over India. The philosophical treatises of the Acharyas are taught in Banaras. Chaitanya in his wanderings in the South is influenced by *Sri Krishna Karnamrita* or Lila Suka, while the northern Mimamsa schools find their best interpreters in Kerala. It is in fact Sanskrit that gives an all-India character to the renaissance of the period.

Though the source of inspiration and the dominant authority is Sanskrit, the popular character of this movement in due to the growth of vernacular languages. Indeed it may be said that the revival of the Hindu mind and the growth of the great vernacular languages are phases of the same great movement. Everywhere at this time we find the local dialects emerging to a position of literary significance. Great writers interpret for the populace the classics of Sanskrit. A new devotional poetry of high quality marks the beginning of this literature, Vidyapati in Maithili, Chandidas in Bengali, Kabir, Mira, Nathaswamy and others lay the foundation of the new literatures. The translation of the great epics into most of the regional languages also belongs to this period and it is significant that they are practically at the same time in every part of India. At the time when the Niranam Panikkars were translating the *Ramayana, Bhagavad-Gita,* etc. into Malayalam, the same process was going on in Kannadiga, Telugu, Hindi, Bengali and Marathi.

The crisis brought about by Islam led undoubtedly to the popularization of religion and literature. Sanskrit scholarship and religious learning had tended in the past to become more and more the monopoly of a limited class and the great achievement of the medieval Renaissance was to make religion popular by enriching the vernacular languages with a vigorous and growing literature. The supreme example of this movement is Tulsidas's *Ramacharita Manasa*. Though a Sanskrit scholar he preferred to write in the vernacular and defending his choice declared that his language was an earthen vessel which contained Amrita while Sanskrit was a bejewelled and rare cup of extreme beauty which held poison. The *Ramacharita Manasa* is not only a magnificent epic singing the great deeds of Rama, but a scripture of the people to which the entire Hndi-knowing world from the Himalayas to the Vindhyas and from Amritsar to Bengal turn for spiritual sustenance, a code of ethics constantly on the lips of all from princes to peasants, and a truly fine expression of poetic genius. As a recent scholar, Kissan Keane, has stated: "It is impossible to exaggerate the influence that the great works of Tulsidas have had on the lives and learning of his countrymen. Above all *Ramayana* as a creation in literature and as an expression of religion stands supreme." In fact Tulsidas's *Ramayana* was the culmination of the great religious movement of which the great lights that preceded him were Ramananda, Kabir and Nanak.

The revival of Banaras as an all-India center of Sanskrit learning was also a feature of the final phase of this movement. A new school of Dharmashastra of which the leading lights were Nanda Pandita, Mitra Mishra and Nilakanta Bhatta established again the primacy of Banaras in the world of Hindu scholarship. It became again under such great scholars as Kavindra Sarasvati and Nrisimha Bharati the radiating center of Hindu culture. Khanda Deva the author of the *Bhattadipika,* Raghunatha Shiromani, the logician and the author of *Didhiti,* and Kamalakara, the astronomer, were but a few of the more notable scholars who proclaimed the revived glories of Hindu learning in Banaras.

It will thus be seen that the period from A.D. 1300 to 1550 witnessed a remarkable revival of the Hindu mind, an astonishing recovery from slough of despondency into which the people of India had fallen as a result of political conquest. It is the religion, philosophy and social thinking that were created during this revival which enabled Hinduism to reassert itself in the period that followed and gradually regain its pre-eminent position in India. It may truly be said that the foundations of modern India's life were laid during this period, and the Hinduism under which the vast majority of the people of this country lives was fashioned during this age of revival. The literature which the period produced was extensive and in many cases of supremely high quality. The period has also left us some magnificent specimens of Hindu architecture, the tower of victory of Maharana Kumbha and the magnificent monuments of Hampi. Nor is the age lacking in great figures in almost every sphere. Hammira, Kumbha and Krishna Deva Raya are men of heroic mould and would have been considered so in any epoch. Sayana, Kulluka and Nrisimha Bharati represent Hindu thought and scholarship at their highest level. An age which produced Vidyapati, Chandidas, and Tulsidas in the north and a host of outstanding writers in Gujarat, Maharashtra and the south must always be considered among the most productive in the long history of India. And yet it is when one comes to the religious life of India that the glory of the period is most resplendent. Ramananda, Kabir, Mira and Vallabhacharya in the north, Chaitanya in Bengal, Madhva, Vedanta Deshika and numerous others in the south give to the religious life of the period a vitality which Hinduism never seems to have enjoyed before. The medieval period may thus justly be acclaimed as the period of Hindu Renaissance, a great era of constructive thought and creative inspiration, without which the re-emergence of the people among the free nations of the world at a later period would not have been possible.

HINDU-MUSLIM ADJUSTMENTS

Hindus and Mussalmans follow different religions and their social life mainly derives its sanction from them. Some of the religious rites and customs which each community follows to all outward appearance are irreconciable. But in some of the most fundamental things the differences between the two communities are no greater than they are among followers of a faith going under one comprehensive name and who admittedly life peacefully and amicably as members of one nation.

The austere simplicity of the inside of a Muslim mosque with only prayer mats and water pots contrasts with the decorated images and paraphernalia of worship in a Hindu temple no more than the inside of Protestant or Presbyterian Church with nothing but seats for the worshippers and a pulpit for the preacher contrasts with the magnificent decoration and the images and paintings and candles of the Roman Catholic Church. Yet no one has claimed that the Protestants and the Catholics of England did not constitute a nation. Among the Hindus also there are sects which are critical of temples, images and many of the rites and ceremonies of other sects, who are also called Hindus.

Spiritual Influence: Apart from outward signs and symbols, rites and ceremonies, however, philosophers and saints, both Hindu and Muslim, have been known to dive deep into the mysteries of life and death and to proclaim the same faith in the Oneness of God.

"The legends of Buddha" to quote Dr. Bhagwan Das "entered into Muslim literature as the type of the saintly man, and Muslim hagiologists assimilated the stories of Ibn Adham to the Buddhist legend. Indian ascetics travelling in pairs and staying not more than two nights at one place were directly known to the Muslim adepts, who took from them their fourfold vows of cleanliness, purity, truth and poverty—and the use of rosary. What wonder then that the conception of Nirvana, the discipline of the eight-fold path, the practice of yoga and the acquaitance of miraculous powers were appropriated in Islam under the names of Tana, Tarika or Saluk, Moragabah, and Karamat or Mujiza" [1]

"But the man who produced the greatest stir in the Islamic world by the boldness of his doctrines was Husainbin-Mansoor Al-

Hallaj.... He travelled about in many lands, among them India, and thrice visited Mecca. At last his activities became so obnoxious that he was arrested in A.D. 922."[2] Mansoor's theories were later worked up in the systems of Ibn-al-Arabi and Abdul Karim Jili and in the poetry of Ibn-al-Farid and Abri Said Ibn Abulkhair and their influence spread to far off countries including India. Jili was acquainted with Hindu religion, for among the ten principal sects he noted the Brahima (Brahman). About them he says that they worship God in his absolute aspects, without reference to prophet or apostle. The scriptures of the Brahmana, according to him, were revealed to them not by God but by Abraham (Brahma); they contained five books, the fifth on account of its profundity was unknown to most of the Brahmanas but those who read it invariably became Muslims. Apparently Jili's fifth book is the Vedanta whose monistic philosophy in the eyes of Jili made it indistinguishable from Islam."[3]

"The Muslim mystic who sets out upon the path of union (*wasl*) or absorption (*fana*) always needs a spiritual guide, "for if a man has no teacher his Imam is Satan." The guide or the preceptor (Pir or Shaikh) is the priest round which the whole machinery of Sufi monachism moves...... The disciple is advised to keep his Murshid constantly in mind, to become eventually absorbed in him through constant mediation and contemplation of him, to see him in all men and all things, and to annihilate his self in the Murshid. From this state of self-absorption in the Murshid the master leads him on through several stages at last to absorption in the Deity. Muhammad taught surrender to God (Islam), Sufism surrender to the teacher who is the representative of God on earth."[4]

Haji Waris Ali Shah whose mausoleum stands at Deva Sharif in Bara Banki district in U.P. summarized the Sufi teachings in a few Persian verses—

"I say Pir is my God. To say this before a *munkir* (non-believer) is a mistake. O man! I ask one question. O believers, answer it. When fuel gets burnt in fire, when thread gets woven into cloth, then should I call it fuel or fire, then should I call the thread cloth or thread? So when my Pir got absorbed in God, the human being disappeared—all became God. I therefore bow to his feet every moment and have dedicated my life and being to his path. Love is superior to all the world inasmuch as it is the *millat* (Bhakti) or God the Great."

Hindu scriptures also abound in references to the necessity of a Guru or preceptor who is to guide the disciple through the difficult and rigorous discipline he has to go through. Without such a Guru progress is practically impossible. In fact "the Guru is Brahma, the Guru is Vishnu, the Guru is Maheshvara, the Guru is Para-Brahma Himself and to that Guru I bow" is a common everyday prayer. It is the duty and ambition of every Hindu to have a Guru and to be initiated by him.

The constructive part of Kabir's mission was to lay out a common path on which both Hindus and Mussalmans could tread together. "In the Pantha (way, sect) of Kabir, the Guru holds the safe position as in any other Sufi order. If it is true of the Sufis that 'among them the worship of God is the same as the worship of man' it is equally applicable here for says Kabir: 'Consider the Guru as Govinda (God)'. Nay more—'If Hari becomes angry still there is some chance, but if the Guru is angry then there is no chance whatever'."[5]

Kabir also attacked with fearless indignation and trenchant language the whole apparatus of externalia which obscured the truth or separated the Indian communities from one another. He spread neither the Hindu nor the Mussalman. The entire teachings of Guru Nanak is but a synthesis of the fundamental principles of both the religions. By birth Kabir was a Mussalman and Nanak a Hindu, yet they are both products of the fusion which was going on despite outward separation.

Grants to Hindu religious institutions: In actual practice *rapprochement* proceeded in many other spheres of life. Muslim kings endowed temples and '*maths*' and granted jagirs to pious Hindus and Pandits.

Students of the history of South India must have come across innumerable instances of such grants, made to Brahmans by Adil Shahi, Kutub Shahi and Asaf Shahi dynasties. Likewise such endowments were made to Muslim places of worship by Maratha rulers even after the political strife with Delhi Emperors.[6] The nucleus of the large Zamindari of the Mahant of Bodh Gaya whose yearly income runs into lakhs was a grant by Muhammad Shah of Delhi, who by a firman granted a village of Mustipur Taradih to Mahant Lal Gir who was the fourth in succession from the founder. Similarly the great Zamindari perhaps the greatest in India—of Darbhanga—owes its origin to a *firman* granted by the Mughal Emperor Akbar to the ancestor of the present Brahman Maharajadhiraj for his learning and piety. To encourage education among his Hindu subjects Sher Shah granted them *wakfs* and allowed them a free hand in their management. For this liberal policy he was liked by his subjects of all castes and creeds.[7]

Sultan Zain-ul-Abdin of Kashmir used often to visit Amarnath and Sarda Devi's temple and had houses built there for the comfort of the pilgrims. The Pathans of Majibabad ruled over Hardwar about 1780. The Nawab built big houses for the comfort of Hindu pilgrims which are still in existence and in possession of the Hindus.

In Hyderabad (Deccan) the Brahman family was the Mutwalli of a Dargah of a famous Buzurg (pious man). The Nizams granted a big jagir to this Dargah and the public also made offerings. They also gave grants to several Hindu temples and Gurdwara. Similar grants and *firmans* from Musalman rulers to Hindu temples are still in existence and in possession of Hindus.

Even Aurangzeb by his *firmans* gave grants to the priests of the famous temple of Maheshvarnath and to priests in the village of Basti. On the other hand, the Hindus even now assemble in large numbers—as large numbers as Muslims—at the Dargah of a Muslim saint or on the occasion of Urs fairs at places like Ajmer Shareef, Bihar Shareef, Maner Shareef and Phulwari Shareef.

Hindu masses have joined in the Muslim celebration of Muharram all over North India. It was not only in the processions that the Hindus joined; they actually observed Muharram like the Muslims in their homes as days of mourning and prayer.

The famous Portuguese historian Fari Souza writes in his *Dakhan-ki-halat:* "There was no discrimination against Hindus, and they used to perform their religious rites and ceremonies without hindrance. The Mussalmans used to show great consideration for the religious feelings of the Hindus".

Sir Alfred Lyall writes in *Asiatic Studies* (p. 289): "But so far were they (Muslim rulers) from converting India that among the Muhammedans themselves, their own faith never acquired an entire exclusive monopoly of the high officers of administration."

Social Life: The influence exerted by the Hindu on the Muslim social life and custom and *vice versa* was no less remarkable. This is illustrated by the rites and ceremonies observed by both the communities in connection with the three most important and significant incidents in human life, *viz.,* birth, marriage and death. At the birth of a child, even in Muslim families, songs are sung as among the Hindus and the mother is considered to be impure for fixed days after the birth of a child.

Though marriage, according to Islam, is a contract, and according to Hindus, a sacrament, the pomp and procession, feasts and festivities, the songs sung by women, the presents, the practical jokes and playful practices are all like in both the communities. In northern India, remarriage of a widow is not looked upon with favour in respectable Muslim families.

The Caste system has not left the Indian Muslims untouched or unaffected. The Syed, the Sheikh, the Pathan, the Malik, the Momin, the Mansoor, the Rayeen, the Qasab, the Raki, the Hajjam, the Dhobi and a host of other caste names may be mentioned to show the divisions among the Muslims.

Though inter-marriages among the Muslim castes are not prohibited, in most cases they take place within the group to which both the parties belong. The Muslim *bhangi* has no higher status in a Muslim society than a Hindu of the corresponding class. This is the influence of environment which the Muslims have not been able to withstand.

Large communities who have been converted into Islam from among the Hindus have carried with them and still maintain many of their Hindu usages and customs, even after a long lapse of time. The Malkhana Rajputs still maintain many old rites and ceremonies which they used to observe as Hindus. Many large groups of Muslims also retained till recently the laws of inheritance which they observed before their conversion into Islam.

Muslims who have come in close contact with the Hindus have not failed sympathetically to understand the Hindu taboos about food and have respected them. They have freely joined Hindu festivities in connection with marriage, child birth, etc. when invited and invite Hindus on similar occasions to their own homes and families. The habits of eating have not stood in the way of free and cordial relationship.

Throughout India we find real and genuine friendship and neighbourliness established between the two communities and a member of the other community being called *bhai, chacha* or *kaka*.

In the old-world economy, each village had its carpenter and black-smith, barber and washerman, potter and bangle-seller, grain parcher and oil-presser, the *mehtar* or *bhangi* and *chamar* and *dom*. Most of them had a part to play on ceremonial occasions for which they got some special reward. Even though some of them might be Muslims, they rendered the same service as their corresponding Hindu professionals an were remunerated in the same way. For instance *the malis,* many of whom are Muslims, supply flowers for all religious functions and for daily worship of the Hindus.

Dress: A villager in Bihar or Bengal or the Punjab or the U.P. wears a dress which is practically indistinguishable from his Hindu compatriot. The pyjamas are worn by Muslims more largely than by the Hindus, but the number of Hindus wearing the pyjamas is not small Muslims as well as Hindus wear *dhoti,* particularly in villages. The ornaments worn by women are common to both communities and many of them have their names derived from a Hindu or Muslim source. The *sari,* is worn by both Hindu and Muslim women. In the north and in the hills, where on account of severe cold, pyjamas are worn, they are worn by Hindus, Muslims and Sikhs.

The purdah is entirely borrowed from the Muslims and yet, from locality to locality the system of purdah varies, but is common to both Hindus and Muslims.

The language that is spoken and understood in northern India, by whatever name we may call it, has undoubtedly been greatly influenced by, if it is not the product of, the joint efforts of Hindus and Muslims. The structure, which is the real frame-work of a language, is common to both forms of the language known as Hindi and Urdu. The difference is mainly in respect of a portion of the vocabulary. Muslim poets have composed devotional songs, the very theme of which is Hinduistic. The *dohas* of Rahiman are household property all over northern India like *sawaiyyas* of Giridhar for their wit and wisdom. Hindus have contributed to Urdu literature. Even today, Hindus constitute a very considerable proportion of the people interested in and devoted to Urdu language and literature. Other provincial languages were also helped and owed not a little to the Persian or Urdu of the Muslim rulers.

"....It was the epics—the *Ramayana* and the *Mahabharata* that first attracted the notice of the Muhammadan rulers of Bengal at whose instance they were translated into Bengali, the language of their domicile. The first Bengali rendering of *Mahabharata* was ordered by Nazir Shah of Bengal (1282-1385 A.D.) who was great patron of the vernacular of the province and whom the great poet Vidyapati has immortalized by dedicating to him one of his songs. ...Emperor Husain Shah was a great patron of Bengali. Haldhar Basu was appointed by him to translate the *Bhagavata-Purana* into Bengali, ...Paragal Khan, a general of Husain Shah, and his son

Chhuti Khan, have made themselves immortal by associating their names with the Bengali translation of a portion of the *Mahabharata.*[8]

Thus Bengali is the language of both Hindus and Musalmans of Bengal. So is Gujarati or Gujarat and Punjabi of Punjab and Hindi or Urdu or Hindustani or by whatever other name one chooses to call it, of northern India including the whole area from the borders of Punjab to the borders of Bengal on one side and from the foot of the Himalayas to the borders of Marathi-speaking and Telugu-speaking provinces in the central and southern India. There is no division of the population in any part of India which coincides both in respect of language and religion. The distribution of language is territorial and not communal or religious.

It is thus clear that in spite of all differences and distinctions that exist between Hindus and Muslims it is idle to deny that both have laboured and lived to develop a joint culture which is the Indian culture and which at once distinguishes an Indian from any foreigner coming from the West or the East, whether from other continents and countries of the Old World or the New World.

REFERENCES

1. Dr Bhagwan Das quoted in Tarachand's *Influence of Islam on Indian Culture,* pp. 66-7.
2. *Ibid.,* pp. 69-70.
3. Tarachand: *Influence of Islam on Indian Culture,* pp. 77-78.
4. Tarachand, *op. cit.,* p. 81.
5. Tarachand *op. cit.,* p. 158.
6. Atulananda Chakravarty, *Call it Politics?* p. 44.
7. Iswari Prasad, *History of Muslim Rule in India,* p. 339.
8. N.N. Law, *Promotion of Learning in India During Muhamadan Rule,* pp. 107-110.

3. India's Religious Renaissance

Those who have sought to describe the history of India's political development have been used to take the year 1885, when the National Congress was founded, as their starting-point and in a sense they have been correct. But when they have gone on to regard the years preceding that date as politically barren, they have surely failed to take account of one immensely important factor. They have not realized and the very intimate connection in India between the political field and the sphere of religious development.

For in India more than any other country we have always to notice those movements which spring directly out of the religious spirit of the people. One writer has even said that Indians are "incorrigibly religious", and there is some truth underlying this extreme expression. For more than anywhere else in the world, politics and religion in India have become mingled together in such a way that they can hardly be separated, however much we may try to do so.

In this, as well as many other aspects, the India of countless villages and hamlets, scattered far and wide over the land, reminds us very forcibly indeed of the Middle Ages in Europe, where the same religious background is met with leading on to great political results. For in those medieval times, when the industrial city life had not yet been established and the country life with its handicrafts was still the center of civilization and culture, this religious mind prevailed. We find great leaders of the Church, like Anselm and

Bernard of Clairvaux, offering guidance in the affairs of State to emperors and kings. So mighty was the power of their spirit among the multitudes that even the royal leaders dare not disobey.

What has been thus stated in the widest terms of India as a whole is perhaps most true of all concerning Hindu India, though in vitally important respects it is correct also concerning Islam. For in Islam, as enunciated by the Prophet, religion actually rules the State. We can see the same tendency at work even in comparatively recent times, for in the north the Sikh Khalsa has shown us how the Indian mind works towards political and social freedom in and through a religious awakening. The history of the Arya Samaj, which will be referred to later, tells the same story, as does the extremely interesting development of the Radha Swami sect at Dayal Bagh.

This noticeable fact of Indian history has not ceased to influence political events even after the foundation of the National Congress. It would be true to say that Swami Vivekananda and Mahatma Gandhi have, each in turn through their own religious inspiration, awakened a love for the Motherland such as no purely political leaders has ever been able to evoke. Their influence on the rise and growth of the Congress itself, as we shall see later, has been paramount. Yet Swami Vivekananda remained a monk to the end and never entered the political sphere, and Mahatma Gandhi has often declared openly in public that he only became a national and political leader in order to carry out his faith in God in the midst of a political age.

The most convenient period from which to trace back the modern movement in the religious life of India, which led on to the Indian National Congress development, would be the very remarkable years, from 1828 to 1833, when Raja Ram Mohan Roy, the greatest religious and social reformer of Bengal, had reached the height of his spiritual powers. In every respect he towered head and shoulders above his contemporaries, both European and Indian alike, in the land of his birth.

He also saw, with unique insight, what was likely to be the course of British power in India, and how its peculiar qualities could best be directed towards the interest both of his own country and Great Britain. By every modern historian of India he is rightly claimed as not only the clearest sighted religious leader of his own age, but also as its most advanced political thinker.

In this connection it is important to notice that the official history of the Indian National Congress corroborates this point of view.* The author goes back to this date of Raj Ram Mohan Roy's supreme influence as the starting-point of the whole national movement of Modern India. He rightly calls the Raja 'the prophet of Indian nationalism and the father of Modern India.' Thompson and Garratt in *The Rise and Fulfilment of British Rule in India* take a similar view and give to Raja Ram Mohan Roy the same place of unique importance as the originator of the remarkable *rapprochement* of two alien races. India and Britain, whereby the Eastern and Western cultures have become intermingled.

In the Congress History the well-known story is repeated at some length how the Raja, on his voyage to England round the Cape of Good Hope, insisted, even though he was in feeble health at the time, on going on board a French ship, which was anchored in Capetown, Harbour. He wished to pay homage from India, his own country, to the great French nation, which had raised aloft throughout the world the banner of revolution against all forms of slavery, and had taken as its watchword—'Liberty, Equality, Fraternity.'

While making this effort, he slipped and badly injured his leg. Indeed, he remained lame for the remainder of his life. But he insisted on performing this symbolic act in order to show, as an Indian political leader, his profound sympathy with the cause of freedom that was dearer to him than life itself.

* *The History of the Indian National Congress* by Dr. Pattabhi Sitarammayya, published in Madras, 1936. This is the authoritative book written for the fiftieth anniversary of the Congress. It has been revised by different Congress leaders.

It is also recorded of him that on another occasion, when he was very greatly depressed at the power of the reactionary forces at work in Great Britain, he determined, if the cause of freedom was defeated, to retire both from Britain and from British India and renounce his citizenship so that he could become naturalized and life in some country where the cause of political liberty still flourished. So far did he put this cause above every other earthly blessing.

This fundamental faith in civil liberty characterized the whole life of Raja Ram Mohan Roy. Herein he was truly the prophet of Indian nationalism, for such a sovereign faith in liberal principles has been the most marked feature of Indian political life ever since. It has led not merely to a persistent struggle to become free from the foreign control, but also to the initiation of internal reforms. For the present movement towards the emancipation of the depressed and submerged classes owes its strongest incentive to this passion for liberty which Raja Ram Mohan Roy created.

The awakening of this new spirit in Bengal at the beginning of the nineteenth century was extended in wider and wider circles till it reached every part of India. It can be historically proved that later movements, such as the Arya Samaj and the Ramkrishna Mission, though quite independent in origin, were greatly helped in their forward progress owing to the pathway which had already been prepared by the wide scope of the Brahma Samaj and its founder Raja Ram Mohan Roy.

On the British side, the same date, 1828-35, has its own significance. For it was the period of the Reform Movement, which produced at last a three-fold result:

(i) The abolition of slavery within the British Dominions.

(ii) The Indian Charter of racial and religious equality.

(iii) The new democratic Parliament in Great Britain.

When Raja Ram Mohan Roy reached England he found that the reactionary powers had been defeated and that all these three reforms were nearly accomplished. The sight of what he found already on its way gave him new hope for the future. The long preparation which had led up to these three simultaneous measures being put forward, one after the other, and embodied in Acts of Parliament, gave a strong assurance to those who remained in India, even after the Raja's untimely death that the liberal policy of Great Britain towards that country would be carried through to the end.

These remarkable years proved to be the period of laying foundations, whereon the whole of the later political side of the reforms was noticeable from the very first, in India for fifty years the religious aspect was most apparent.

If this religious background, which intimately touched the masses and not the intellectuals only, had not been firmly established by arduous years of incessant labour; if great personalities had not arisen, one after the other, proclaiming a religious message to the whole of India, the National Congress movement on an all India basis would never have become possible. It would not have reached the masses; nor would it have been vigorous enough to withstand all the shocks of division, rivalry, and party strife, which are inevitable at the beginning of a great political advance. It was only when movement reached the village people, through the medium of the supreme personality of Mahatma Gandhi, that its strength became irresistible and its range of action wide enough to cover the whole of India.

For this reason, among others, it is vitally necessary to deal in some detail with the main religious reforms which have arisen in India during the nineteenth century, and to explain how they have always been associated in public memory with commanding moral and spiritual personalities. These religious movements have one remarkable characteristic. Although they started from a single province and a local area, they reached out in wider and wider circles in order to touch, if possible, every part of India. Thus they made much easier the realization, when the right time came, of an all India political organization such as the Congress.

One more fact needs explanation before taking in detail these wide movements of religion which characterized the nineteenth century. The starting point was Bengal. It was a natural and almost inevitable mode of advance, because Bengal was the first part of modern India to come into closest contact with the West, as the focus and center of British rule. Furthermore, the intellectual atmosphere of Bengal, early in the nineteenth century, which encouraged the fullest freedom of thought, made the order of progress, from that province to other parts of India, natural. Bengal had peculiar gifts whereby the assimilation of Western thought became comparatively simple. For such a process demands high imaginative power as well as intellectual capacity, and both of these qualities the cultured people of Bengal possessed in full measures. But while this starting-point is a matter of history, the part played by the other provinces of India as the century advanced was no less important. This will be made clear later.

In earlier centuries there had already been close contact between India and the West. For instance, in the days when the military and naval power of Portugal was established at Goa, men of remarkable genius had come out to India. The names of Vasco de Gama, Albuquerque, Camoens and Francis Xavier have attained a notable place in world history. But no creative period in Indian thought and life followed from this contact with the Portuguese, even at the height of their literary fame. There was no real blending of cultures.

But when Warren Hastings, Sir William Jones, H.H. Wilson, and others settled in Bengal, in the latter half of the eighteenth century; and Carey, Hare and Duff followed in the early nineteenth they were able to carry over to the West much of their experience of the East; and Ram Mohan Roy, Dwarkanath Tagore, and others brought from the West much of European thought in return. The earliest instance of this interchange of thought is Warren Hasting's well-known appreciation of the Gita. The time was ripe for such a cultural approach, and a fertilizing soil had been found.

Europe thus received during this germinative period precious seed thoughts from the East, especially concerning the inner life of man Asia, in its turn, learnt something of the advance of modern science in Europe.

One of the principal reasons for this remarkable renaissance in Bengal at the beginning of the nineteenth century was undoubtedly the French Revolution. The intellectual and spiritual change which was passing over Europe had its repercussions in India. The social and political ideas of the seventeenth and eighteenth centuries before the French Revolution had a certain uniformity about them, both in the West and the East. But those new conception of social justice which the Revolution of 1789-93 brought with it were startlingly fresh and strange. They created a different attitude of mind. While the rest of India was still only slightly conscious of this new movement of human thought which had come to the West, Bengal was acutely awake. The hard mould of centuries had been broken and the new ideas of human progress found in Bengal their most congenial soil.

Note. Considerable latitude concerning the spelling of Indian name is observed by authors whom we have quoted, and it is difficult to maintain strict uniformity. Thus, Muhammadan, Mahomedan, and Mohamedan have all found their way into English texts, together with Moslem and Muslim. In the same manner Ghosh and Ghose, Dayanand and Dayananda are almost equally common.

THE BRAHMA SAMAJ

During the earlier days of British rule in India the two most important groups within Bengali Hindu society were at Vaishnavas and Saivas, who worshipped Vishnu and Siva as the one supreme lord of creation. They were both equally orthodox in their rigid observance of the traditional laws of Hindu conduct which were embodied in the caste system. They both recognized all the lesser divinities of the Hindu pantheon. Each group claimed to follow closely the Vedanta philosophy, interpreting it according to its own tradition.

But there was little clarity of vision. Four Hinduism itself was at this time in a pitifully moribund condition. The subjugation of the Hindus by the Muslims, which had now lasted for many centuries, seemed to have destroyed initiative. Vast multitudes in East Bengal had become Muslims, though the old Hindu background of thought and life remained. Thus, historically, when the East India Company began to consolidate its power the Hindu community had almost reached the point of exhaustion.

Furthermore, Islam itself, owing in a great measure to the large numbers that had come under its way, had become rigid and lifeless in its turn. There was neither any active movement of religious thought nor any outstanding spiritual leader. Like Hinduism, Islam had lost its old religious fervour. It was content with keeping its own ceremonial traditions.

The question, which has been already stated, needs to be put in another form: Why did the religious awakening in Bengal begin in the early nineteenth century? Why did the European influence before that date produce such very feeble results? If it is accepted that a renaissance in Indian thought and life was produced by contact with Western ideas, why did it not begin at an earlier date?

Farquhar, in his book on *Modern Religious Movements in India,* suggests that the two forces which quickened that spirit of Bengal into new life were the impact of British rule and the intellectual stimulus caused by the Christian missions. The later of these two forces was not felt to any great extent before the nineteenth century was well on its way. A third factor was the great work of the European Oriental scholars, whose publication of noble Sanskrit texts created a wide interest both in India and the West, Farquhar states that when Carey settled down at Srempore, the more farsighted Englishmen, both in the Mission's and in the Company's service, realized the need of close co-operation in order to accelerate the progress of Indian education. Thus the further study of the East and the new experience of the West went on side by side.

One of the most interesting and romantic incidents of these eventful days was the arrival in Paris, under arrest, of an Englishman named Hamilton, in 1803. During his forced detention he taught Sanskrit to several French scholars and also to Friedrich Schlegel. The latter was deeply impressed by the Sanskrit literature, which was thus opened out to him for the first time. He translated some texts into German. It was a period when patient research was being made in the science of language. These translations made a great sensation in academic circles. Afterwards a number of European scholars continued to take an increasingly sympathetic interest in India and Indian affairs, creating thereby an enthusiasm for Indian culture and religion quite unknown before.

These were the years (1800-28) which shaped and formed the political and the religious ideas of the founder of the Brahma Samaj—Raja Ram Mohan Roy (1772-1833). Born of an old Brahmin family, he was educated at Patna, in Bihar, at that time a well-known center of Islamic studies. It was been said of him that throughout his life the Raja remained profoundly influenced by his early education, both in his habits and tastes. On his return home from Patna at the age of fifteen, he found that the difference of opinion with his father on the question of idolatry had become so acute that he was unable to live with him any longer. He therefore left his ancestral home and, after wandering about in India and even visiting Tibet, settled down in Banaras in order to study Sanskrit and the Hindu scriptures. In his early youth he was said to have had a great dislike for the English, but after a favourable experience in the service of the East India Company, and close contact with worthy Englishmen like Mr. Digby, he began to alter his opinion. As a man of affairs, he gradually saw that as the British rule had come to stay it was right to make terms with it and to utilize the contact with the West for the good of the Indian people.

On the death of his father in 1803 he moved to Murshidabad, in Bengal, and published in 1804 a pamphlet in Persian called the *Tuhfat-ul-Muahhidin* or *A Gift to the Deists,* expressing very strong views against idolatry and polytheism. Soon after his retirement from the service of the Company in 1814 he settled down in Calcutta and established in 1815 a society called the "Atmiya Sabha" or the Society of Friends. He also came into contact with the Serampore missionaries, and took up the study of Hebrew and Greek in order to understand the Christian scriptures. In 1820 he published a notable pamphlet called *The Precepts of Jesus: The guide to Peace and Happiness*. Before that he had already attracted public attention by publishing in English a statement of his own views on religion in a book called *Translation of an Abridgement of the Vedanta, or the Resolution of all the Vedas* (1816).

But the Raja's activities were not confined to controversial discussion of the different religions. He was equally interested in education and social reform, slowly building up at the same time his own religious convictions. He was one of the many Indians who took an active part in the establishment of the Hindu College, which was founded in Calcutta in 1819. His efforts towards social reform were equally fruitful. He championed the agitation against the burning of widows, and it was very largely through his great influence in Bengal that Lord Bentinck was able to abolish *Sati* by an order of the Government on December 4, 1819.

Although Raja Ram Mohan Roy's manifold social reforms were of great importance, it was in religion that his contribution had the most far-reaching effect. In 1828 he founded the Brahma Samaj, a theistic society opposed to polytheism, mythology, and idolatry. This proved to be the first influential religious movement of the nineteenth century in India.

The Samaj held its first meetings in a house in Chitpur Road, Calcutta. The word "Brahma" is derived from the Sanskrit "Brahman"—the name for God in the Upanishads. "Samaj" means a society or association. Throughout its long history the Brahma Samaj has remained rigorously theistic and opposed to idolatry and has always advocated progressive social reform. While its roots have been grounded deep in the Hindu religion, the Raja, as well as the early founders of the Brahma Samaj, derived inspiration and stimulus from keen intellectual controversies with the Christian missionaries. In fact, the impulse which proved most creative in Ram Mohan Roy's mind was the desire to found a form of religion capable of meeting the missionaries' attacks on Hinduism in a manner which would conform with the scientific spirit of the age.

Yet in spite of the great personality of the Raja and his friends, the progress of the Samaj was slow. It did not create immediately a widespread enthusiasm even among educated people. Nevertheless it released forces, both favourable and hostile, of remarkable intensity, which developed into many different social and religious movements all through the nineteenth century. People were roused from their old lethargy, either to defend or to attack it. Bengali society was rocked with religious discussion, the outcome of which was a saner conception of religion, a more well informed attitude towards the question of morals, and, above all, a more determined effort to secure justice and liberty, both for the individual and the people.

The first name chosen for the newly formed Church was the Brahma Sabha, but very soon this was changed into Brahma Samaj. The Samaj used to meet every Saturday evening from seven to nine in a hired house in Calcutta. At first there was neither a well-established organization nor any regular membership. It was weekly gathering, where people met to pray and worship. Ram Mohan fervently believed that he was reviving the ancient character of the Hindu religion. The simple ritual and the spirit of devotion which pervaded the atmosphere of the gatherings represented to him a return to the ancient form of Vedic worship.

The Raja left for England in November 1830 and remained there until his death, in Bristol, on September 27, 1833. While during his stay in England he was engaged in many social and political activities, his contact with the British Unitarians and men like Roscoe and Bentham gave him a greater opportunity of understanding liberal Christian thought. He was impressed by the rational attitude which certain Christian denominations were adopting and he was eager to do the same for Hinduism. A man of unbounded energy and great patriotism, he was born at a time when the civilization of the West with its philanthropic enthusiasm came into close touch with Hinduism through his own interpretation of it. A profound spiritual ferment had been created. It needed a man of large imagination and keen intellect to harmonize these diverse influences and turn their direction towards a positive outlook upon life.

Ram Mohan had thus to perform a double task. He had to challenge Hindu orthodoxy and also to turn in a new religious direction the negative, sceptical spirit of the first generation of English educated Bengalis. Miss Collet quotes from an article in the *Asiatic Journal* (1833): "The Raja often deplored the existence of a party which had sprung up in Calcutta, composed principally of imprudent young men, some of them possessing talent, who had avowed themselves sceptcis in the widest sense of the term. He described it as partly composed of East Indian and partly of Hindu youth, who form education had learnt to reject their own faith without substituting any other. These he thought more debased than the most bigoted Hindu and their principles the bane of all morality."

Because of his high courage and vast scholarship and comprehension of other religions, the Raja was best fitted to accomplish a union of the spiritual forces of the East and West which had met in India. His success was further made possible by the new temper of the politically minded Indians, who were beginning to question the supremacy of England. The Brahma Samaj, therefore, did not merely establish a new Church; it also brought a reconciliation within Hindu society which led on to progress.

Soon after the death of the Raja the affairs of the Samaj came into the hands of the Maharaja Ramnath Thakur and Prasanna Kumar Thakur, who were not able to give much time to its supervision. Then Ram Mohan's eldest son took it up in his own hands. But he was soon involved in his private affairs and left the Samaj in a very disordered state. Then Dwarkanath Tagore took charge of it. But as he left for England very soon afterwards, its work again began to decline, until his son, Debendranath Tagore, joined the Samaj in 1842. His power of organization and his saintly life once again restored the Samaj's usefulness, which had suffered after the death of the Raja. He published in 1848 a series of extracts from the Hindu scriptures called the *Brahma Dharma,* and its publication satisfied all the different elements of the Samaj. Debendranath remained with the Samaj until 1872, when he finally handed over its affairs to his son Dwijendranath. During the 30 years of Debendranath's stewardship its prestige had grown and many branches were started in different parts of India. He steadfastly believed that original Hinduism was a spiritual theism and that India had no need of any other religion. He showed in his attitude towards redical social ideas a decided disinclination to adopt any newer patterns which he thought were not rooted in the body of Hindu thought and tradition.

In 1857 Keshav Chandra Sen joined the Samaj. Born of a well-known Yaidya* family of Calcutta, Keshav very early showed great powers of oratory. Amongst his friends he was regarded as a coming religious leader. Soon, by his gifts of speaking, he became a leading light. He founded in 1860 a society called the "Sangat Sabha" or the "Believers Association" for the discussion of social and religious reforms and particularly for the abolition of the caste system. In 1861 he resigned his position in the Bank of Bengal in order to become a whole time missionary of the Samaj, and shortly after his resignation he was formally ordained as a minister of the Samaj, with the title of "Acharya." But very soon afterwards, because of his radical ideas about the caste system, serious differences of opinion arose with other leaders and he retired from his position as the secretary of the Samaj in 1863. His advocacy of inter-marriage and his objection to the wearing of the sacred thread† were two of the most vital objections against him.

---

* The Vidyas of Bengal are supposed to have descended from the Brahmin caste.

† The higher castes amongst the Hindus are required, according to ancient customs, to wear cotton threads next to their skin after they have been initiated to the Hindu doctrines at an early age.

Keshav, finding that his radical ideas were not supported in Calcutta, made a tour of the whole of India in 1864, as a result of which the "Prarthana Samaj" in Bombay and the "Veda Samaj" in Madras (now called the Brahma Samaj of Madras) were founded. During this tour Keshav had gathered round him a group of younger men who shared his views on the question of a more radical programme of social reform within the Samaj. But these opinions were not shared by any other leading members, and it became therefore inevitable that a schism should take place. Debendranath made repeated attempts to bring about a reconciliation, but Keshav and his young friends were determined to fight out the question of the caste system and they consequently left the Samaj in 1865.

In November 1866 Keshav formed a new society called the 'Brahma Samaj of India,' and very soon afterwards a selection of theistic texts from different religious scriptures was published for use in the services of the new Samaj. A little which afterwards he met Ramakrishna and began to use frequently his sermons the word *Bhakti,* a term borrowed from the Vaishnava tradition of Bengal. He also introduced many ceremonies of the Hindu religion, which caused great dissatisfaction among many of those who had sided with him in respect to social reforms. The actual schism took place in 1878, when he consented to give his daughter in marriage to the ruling prince of Cooch Behar, although both the bride and the bridegroom were still under age. In a public statement* Keshav justified his action. He did no, however, satisfy a large body of influential members, who left the Samaj as a protest against his action. He afterwards formed the "Nava Vidhan" or the "New Dispensation." He died on January 8, 1884.

The majority of the provincial Samajists and the body of influential members in Calcutta who seceded from the new Samaj formed afterwards the "Sadharan Brahma Sakan" in 1878. Its organization was framed in such a way that one single person could

* Keshav published a statement defending his action in the *Indian Mirror* of April 6, 1878.

never dominate its affairs. Pundit Siva Nath Sastri, a leading and respected Brahma preacher, also joined the Samaj and on January 22, 1881, a new house for services was opened in Cornwallis Street, Calcutta. Since then the Sadharan Brahma Samaj has made continued progress. Its influence has been very widespread and it has given to the National Congress some of its noblest leaders. In its earliest days it had stood for a complete modernization of the Indian way of life. But the Hindu devotional instincts, which were always latent in its members, soon found expression. In addition to giving the different reform movements the necessary stimulus, it also helped to leaven Hindu society generally.

Thus from whatever angle we start we are led back to the conclusion that the greatest changes in Indian society originally sprang from the commanding spiritual genius of Raja Ram Mohan Roy. At the same time the contact at close quarters with such personalities among the missionaries as Carey and Duff afforded a constant stimulus to the leading members of the Brahma Samaj to reform Hinduism from within. This brought with it a wider study of the religious and political thought of the West.

THE ARYA SAMAJ

By the year 1870 the Brahma Samaj, especially among its younger and more advanced members, had brought about within the Hindu community itself a deep desire to carry through certain social and educational reforms on purely western lines. The majority of educated Indians were thus becoming cut off from those who had not received a western education. It became the fashion even in the smaller things of life to imitate the West. Though no religious change was contemplated, the West was morally and intellectually all-pervasive. There was no outstanding Indian leader as yet who was strong enough to challenge this process altogether.

Nevertheless, a natural reaction had already begun to set in. A very large section of Hindu society began to cast grave doubts on the wisdom of breaking away so completely from old Hindu traditions and neglecting their own religious philosophy.

This Hindu reaction often took extravagant forms. But gradually it found a certain balance, and while it fostered at first a spirit of somewhat narrow nationalism, it gave to educated Indians a new self-respect as they took legitimate pride in their ancient cultural heritage.

Bepin Chandra Pal, who was a member of the Brahma Samaj, writes in his memories as follows:

"When in 1879, I left the University and went to Calcutta, the Brahma Samaj was still a great intellectual and moral force in the country. The middle nineteenth-century rationalism and individualism of European culture were still the dominating ideas in the life and evolution of modern Begal. But the conflict of political interests between the new generation of English educated Indians and the British officialdom in the country and the more fundamental cultural conflict between European modernism and Indian medievalism soon provoked a new revolt against the foreign domination, in the wake of which followed a new national self-consciousness which in the first flush of its new-found pride of race and culture commenced to repudiate whatever was foreign irrespective of the intrinsic reason and value of it and set up a new defence even of those social institutions and religious and spiritual tendencies that had previously been openly repudiated as false and harmful."

An intellectual basis was provided by the Bengal novelist, Bankim Chandra Chatterjee. In a series of brilliant articles in the *Banga Darshan* he interpreted Hindu ethics and religion in accordance with the new rules of criticism accepted as valid in the West, re-explaining and re-assessing the whole content of Hindu belief and traditions.

In Northern India a similar movement had been started by Dayanand Saraswati, a Hindu monk and preacher, who was born in 1824 in the small town of Tankara, in the Kathiawar State of Morvi. Even as a boy he often doubted if the Hindu idols which people worshipped contained any divinity. His parents were disturbed by his attitude and wanted to get him married, thinking that marriage would alter his views. But Dayanand, being unable to share the opinions of his parents, fled from home. Then began a period of wanderings throughout India, during which he met many ascetics, practised *yoga,* and studied the Vedanta with a teacher in Mathura. In 1863, when he thought that his studies were completed, he started preaching his doctrines and began to publish books and pamphlets. He went about all over the country and at last in 1875 conceived the idea of founding the Arya Samaj. It was linked up for a very short time with the Theosophical Society, but the union was soon broken off in 1881. Dayandnad died on October 30, 1883, at the age of fifty-nine.

Unlike the leading members of the Brahma Samaj, Dayanand never learnt English. He wrote in Hindi. This made him more intelligible to the masses in Northern India, and the Arya Samaj became, broadly speaking, a mass movement. His followers were attracted by the truly Indian character of his teachings. His idea of going back to the Vedas was shared by many at the time, who were now becoming eager to challenge all the doctrines of the West.

Dayanand held fast to the belief that there was only one God, who was to be worshipped not by images, but as Spirit. He preached that the Vedas contained all the knowledge imparted to man by God and that the essentials of modern science were contained in them.

The popular Hindu doctrines of transmigration, *karma,** and the sanctity of the cow were upheld by him. Thus he had his immediate appeal to the common people even while advocating drastic reforms in the social system. The dynamic of his personality and his typically Indian approach to the question of religion brought to him many adherents. He represented the temper of a whole generation and symbolized in his person the political attitude of a

* The Hindu belief that a man's future is inevitably determined by the deeds he performs.

large number of Indians of the latter part of last century. Raja Ram Mohan Roy and the Brahma leaders had taken their stand on an enlightened reason when they denounced the evils of caste system, child marriage, etc. But Dayanand based his own position on the Vedas and proved to the people that these evils had no sanction in their own scriptures.

The Arya Samaj accepted the permanent existence of the four castes and retained the sacred thread for the three superior castes. On the other hand, it opposed child marriage and encouraged window remarriage. Thus its tenets represented an intermediate stage between conservative orthodox Hinduism on the one hand and an entirely modern critical outlook on the other. The followers of Dayanand sought to retain modern ideas about science without abandoning either the ancient Vedas or the equally ancient "caste" basis of society. From this standpoint a reform movement spread far and wide over the whole of the North of India and even up to the present day its spirit is active in the villages as well as in the towns.

Thus the lesson of all political advance in India is made clear by Dayanand's remarkable success. For starting from the realm of pure religious truth, he was soon caught up in the current of rising national feeling. By coming into contact with those who were eager to reform Hindu society, he imbibed their keen enthusiasm. As a great visionary, he saw the future of his country blessed with a true faith and reaping the fruits of modern science. Such a people would be fit for self-rule and would occupy an honoured place among the nations of the world.

THE RAMAKRISHNA MISSION

A third movement differing remarkably in its inspiration from the Arya Samaj was started by Ramakrishna Paramhansa in Bengal. Ramakrishna, a simple village priest, had neither the learning nor the ability of Dayanand. Yet the entire middle class, western-educated Bengali community made him their national hero. Men like Keshav Chandra Sen, the Brahma leader, Bankim Chandra Chatterjee, the novelist, and Girish Chandra Ghosh, the dramatist, recognized his greatness and regarded him as a saint. It is strange that Ramakrishna, whose early upbringing had been amongst people untouched by English ideas, should stand out as the inspirer of a whole generation. One main reason was that these highly educated men put forward this simple village mystic and genius as the symbol of their revolt against English cultural superiority. They felt instinctively that they had been in danger of going too far and losing their own souls.

Ramakrishna was born in the village of Kamarpukur, in the Hooghli district of Bengal, on February 18, 1836. His parents, who were priestly Brahmins, soon found him a post as assistant priest in a temple at Dakhineswara, near Calcutta, in 1855. Even when he was an ordinary temple priest he would very often pass into a form of trance and remain unconscious for a long time. As in the case of Swami Dayanand, his parents, thinking that marriage would make him more like an ordinary man, had him married in 1859. But this did not stop his mystical mediations. He would very often fall into *Samadhi* (Yogic trance), from which he would return after a long period. It was about this time, when most of his acquaintances felt baffled with him, that he met a Brahmin nun, who came to him saying that she was sent by God. She helped him much at this early stage of his religious life. Later on he met an Indian monk called Totapuri, who taught him the monistic *Vedanta,* as preached by the great Sankaracharya, and also many Yogic practices, specially the "Nirvikalpa Samadhi," in which the devotee loses all trace of consciousness.

After Totapuri had left, Ramakrishna tried to attain the *Vaishnava* idea of love for God, which is characteristic of Bengal. The next phase of his inner life consisted of a struggle against his own hesitation in matters of caste. After he had succeeded in removing his prejudices against other religions, he met Christians and Muslims and held discourses with them and eventually came to the conclusion that all religions were equally true and that they were various paths leading to the same goal.

The story of his mystical life now began to be spread abroad, and many people came to see him and here him. Dayanand himself visited him towards the end of 1872, but the meeting was unsuccessful.

It was his contact with men like Keshav Chandra Sen and Girish Chandrá Ghosh and other which made him realize what was going on in the minds of the educated people. They spoke and taught in a language which he could hardly understand at first. Yet he was never embarrassed by his ignorance. His natural goodness and enlightened consciousness made him appreciate things which people never expected from him. In spite of his orthodox upbringing the largeness of his mind made him sympathize with the intellectual dilemma of educated people. His broad sympathy, saintliness of character and radiant personality disarmed al opposition and he guided and advised people even without knowing it.

Ramakrishna's success with the educated people of his age was also due to the weakness of their intellectual belief. For, very many had found it impossible to reconcile the condition in which they were born with the ideas they had imbibed. Their aspirations remained unfulfilled and the answers they had gained from modern science were also inadequate. So they wanted a symbol or focus for all their inner conflict. Ramakrishna, who was mentally their exact opposite, become their ideal. It is worth noticing that most of the men who surrounded Ramakrishna belonged either to the aristocracy of Bengal or else had come from the newly rising upper middle class. M. Romain Rooland mentions the fact that except Latu (a servant) all the men close to Ramakrishna came from the upper stratum of Bengali society.

The movement which Ramakrishna thus set in motion is important because he justified the claim of the Hindus that God can be worshipped and realize by following the traditional methods of India, which the Christian missionaries had characterized as superstitious. This fact gave the rising nationalist consciousness a weapon with which to fight the West. Indian could now claim that their religion was good enough for them. Since they did not want any other religion, they were capable of looking after themselves.

In the same way, politically they were quite capable of governing themselves without foreign interference.

Ramakrishna also created a movement for social reform, which carried political consequences with it. The cult of "Bhakti," on devotion, had always had a special appeal to the Bengali mind. The Bengalis of the late nineteenth century had left puzzled with their new-found race-consciousness, and it was Ramakrishna who showed them the way towards self-expression. The restlessness of the Bengali mind, gradually manifesting itself both in a new outburst of literature and in grave religious doubts, had reached a stage when it was marked by an inner agony that could not be controlled. An unsympathetic foreign Government, unable to realize the depth of these emotions, only exasperated the youth of Bengal. Together with an almost complete disbelief in religion, there had come something of the helplessness of despire. The stirring call for social service made to the young men by the Ramakrishna movement gave an outlet to this pent-up feeling of dissatisfaction. Many came forward and took vows of celibacy and dedicated their lives with joy to the service of the poor and the needy.

Behind this great movement the figure of Ramakrishna remained enshrined. His childlike tenderness, his homely wisdom and his engaging simplicity had so won the hearts of Young Bengal that they refused any longer to be impressed by the glamour of western learning. The merit of this movement lay in the fact that although Ramakrishna had never gained any scholastic distinction it became stronger and grew in importance among the educated classes. The steadiness with which it spread not only in India, but also abroad, was a thing of wonder. Ramakrishna, by being what he was, achieved these remarkable results.

After his death on August 15, 1886, his favourite disciple, Vivekananda (1863-1902), became the chief exponent of his teachings. He had a character altogether different from that of his master. He was forceful and uncompromising. By his remarkable energy he made the cause of Hinduism known in many parts of the world. His appearance in the Parliament of Religions at Chicago in 1893 was epoch-making for Indian religious thought. He was a scholar with a remarkable knowledge of other religions. His organizing ability soon made him the leader of the Ramakrishna Mission.

The activities of the Ramakrishna Mission itself remained predominantly reformist in the sphere of social service, but Vivekananda by his eloquent appeals had also given a new stimulus to the wider political aspirations of young India. He came back as a national hero from America and was welcomed as such. His success had increased the self-respect of the Indian people in face of the world at large. The time had passed when merely petitioning the British rulers to remove the manifold grievances and ills of foreign rule was all that the Congress could achieve. Vivekananda struck a new note, and among the young it found an immediate echo and response. Therefore when he asked his own countrymen not to blame the English people, but *themselves* for their suffering and degradation, he was voicing their own inner feelings. "I ask myself," he exclaimed, "who is responsible?" And the answer comes every time, "Not the English, no, they are not responsible: it is *we* who are responsible for all our misery and all our degradation, and we alone are responsible."

As to the causes of this degradation he went on as follows: "It is simply due to your having despised the masses of India that you have been living a life of slavery for the last thousand years; it is therefore that you are objects of hatred in the eyes of foreigners and are looked upon with indifference by your countrymen."

Ramakrishna had taken very little active interest in any particular political question. But Vivekananda, from his youth, was vitally interested in the political future of his country; and because of his wide travels and still wider acquaintance with people of many countries he had formed clear opinions regarding the needs of political freedom. Although he did not take any active part in the deliberations of the Congress, he was keenly observant of all that was happening. Many prominent Congress leaders sought his counsels, and he even knew personally some of the younger men who afterwards joined the revolutionary movement. On one occasion, on being asked why he advised a friend not to take part in politics, he said, "What does X know of politics? I have done more politics in my life than X. I had the idea of forming a combination of Indian Princes for the overthrow of foreign yoke. For that reason, from the Himalayas to Cape Comorin, I have tramped all over the country. But I got no response; the country is dead"*

Thus Vivekananda urged his countrymen to work out their own salvation. He wanted them to learn to do things for themselves without blaming other people or depending on them. It was for this reason that he concentrated on his work at the Ramakrishna Mission, where he intended to turn out a band of workers devoted entirely to the cause of national service.

As a result of his continued efforts, homes of social service and religious discipline were built at Belur, near Calcutta; at Allahabad, in Uttar Pradesh at Mayavati, in the Himalayas; and at Bangalore, in South India. These are used for the monks who are made to go through a period of training and discipline before they are permitted to be initiated into the order. Charitable institutions called *Seuasrams* have grown up all over the country, of which the most important are at Benares, Hardwar, Allahabad, and Brindaban. Educational work is also done in some places but Vivekananda's idea of building up a great center of learning on Indian lines was never fulfilled.

In April 1898 the building of the headquarters of the order was begun at Belur, near Calcutta. The dedication took place on December 9, 1898, and the final occupation on January 2, 1899. Its functions were divided. (i) The Ramkrishna Math is a purely monastic body with a retreat for the monks, having as its avowed object the maintenance of a universal religion. (ii) The Mission exercise jurisdiction over all works of public utility, both philanthropic and charitable. It is open both to the laymen and the

* *Swami Vivekananda, the Socialist,* by Dr. Dhupendranath Dutta (Khulna, Béngal), 1929, p. iv.

monks. It was legally registered in April 1909, a few years after the death of Vivekananda.

The Ramakrishna Mission differed from other social and religious movements in this respect that it put emphasis on that aspect of *Vedanta* which encourages universalism in its religious conception. Dayanand was never consciously drawn to a universal conception of religion, although some of his disciples claimed that the Arya Samaj was meant for the whole of humanity. But Ramakrishna and Vivekananda, because of the cult of *Vaishnavism* in Bengal, were fitted to evolve, each in his own way, a conception of religion which became universal. Vivekananda specially, by his new interpretation of Hindu religion, raised it to a universal status.

Above all, Vivekananda's intrepid patriotism gave a new colour to the Nationalist movement throughout India. The monk and the patriot were curiously blended in him, and Sister Nivedita has recorded in her reminiscences how very often he passed from one mood to the other. Mrs. Besant had described him as the warrior monk; and it is true that he had been deeply influenced by the political thinking of his time. His preachings of Hinduism had more references to the immediate condition of the people than those of Ramakarishna. Ramakrishna was like a gentle wind. He saw truth and spoke about it in the immemorial manner of ancient India. But Vivekananda was like a storm sweeping away all obstacles from the path of India's future greatness.

The year 1895 was the date of Vivekananda's return from America after his successful vindication of the Hindu religion in that country. More than any other single individual of that period, he had made his own contribution to the new awakening of India. As we read his biography we realize how, even without being connected with the Congress, he very largely shaped its policy and promoted its evolution.

THE ALIGARH MOVEMENT

By far the most outstanding figure in the Muslim world of India during the nineteenth century was Sir Syed Amed Khan, the founder of the Muhammadan Anglo-Oriental College at Aligarh, which has now become the Muslim University and accepts students from all over India and from other lands in the East.

The story has never yet been fully told of the remarkable revival of Islamic culture at Delhi from 1835 to 1857 as it came in touch with western learning. This renaissance in the north-west of India presented a remarkable parallel, in many directions, to the revival of learning in Bengal. The innate beauty and flexibility of the Urdu language—as it retained its near kinship with Persian literature on the one hand and absorbed new idea from the culture of the West on the other—afforded an admirable medium for this revival of learning in the north-west just as the Bengali language was the true medium in Bengal. If Rabindranath Tagore has given the fullest expression in poetry to the Bengali revival, Muhammad Iqbal has done the same thing through his Urdu and Persian poetry for the Punjab.

Even as late as the year 1908 there were those still living at Delhi who had taken part in their youth in this efflorescence of Urdu literature under the last of the Moghul emperors. Munshi Zaka Ullah and Maulvi Nazir Ahmad were two of these; Altaf Husain 'Hali' of Panipat was a third. The results of this early cultural contact between India and Britain in the north-west provinces were remarkable. Professor Ramachandra, an eminent Hindu scholar, who became a Christian, was one of the first-fruits of this contact. He was, in his own day, a mathematician of very high repute. There were also poets and writers in Urdu, who gained much of their inspiration from a study of English authors. Perhaps the most interesting fact of all is that this renaissance flourished, not through learning to speak and write English, but through the mother tongue, Urdu. It remained wholly indigenous. Those who were its highest exponents never used English as a medium of conversation, though they read and studies English books. They also refused to adopt English customs.

To give one example, Munshi Zaka Ullah made an immensely laborious effort to reproduce the science and mathematics of the

West in an Urdu form. He also wrote modern history and geography in the same manner. These books were steeped in Western culture, although the author never spoke English, but only read it in books. He greatly lamented, in his later life, that Urdu had not been made all along the medium of instruction in the new universities of northern India instead of English.

All this remarkable revival of learning went on in Delhi right up to the outbreak of the mutiny of the sepoys at Meerut on May 11,1857. These troops marched into Delhi in the course of a few hours, and from that time forward modern education and culture ceased. Those who had received the western learning were all suspected by the mutineers. Professor Ramchandra and many others barely escaped with their lives. For many years after the siege and capture of Delhi every sign of the earlier education had vanished. Only very slowly did it return and it never reached in later days the glory of its first efflorescence.

The community that suffered most at the hands of the British when the mutiny had been quelled was that of the Muslims. The rebellion was regarded, quite unjustly, as having had its origin among *them.* The truth seems to be that discontent was universal both among Hindus and Muslims alike, and the sepoy rebellion fanned the flame into open revolt. But the theory somehow got abroad, and was very widely held by British administrators, that the whole outbreak was the last bid for power on the part of Muslims, who had thus sought to restore at Delhi the throne of the Great Moghuls.

On this account, because they were so suspected even after the rebellion had been crushed, The Muslims steadily lost ground, both in education and in Government favour. Some of the noblest families were brought to the verge of ruin, and in many parts of the north of India the plight of the Muslims became almost desperate. In Delhi itself even the direct descendants of the royal family lived in miserable destitution. As late as the early years of the twentieth century this state of things continued. Illiteracy among the Muslim population soon reached a far higher percentage than among the other communities, and in spite every effort that is now being made to recover lost ground, this deficiency still remains.

The one man who broke the spell of this desperate state of affairs was Sir Syed Ahmed Khan. He had passed through the dreadful days of the revolt with a record of service to the Government which gave him a right to speak on behalf of his own Muslim community. His life during those terrible days read like a romance. He made his appeal just at the time when the official world had begun to be seriously alarmed at the backwardness of Muslim education and to realize the danger to political affairs if this increased still further. There were enlightened educationists also among the officials to whom Sir Syed Ahmed appealed in the name of justice as well as of high expendiency.

Thus he struck the right note a the right time by his public pronouncement that his own Muslim people had been unfairly treated. His appeal went home because it came from the depths of his own heart. Strangely enough, as we look back today, the greatest opposition which he had to face came from within his own community. For, there were men of deep piety and ancient learning among them who regarded Western education itself as leading to irreligion and atheism. They were content to go on with Arabic culture alone, while turning their backs on all the new knowledge which the West had brought into the world.

But this reactionary educational policy was entirely contrary to the true spirit of Islam. For the Prophet had urged his followers to get knowledge wherever it could be found and had encouraged learning of every kind. But one of the results of the long and studied neglect of the Muslims by the ruling power had been to drive their thoughts and sentiments inward, until the new learning which was so rapidly coming into India from every side became regarded as *harām*—an unclean thing.

No one but a giant in intellectual power and vigorous personality could have overcome this obstacle so completely as to make the leading Muhammadan families, on whom success really depended, ready to defy the anathemas of their own religious leaders and send their sons to a college which had already been condemned as leading to atheism.

In an almost superhuman task of removing obstacles of this kind out of the way and obtaining the necessary funds, Sir Syed Ahmed was helped most of all by those at Delhi of his own age and standing, who had already received Western education before the outbreak of 1857, and yet had in no way changed their manner of life or dress of thrown over their religion. Maulvi Nazir Ahmed was a stalwart champion whose name was known everywhere in the Punjab and Uttar Pradesh for his brilliant Urdu prose. It was true that many were afraid of him as a 'free-thinker' in certain matters of religion, but no one could deny either his life of strict piety or his championship of the Muslim faith. His Arabic learning also was almost unparalled. He became one of the ardent followers and lieutenants of Sir Syed Ahmed Khan.

It may be well to give at this point the carefully considered verdict of one who knew Sir Syed intimately and had worked with him in his great enterprise at Aligarh from the very start. Sir Theodore Morison writes: 'Sir Syed was first and last a religious reformer; he summoned his people to return to the sanity and simplicity of primitive Islam. He denounced the superstitions and bigotry with which their faith had become encrusted; he told his people that the only instrument which could accomplish this regeneration was education and that education must be on Western lines; there was nothing contrary to the principles of Islam, he said, in the acquisition of Western learning—as the Maulvis ignorantly proclaimed. Had not the Prophet said: 'Go even to the Walls of China for the sake of learning......' Sir Syed was violently attacked for his courageous opinions and suffered much social persecution, but no persecution could daunt his leonine courage; his great personality prevailed at length over opposition and misrepresentation, and in the last years of his life he exercised a marvellous ascendancy over Muslim opinion. When he was laid to rest by the side of the mosque of the college in Aligarh, a lifelong friend of his said to me: 'Other men have written books and founded colleges; but to arrest, as with a wall, the degeneration of a whole people—that is the work of a prophet!' That remark conveys, in my opinion, a correct judgement of Sir Syed's personality and of the quality of his work. For myself I can say that I have never met another man so great as he.'*

The Aligarh movement, which was thus started by its founder Sir Syed Ahmed, has had its times of depression as well as its remarkable successes. Much depended on the English principals of the M.A.O. College, who were carefully chosen by the board of trustees with the help of friends of the movement in England. In Beck, Morrison and Arnold, three well-wishers of Islam were chosen in succession, and this helped to set the tone of the College and to create public confidence among the leading Muslims in its favour.

The movement was by no means confined to Aligarh, though that was made its center. For in every city of the north India, and in other parts of India also, the new spirit spread rapidly. Schools and colleges sprang up where the Muslim culture was taught side by side with the learning of the West. If today the Muslim community has made up which of the leeway that it had lost during the latter half of the nineteenth century, it is in a very great measure due to that spirit of Islam which Sir Syed Ahmed rightly declared to be the friend of all human culture and science in whatever part of the world it may be found. We shall note in a later chapter the effect of the Aligarh movement upon the political life of the Muslim community after the founding of the National Congress in 1885.

OTHER RELIGIOUS MOVEMENTS

The Sikhs, who are to be found chiefly in the Punjab, have a romantic history of their own which has been told in story and song. They form a community based on religion which traces back its origin to Guru Nanak, who was born in the Pubjab in A.D.

---

* *Political India,* p. 88. by (Oxford University Press).

1469. He was a devotee of the Bhakti school of religious devotion and also a social reformer. His followers were given the name of 'Sikh', which means 'disciple'. During the persecutions of this new religion by the Moghul Emperors at Delhi, the community was welded together and grew in strength and also in political importance. This came to a head in the martyrdom at Delhi of the ninth Guru, Tegh Bahadur, and the organising ability of his son, Guru Govind Singh, who transformed the Sikhs into a militant body called the 'Khalsa'. He gave to every member the name Singh, which means Lion, and constituted sacraments which bound the religious members in one brotherhood. The body of scriptures called the *Granth Sahib* was completed and a central shrine was built at Amritsar, which was named the Golden Temple. The city of Amritsar thenceforward became the center of the new faith.

The remarkable reign of Ranjit Singh, who conquered the Punjab in 1820, gave to this religion a political importance which it had never had before. But when the maharaja died in 1839 this military sovereignty in the north-west of India fell to pieces. In the revolt of 1857 the Sikh troops were enlisted on the side of the British and this fact kept the revolt from spreading in the north-west beyond the city of Delhi.

The great revival among the Sikhs came after this outbreak was over. A strong communal spirit developed which sought at the same time to purge the Sikh faith from many abuses. These made it in some danger of relapsing into Hinduism once more in matters of caste and idol-worship. The reformers sought to purge the Sikh *Gurdwaras* (temples) of anything idolatrous and at the same time to set up in them abbots, called *mahants*, whose lives were lived in accordance with the religion they professed.

Along with these reforms in worship, education was carried forwards by means of a remarkable number of Sikh schools and colleges. No outstanding personality can be mentioned separately, but what is all the more noticeable has been the large number of religious reformers who have devoted themselves to the good of the community. The Sikhs have also traveled more widely to every part of the world than any other body among the people of India, and they have formed, since the Pubjab came under British control, an important and celebrated section of the Indian Army. In the political development of India they have also taken a prominent part and have given progressive and enlightened leaders to the Congress movement.

The Christian Church

An the beginning of the nineteenth century the Christian Church in India, in its ancient forms of orthodoxy, had lost much of its inner power of reformation and revival. Like Hinduism and Islam, it had suffered for many centuries from a slow decline which had reached its lowest point as the eighteenth century drew to an end.

The ancient history of Christianity in India forms a profoundly interesting study. Its origin is said to have dated back to the Apostle, St. Thomas, and the record of his name is still preserved in San Thome and St. Thomas's Mount, which lie just outside the city of Madras. Early in the fourth century (the date is still uncertain) large numbers of Syrian Christians from the Near East found a haven of refuge from persecution along the Malbar and Coromandel coasts of southern India. They were very hospitably welcomed by the ruling princes of those day and were given at a later period their own place in the body politic.

Much later, in the fifteenth and sixteenth centuries, a second influx came with the Portuguese, who made Goa the center of their new maritime empire. Very soon conversion to the Christian faith was made an integral part of their imperial rule and large numbers submitted to the invaders and became baptized. At the same time St. Francis Xavier, by his marvellously saintly life, raised the Christian ideal in India to an altogether higher level. The missionaries who followed him literally laid down their lives for the truth they taught. St. Francis Xavier himself died young owing to his fervour of religious devotion. Rarely has such a noble Christian apostle come to the East. His tomb at Goa is a center of pilgrimage, not only for Christians, but also for those of other faiths.

With the decline of the maritime empire of Portugal in the East, the Catholic Church in western India, which owed allegiance to Rome, lost most of its imperial support. But missionaries who lived saintly lives still came out from Europe and kept alive the Christian faith among those who were living along the western coast. They also built up congregations of Christians in the south. Nevertheless a slow decline had set in towards the end of the eighteenth century, as has already been stated.

The new impetus at the beginning of the nineteenth century came first of all in the south from the reformed Churches of Europe. The Lutherans and other missionary bodies began their memorable work chiefly among the untouchables, and vast numbers of these unfortunate and despised people embraced the Christian religion. Very soon these outcasts of humanity began to show the power within themselves of rising to a new life which they had received from their Christian faith. This gained for them a respect from those who had treated them before as unworthy even to be touched or approached, and had regarded them almost as sub-human.

It would be difficult to exaggerate the effect of this in the long run on the rising political and social life of India in the nineteenth century. It meant the future emancipation of a large part of the population from a condition almost worse than slavery. That emancipation has not even yet been accomplished, but this was the first step towards it.

One other factor needs to be mentioned which broke down barriers of a different kind and led to important political results. Western education was introduced into India at the very first in a large measure through Christian colleges and schools. The most noticeable feature in this respect was the moral basis and the personal influence of noble self-sacrificing lives upon the students. This produced an idealism altogether different from the purely secular and professional teaching which was given in Government institutions. Thus the Christian education helped to build up character among those who were non-Christians as well as among Christians and served to direct their minds towards the most urgent social reforms. If the political life of India were to be built up on strong and secure foundations, these social injustices had to be eliminated, and here the Christian colleges, whose doors were open to all, played a notable part. To take one example only, the life-long work of a great principal, such as Dr. Miller, of the Madras Christian College, shows in a striking manner the value to the national movement of an education carried out on so broad a Christian basis.

Added to these more general results of the modern movement in the Christian Church their must also be reckoned a revival in the south of India among the more ancient Christian Churches—both Syrian and Roman. It has been already explained how these had become integrated with the life of India itself, since they could trace back their own history for many centuries. Their revival was an asset to Indian politics, and it is noticeable today that some of the ablest leaders, such as Mr. George Joseph and Mr. Johan Baptista, have come from these ancient Churches. It is equally noticeable that others, such as Kali Charan Banerji, S.K. Rudra, K.T. Paul and S.K. Datta have come from the reformed Churches.

The Parsees

The Parsees in India have a history that runs parallel in remarkable ways to that of the ancient Christian Churches. For the Parsees also sought for a refuge from their own mother country, many centuries ago, and they found it in India. They eagerly \accepted the hospitality that was offered to them and sent for others who had remained in Persia. What is now the Maharashtra State became their new home and they have clung to it ever since.

Again, we note how with them, as with the Christian exiles from Syria, the original purity of their faith became in the course of many centuries overlaid with meaningless forms and ceremonies.

These had gradually taken the place of living religion in the hearts of the people. Thus the nobility of the faith of their founder, Zarathustra, was being threatened. Nothing short of a revival from within could have saved it from ultimate extinction.

That revival came during the whole period of the nineteenth century. It does not seem to have been due to any single personality or religious leader. It was due rather to the innate virtues which had been developed within the community itself. Through these it was able to withstand the shocks of time and even the onset of decay. For the religious instinct within the heart recovered speedily when brought into contact with the new learning which had come from the West. The Parsees were able to assimilate it without losing their own identity. In many of their social customs they stood out conspicuously for conditions which were altogether healthy and sound, as compared with those around them. The position of women was dignified; marriage was celebrated at a mature age; all members of the community shared a common religious equality: those who were poverty-stricken or otherwise distressed were generously supported. Thus they instinctively appropriated the best that could be offered in the Western education that they now received with its democratic background. Their social life was not out of harmony with it. In the business of everyday life the Parsee community has shown outstanding capacity, and the great city of Bombay owes very much of its advance in modern methods of administration to its energy and enterprise.

From the very first the Parsees have been prominent in the great work of national reconstruction which the political movement has brought about. To mention three names only, the early history of the Congress during its first phase is bound up with the three outstanding figures of Dadabhai Naoroji, Sir Pherozeshah Mehta, and Sir Dinshaw Edulji Wacha. Their presence within the Congress ranks in its early days was indispensable. Not merely were they outstanding personalities, but they had also that splendid business capacity which was sorely needed if the Congress was to be carried forward on sound practical lines. It will be explained also in a later chapter how the Congress in its early days owed more to the faithful work of Dadabhai Naoroji in London than to any other single person. Thus as compared with their almost insignificant numbers in the vast Indian population the Parsees have provided a very remarkable array of Congress leaders, and it may also be stated that all through the period with which this volume deals their reputation remained at this high level.

Jains and Buddhists

In this summary of religious movements throughout India the Jains and Buddhists have not as yet been mentioned in any detail. Buddhism is almost entirely confined to Burma, which has now been separated from India and even in earlier days naturally stood apart from the Indian Continent as a distinct geographical area. The Jains are to be found in many parts of India, especially as a commercial body engaged in banking and industrial affairs. They have shared along with Hinduism the national and social awakening and have produced men of very great eminence in the business world. In this way they have made their own deep impression on the national life as a whole, but in the purely political field they have not taken much active part. At the same time their religious faith has been quickened by the recovery of their ancient literature, and the principle of non-violence for which they have stood out so firmly through all the centuries has been made one of the greatest factors, under Mahatma Gandhi's leadership, in the programme of the National Congress.

—*C.F. Andrews*

4. *Influence of Renaissance and Reformation*

The battle of Plassey (23 June, 1757) sowed the seeds of British political supremacy in Bengal, which was extended throughout India during the hundred years following it. The expansion of the British dominion in India, and the development of an Indo-British administrative system as a corollary to it, naturally conducted India through manifold process of transition,—political, economic and social. This for diverse reasons, generated fumes of discontent among various sections of the people in different parts of India, which burst into flames in the movement of 1857-59[1]. The Movement of 1857-59 was no doubt suppressed by the Government. But it produced significant consequences for India and its memory recalled in the subsequent years certainly worked against British imperialism.

The post-1859 period was marked by the development of some new forces in India destined of effect transformation in the various phases of her life. Cultural renaissance and the Reformation movements in India during the second half of the nineteenth century were then producing a new awakening in Indian minds. The political development of modern India has been an aspect of a general renaissance pervading different spheres of life,—religion, society and culture—and producing momentous consequences in each. The inevitable penetration of its spirit into the field of politics generated there a commotion which gathered an irresistible momentum defying all the weapons of an aggressive imperialism.

It is true that growing acquaintance, through the medium of western education, with the progressive political thought of the West and the stirring achievements of the revolutions of modern Europe resulting in the triumphs of nationalism and democracy saturated the minds of some educated Indians with the ideas of liberalism, civic liberty and freedom. But this by itself could not have produced and fostered a truly Indian national movement if there had not been at the same time a genuine urge from within, a spirit of renaissance aiming at the revival of what was noble and elevating in India's past and also at the redemption of her people from the crushing load of unreason, social abuses and political servitude.

Indeed, discovery of India's past through the honest endeavours of scholars, poets and social or religious reformers proved to be a highly fertile source of inspiration generating in the minds of many a feeling of regard for the motherland. Indian nationalism has been, remarks Ramsay Macdonald truly, "the revival of her historical tradition and the liberation of the soul of a people." "Indian Nationality is," in the words of Annie Besant, "not a plant of mushroom growth but a giant of the forest with millennia behind it".[2]

The establishment of the Asiatic Society in Bengal was a significant landmark in the history of cultural renaissance in modern India. The researches of many zealous antiquarians, Indian as well as European, revealed the majesty and glory of India's old civilization, which served to inspire generations of people in this land. No doubt the pioneer workers in this respect were a number of European scholars like Jones, Prinsep, Wilson, Colebrooke, Rosen, Roth, Burnouf, Schelegel, Bopp, Max Muller and some others. But it is highly gratifying to note how for this supremely important task of rediscovering and reinterpreting India's past we owe a heavy debt to our distinguished countrymen like Rammohan Roy, Radhakanta Dev, Rajendra Lal Mitra, Vishwanath Narayan Mandlik, Mani Shankar Jatashankar, Bhau Daji, Bhagwan Lal Indraji, M.G. Ranade, B.G. Tilak, R.G. Bhandarkar, K.T. Telang,

R.C. Dutt, Manamohan Chakravarty, Haraprasad Shastri and some others.

At first "the new wine of Western learning" went to the heads of young Bengal producing "denationalizing tendencies"[3] in the minds of many of those who tasted it. But the Indian religious and social reform movements did much to arrest the evil effects of the blind imitation of what was apparently glittering in an imposing exotic civilization and to maintain the dignity of our national culture. Rajanarain Bose, a progress Bramho who had drunk deep of Western education, stood undauntedly to uphold the superiority of our culture at a time when some of our countrymen, receiving new education, were growing prejudiced against it. To check denationalization Rajnarain started in 1861 a Society called the *Society for the Promotion of National Feeling among the Educated Natives of Bengal* and issued a prospectus for it in the form of a pamphlet containing its aims and objects.[4] Bipin Chandra Pal writes that Rajnarain's lecture in Bengalee on *Hindu Dharmer Shresthata* or 'the superiority of Hinduism' was 'really first public protest of the age-long Nation-spirit of India against the threatened domination of our thought, and life by the aggressive and colour-proud civilization of Europe."[5] This view was more emphatically Ranade and Vivekananda to nourish our early nationalism.

We should also note how a galaxy of inspired geniuses produced literature of a highly creative nature, marked by a marvellous fusion of the old and the new, a grand intermingling of the best literary traditions of old India with the good features of the culture of the modern world outside, by feelings of deep adoration for the motherland, and by profound emphasis on the virtue of patriotism. Influence of literature of this kind in stimulating dormant souls can hardly be over-estimated R.W. Frazer very significantly observes: "Men such as Rammohan Roy, Keshab Chandra Sen, Michael Madhusudan Datta, Bankim Chandra Chatterjee, Kashinath Trimbak Telang, are no bastard bantlings of a Western civilization; they were creative geniuses worthy to be reckoned in the history of India with such men of old as Kalidas,

Chaitanya, Jayadeva, Tulsidas and Shankaracharya and destined in the future to shine clear as the first glowing sparks sent out in the fiery turmoil where old and new were fusing."[6]

In 1860, Dinabandhu Mitra produced in his work, entitled '*Nila-Darpan" (Mirrors of Indigo),* a scathing satire on the indigo-planters of Bengal, whose dealings with the local ryots form a tale of unspeakable tyrannies. Hem Chandra Banerjee (1838-1903) 'voiced in his national lyrics the sense of impotence of his people to assert their legitimate rights and self-respect against their British master'[7] Bipin Chandra Pal thus describes Hem Chandra Banerjee's influence upon him; "Hem Chandra, however, was our special favourite. The intense patriotic passion that breathed through his poems captured our youthful minds in a way which no other Bengalee poems had done. The new generation of English-educated Bengalees had already commenced to advance themselves to positions of trust and responsibility in the new Administration. In the learned professions of law and medicine also, they were gradually asserting themselves as against the British members. A new spirit of independence and self-assertion was increasingly manifesting itself in the conduct and conversations of the English educated Bengalee. All these had already commenced to provoke a racial conflict in the country. Hem Chandra was, in a special sense, the poet of this new conflict and of the racial self-respect and sensitive patriotism, born of it."

Hem Chandra expressed in one stanza of his '*Bharat Sangeet'* or the 'Song of India':

"Sing, O my clarionet! Sing to these words:
Every one is free in this wide world.
Every one is awake in the glory of science,
India alone lieth asleep."

We read also in the same song:

"China and Burma, and uncivilized Japan,
Even they are independent, they are superior,
India alone knoweth no waking."

Another national song contained the following heartrending note:

'O, India, weep, weep Thou,
As long as thy polluted atoms have not been washed away into the waters of the ocean,
So long weep thou, so long weep.'

Ranglal observed in his ode to Liberty: 'Breathes there the man, who would like to live, though shorn of liberty".

Govinda Chandra Roy, a nineteenth century Bengalee student of Agra, gave expression to his feelings of patriotism in some of his most touching songs. In one of these lie said:—

'How long will it take thee, Oh Bharat,
to swim across this ocean of misery?
Or, sinking and sinking in depression,
Wilt thou enter the nether regions for ever?
Having gladly offered thy jewels to the
Stranger, thou carriest now only an iron chain
On thy breast!
There are rows of light in thy cities (owned by
the stranger)
But thou art in darkness all the same.'

In another song the author pathetically noted:
'O India, gloomy is thy face, beautiful that
was as the moon;
Day and night tears flow from thy eyes.'

The writings of Bankim Chandra Chatterjee revealed remarkably the inward spirit of Indian life and thought."[8]

Their lessons penetrated into the hearts of our countrymen and stirred them to their very depths. He was not only a 'propnet'[9] of Indian cultural renaissance, but also, as Shri Aurobindo puts it, 'a seer and a nation-builder' and one of the 'Makers of Modern India.'[10] It is well known how greatly stimulating has been the influence of the famous *Anthem 'Bande Mataram'* recorded in his classic work *Ananda Math*. The *'Bangadarshan,'* which began to be published as a weekly paper in Calcutta from April 1872, proved to be a very effective organ in contemporary Bengal for the expression of thoughts of her educated youths on the varied problems of life and society, and this facilitated the growth of our early natioinalism. We read as follows in the Hindi drama *'Bharat-Durdasa'* written by Harish Chandra in 1880:

'O Brother Indians, come and let all of us weep;
Alas, alas, the misery of India is not to be witnessed.
The one whom God granted first of all wealth and power,
The one who was made civilized by the Creator first of all,
The one who bathed first of all in beauty, colour of *rasa*
And the one who first of all caught the fruits of learning,
Is now seen last of all.
Alas, alas, the misery of India is not to be witnessed.

* * * *

The British Government has arranged all big comforts:
But that this wealth goes away to foreign land is pricking,
And even then dearness, famine and diseases are spreading.
Oh, oh, God gives troubles doubly day by day:
And over all the catastrophe of taxation is come.
Alas, alas, the misery of India is not to be witnessed.

A powerful dramatic literature, coming out of the pen of D.L. Roy and some others also contributed to stir national feeling. For about half a century Rabindranath's works interpreted in a unique way the true spirit of Indian culture and civilization. "Tagore's Poetry," remarks Ramsay Macdonald significantly, "is India. It is the product of his devotion of Indian culture. It is the soul of a people, not merely the emotion of a man; a systematic view of life, not merely a poetic mood; a culture, not merely a tune".[11] A mighty stream of inspiration has flown out of the stirring speeches and writings of Sarojini Naidu, Sarala Devi, and some other highly gifted ladies of India.

Spiritual idealism has been also a highly potent factor in promoting the progress of nationalism in modern India. The Indian social and religious reform movements of this period have undoubtedly exercised much influence on the course of our national development. Referring to India's new awakening. Rev. C.F. Andrews wrote about 1912: 'But this awakening would have been wholly insufficient to usher in a new era if it had not been combined with a second and even greater change. A religious Reformation has been advancing side by side with the new renaissance."[12] Rammohan Roy, Devendra Nath Tagore, Ishwar Chandra Vidyasagar, Keshav Chandra Sen, Dayananda Saraswati, M.G. Ranade, Bal Gangadhar Tilak, Ram Krishna Paramahansa and his great disciple Vivekananda and Shri Aurobindo impressed on the minds of our countrymen the profoundness and sublimity of our ancient thought and created therein an indomitable urge for national regeneration on the basis of the best in Indian culture. Rammohan Roy was not only the "first earnest-minded investigator of comparative religion and truth" and the pioneer social reformer in modern India, but also an ardent champion of freedom. William Adam, a Baptist Missionary associated with him for some time, remarked: 'He would be free or not be at all......Love of freedom was perhaps the strongest passion of his soul.' In his latter to Buckingham, dated the 11th August, 1821, Rammohan expressed his strong conviction in the following words; 'Enemies to liberty and friends of despotism have never been and will never be ultimately successful. Particularly significant in this respect was the influence of the reforming activities of India during the second half of the nineteenth century and the early years of the present century. Famous Theosophists like Colonel Olcott and Mrs. Annie Besant, who were themselves great admirers of India and helped the cause of Indian nationalism through their writings and speeches, tell how Swami Dayanand exerted 'great nationalizing influence.'[13]In his numerous speeches and writings Swami Vivekananda impressed upon his countrymen as well as upon some foreigners the capacity of India's inborn spiritual genius, her rich cultural heritage, taught them self-confidence and trust, and thus immensely stimulated

Indian nationalism. "The queen of his adoration," says Sister Nivedita, his brilliantly gifted Irish disciple, "was his motherland." "Oh India! Wouldst thou attain," he exclaimed, "by means of thy disgraceful cowardice, that freedom deserved only by the brave and the heroic? Oh India! Forget not that the ideal of thy womanhood is Sita, Savitri, Damayanti, forget not that the God thou worshipest is the great ascetic of ascetics, the all-renouncing Sankara, the Lord of Uma; forget not that thy marriage, thy wealth, thy life are not for sense-pleasure, are not for thy individual personal happiness; forget not that thou art born as a sacrifice to the Mother's altar; forget not that thy social order is but the reflex of the Infinite Universal Motherhood: forget not that the lower classes, the ignorant, the poor, the illiterate, the cobbler, the sweeper are thy flesh and blood, thy brothers. Thou brave one, be hold, take courage, be proud that thou art an Indian, and proudly proclaim: 'I am an Indian, every Indian is my brother'. Say: 'The ignorant Indian, the poor and destitute Indian the Brahman Indian, the Pariah Indian is my brother'.

Thou, too, clad with but a rag round thy lions proudly proclaim at the top of thy voice: 'The Indian is my brother, the Indian is my life, India's gods and goddesses are my God, India's society is the cradle of my infancy, the pleasure garden of my youth, the sacred heaven, the Varanasi of my old age. Say, brother: The soil of India is my highest heaven, the good of India is my good, and repeat and pray day and night; 'O Thou Lord of Gauri, O Thou Mother of the Universe, vouchsafe manliness unto me. O Thou Mother of Strength, take away my weakness, take away my unmanliness, and make me a Man."

The thoughts and activities of Bal Gangadhar Tilak, Shri Aurobindo and some others richly fed this current of inspiration. The conception of India as the 'Mother' originated with Bankim Chandra, who, in a moment of inspiration, first 'uttered' in his *Bande Mataram* the *'Mantra* of an awakened nationalism." To Shri Aurobindo India was the eternal and infinite Mother, and love of her was a spiritual experience. 'Patriotism', he wrote, cannot be anything sort of a desire to redeem one's country. It cannot bear to look upon the country as a sepulchre though it may seem so. It feels the immortality shining beneath these ruins with which subjection has overspread the country. It feels the pulsations of the immense eternal life of the country through the artificial crust with which the great sleeper has been covered as with a shroud."[14] He once wrote in the paper, *Bande Mataram:* "The work of national emancipation is a great and holy *yajna* of which boycott, Swadeshi, national education and every other activity, a great and small, are only major and minor parts. Liberty is the fruit we seek from the sacrifice and Motherland the goddess to whom we offer it; into the seven leaping tongues of the fire of the *jajna* we must offer all that we are and all that we have, feeding the fire even with our blood and lives and happiness of our nearest and dearest; for the Motherland is the goddess who loves not a mained and imperfect sacrifice, and freedom was never won from the Gods by a grudging giver."[15] The new nationalism of the early years of present century was characterized by an intense religious conviction as Shri Aurobindo expressed in this passage. Another prominent Indian leader of the time, Shri Bipin Chandra Pal (one of the trio *Pal-Bal-Lal*), significantly refers to it in the following words: "All those old and traditional gods and goddesses who had lost their hold upon the modern mind have been reinstalled with a new historic and nationalistic interpretation in the mind and soul of the people. Hundreds of thousands of our people have commenced to hail their motherland today as Durga, Kalee, Jagadhatree. They are no longer mere mythological conceptions or legendary persons or even poetic symbols. They are different manifestations of the Mother. The Mother is the spirit of India."[16] In an article entitled *The Age of Gita again in India,* Barindra Kumar Ghose expounded the gospel of their movement by writing: "Shri Krishna has said in *Gita* that whenever there is a decline of righteousness and a rise in unrighteousness there shall be a reincarnation of God to rescue the good, to destroy the wrong-door, and to establish righteousness. At the present moment righteousness is declining and unrighteousness is springing up in India. A handful of alien robbers are running the crores of the people of India by robbing the wealth of India. Through the hard grinding of their servitude, the ribs of their countless people are being broken to pieces......Fear not, oh Indians, God will not remain inactive......He will keep his word. Placing firm reliance on the promise of God, invoke His power......When the lightning of Heaven flashes in their hearts, men perform impossible deeds."[17] Mahatma Gandhi's own conviction in this respect was thus expressed by him: To see the universal and all-pervading Spirit of Truth face to face one must be able to love the meanest of creation as oneself. And a man who aspires after this cannot afford to keep out of any field of life. That is why my deviation to truth has drawn me into the field of polities; and I can say without the slightest hesitation and yet in all humility that those who say that religion has nothing to do with politics do not know what religion means."[18]

REFERENCES

1. Sashi Bhusan Chaudhuri, *Civil Disturbances During the British Rule in India* (1765-1875); K.K. Datta, *The Santal Insurrection of* 1855-57.
2. Annie Besant, *How India Wrought For Freedom,* L.
3. Ronaldshey, *The Heart of Aryavarta,* p. 47.
4. For full text of it, vide *Modern Review, January-June,* 1944.
5. Bipin Chandra Pal, *Memories of My Life and Timee,* I., p. 262.
6. Frazer, *Literary History of India,* pp. 416-447.
7. Bipin Chandra Pal, *Memories of My Life and Times,* 1, p. 252.
8. Frazer, *op. cit.*, p. 420.
9. Bepin Chandra Pal, *Memories of My Life and Times,* I, p. 226.
10. Shri Aurobindo, *Bankim, Tilak, and Dayananda,* p. 9.
11. Ramsay Macdonald, *Government of India,* p. 245.
12. C.F. Andrews. *The Renaissance of India* p. 11.
13. A.C. Mazumdar, *Indian National Evolution,* p. 23.

14. Quoted in *Sri Aurobindo and Indian Freedom by Sishir Kumar Mitra,* pp. 47.48.

15. *Ibid,* p. 49.

16. Bipin Chandra Pal, *The Soul of India* (1916), pp. 187-18.

17. Quoted in Chirol, *Indian Unrest,* pp. 90-91.

18. *Autobiography,* p. 615.

5. The Renaissance in British India and its Effect

The marvellous transformation and modernisation of our vernacular literatures: its stages

The first effect of the Indian Renaissance was felt in our vernacular literatures, which have undergone a complete change and at the same time approximated to one parent standard, namely, English literature. The work of centuries has been crowded into a few decades in this evolution of our modern literatures. My illustrations are all taken from Bengal.

The first generation of Indians educated in English accepted European literature philosophy and history, and to a lesser extent science,—with enthusiasm and tried to diffuse them among their countrymen by translation, while attempting little or no original composition of their own. They did not display any literary genius except in manipulating the language for a new need. To this earliest generation belonged Krishna Mohan Banerji (1813-1885), Rājendra Lāla Mitra (1821-1892), Peāry Chānd Mitra (1815-1883) and Pandit Ishwar Chandra Vidyāsāgar (1820-1891). They wrote translations, adaptations and epitomes of English works, and did not create any revolution in Bengali thought or style.

A little later came another group of authors, who introduced the new order in its full majesty. They were Michael Madhusudan Dutt the poet (1824-1873), Dinabandhu Mitra the dramatist (1830-1874),—each of whom reigned over one branch of literature and turned it into a new channel, where it has since flowed at his bidding. Their work has been continued by their successors, notably by Hem Chandra Banerji (1838-1902), Nabin Chandra Sen (1847-1908), and Rabindra Nāth Tāgore (1861-1941). In their writings the influence of English literature is unmistakable, but equally unmistakable is their success in adapting the foreign spirit and literary model (and even technique) to the Indian mind and tradition. The best specimens of this new vernacular literature are European in spirit, in outlook, in literary devices, in the choice and treatment of subjects; but they retain a close connection with the best in the literature and life of ancient India. They represent the spirit of England clad in a half oriental garb. There has been no wholesale borrowing, but an assimilation of foreign models, while retaining a surprising amount of originality.

How the style has been changed

Our vernacular languages have been wonderfully developed and in some cases almost revolutionized by the example of English style and the needs of the modern world. Our literary language has become both simpler and harder at the same time. It has acquired an unwanted flexibility, variety and naturalness of movement, while the vocabulary has been greatly amplified. Madhusudan Dutt and Ishwar Chandra Vidyāsāgar, (middle 19th century), greatly modernized the Bengali tongue and made it a proper vehicle for expressing the varied thoughts and feelings of the present day. Both followed the classical style, *i.e.,* They used Sanskrit words by preference and avoided colloquial or homely expressions. But at the same time there is no stiffness, no pedantry, no obscurity in their style, and their genius was shown in combining clearness, sweetness and beauty of expression with strength and purity of diction and a certain music of sound. The Indian drama has been completely transformed since the middle of the 19th century, and is now really a close imitation of the modern European drama. Our greatest divergences from our older literature have been in the departments of the drama and the novel, in which we have been wholesale borrowers from the West. And this has been the case in every Indian vernacular.

The influence of Europe has also enriched our literature by kindling the patriotic spirit and developing a regard for our historic past. This awakened sense of nationality has added a manly and noble element to the Indian literature of our day. Here the Tagores showed the way.

In the days before our Renaissance all Indian vernacular literatures dealt only with religious subjects, erotics, and mythological or heroic narratives. Poetry was the only medium employed, except for pithy sayings and business correspondence. Worst of all, there was an absolute lack of suitable text-books which could be placed in the hands of boys and girls at school, by reason of their purity of tone and gradation of lessons. Even for grown-up readers fiction and history of the type popular in Europe for centuries before 1850 were unknown among us. All these types in our midst today are the creation of the English age. The creators of our modern vernacular prose literature began with the translation of English books (*like Rasselas, the Vicar of Wakefield, etc.*), then advanced to adaptations and colourable imitations of their English models, and finally produced original works of the same *genre* as their foreign prototypes.

The net result of this literary revolution has been that the best pieces of modern Indian literature do not appear foreign or grotesque to European readers, they really approximate to the spirit of Europe in plot, in treatment of the subject and in the general characteristics of style. This fact is recognised by the best of our nationalist writers. Rabindranāth Tagore thus replied to Chandranāth Bose, a literary champion of orthodox "Aryan" ideals, in August 1891: "You say that my writings betray the European type to mind and not the Hindu mentality .....When our social revolution has come to a close and we are able to think calmly, it will be found that there is no real conflict between the Hindu mind and the European mind, and that it is the lifeless orthodoxy and fantastic perverted Hinduism of present-day India in her degradation, that are truly un-Hindu."

Then, again, in the 19th century we recovered our long-lost ancient literatures, Vedic and Buddhistic, as well as the buried architectural monuments of the Hindu days. The Vedas and their commentaries had almost totally disappeared from the plains of Aryāvarta (Northern India), where none could interpret them, none had even a complete manuscript of the text. The English printed this ancient Scripture of the Indo-Aryans and brought it to our doors. A similar restoration of the ancient literature of Buddhism to the land of its origin has taken place thorough the enterprise and scholarship of Europeans. From Nepāl, China, Central Asia, and Japan English French and German scholars have sent the lost Buddhistic works to Europe and Europe has printed them and made them available to us.

But the mere study of a foreign or long-lost literature does not constitute a Renaissance. There must be a new birth of the spirit, there must be reforms in society religion and morals, following the intellectual awakening, before we can truly call the movement a Renaissance.

Social Reform an Effect of the Indian Renaissance

As surely as the Renaissance in Europe was followed by the Reformation, so in India too a modification of our social relations, our general outlook upon life, and our religious doctrines and practices was bound to result from the action of English education. Attempts at Hindu social reform began to take shape from 1855, under Pandit Ishwar Chandra Vidyāsāgar (1820-1891) who fought for and obtained legal sanction to the marriage or Hindu widows (1856) and tried (though without success) to forbid polygamy. Schools for Hindu girls began to be founded at this time, the Christian missionaries having opened schools for their converts' daughters 30 or 35 years earlier. But social reform received its greatest impetus and spread outside Calcutta to the country districts after the Sepoy Mutiny, from the personal magnetism and organizing genius of Keshav Chandra Sen (1838-1884). In addition to spreading female education and widow marriage, he organized temperance associations, night-schools, "uplift work" for the lower classes, intercaste marriages, the creation and diffusion of cheap and pure popular literature, famine relief, and other forms of social service. In Bengal, the most conspicuous followers in the path thus marked out were Shiva Nāth Shāstri (1847-1919) and Anand Mohan Bose (1847-1906); immediately after Keshav.

The Reform movement in England which drew its inspiration from Bentham and Mill and which began to bear fruit from 1832 onwards, first made itself felt among the Indian people about 25 years later, as was until recently the case with all our borrowings from Europe. In England it was dissociated from religion, but the Indian movement went hand in hand with religious reform and was the direct offspring of the latter force.

The Renaissance continued unchecked and in full swing for more than one generation crowded with events, and everything old or purely indigenous seemed to go down before it. But the very completeness of the victory of the new light led to a reaction in favour of orthodoxy, which was as curious in its nature as it was grotesque in its garb. At the first flush of the Renaissance, our ardent youths had been drawn to Christianity, because the inner spirit of Hinduism had never been taught to them and they could find nothing but unreason and repulsiveness in the externals of Hinduism as practised in their day. To them the reform of such religion seemed an impossibility. This explains the conversion to Christianity of Krishna Mohan Banerji (1813-1885), Lāl Behāri De (1826-1894), Govinda Dutt (the father of the poetess Toru Dutt) and several other highly educated Bangalis of the pre-Mutiny days. Other English-educated Indians remained in the fold of Hindu society, but with hardly concealed scepticism about its faith and practices.

The Brāhmo Samāj: its internal history and achievement

Then the Brāhmo Samāj—which, first founded in 1828, had remained dead or somnolent for twenty-five years, was revived by Devendra Nāth Tāgore (1818-1905), and began an active propaganda in and outside Calcutta under the leader ship of young Keshav Chandra Sen about 1860. Its intellectual appeal, refined spirituality and active social service brought many converts to it. The purely philosophical and aristocratic section of the educated Bengalis were attracted to the Adi Brāhmo Samaj as conducted by Devendra Nāth Tāgore.

Thus, Brāhmoism rose up to arrest the conversion of educated Hindus to Christianity. But Brāhmoism proved only a halting place for the straying Hindus of the new school. Hinduism again asserted its marvellous assimilative power, and changed its colour like the chameleon. Internal reforms were carried out and age-old abuses were removed in Hindu society, silently under the pressure of public opinion on the part of the rapidly increasing educated Hindu Population. And then, early in the eighties of the 19th century began the modern Hindu revival. Champions sprang up to defend its philosophy and ritual and proclaim them to the world as the perfection of human thought!

The Hindu Revival

An "aggressive" Hinduism replaced the shy passive creed that formerly used to be almost ashamed of itself and to stand ever on the defensive amidst growing foes and a diminishing number of adherents. The conversion of educated Hindus even to Brāhmoism ceased. The first philosophical exponents of this new or aggressive Hinduism in Bengal were Pandit Sasadhar Tarka-churāmani (c. 1840-1823) and Bankim Chandra Chatterji. The former called called science to his aid to prove that Hindu religious practices surcharged the body with electricity drawn from the atmosphere and the earth. It was pseudo-science, no doubt, but his audience knew no better science. He proved to his own satisfaction and to the exultation of his half-educated audience that the perfect development of a man's mind and body is possible in India only, because here the succession of seasons is so regular, the climate is so free from extremes, the land is so fertile and well-watered. There are, he held, two opposite currents of electricity, one upward and one downward, through the universe, and the tuft of long hair at the back of the orthodox Hindu's head enables him to purify and invigorate his mind by helping the passage of these electrical currents through his body, for had not his hearers seen a horse-hair brush used for carrying away electricity in laboratory experiments? Therefore, all other religions and civilizations were defective, unscientific, and harmful in comparison with Hinduism.

These theories may raise a smile today, but their effect was extraordinary. The pandit had no natural gift of eloquence or charm of voice, his subject was new and not yet popular or familiar. But hundreds of clerks, schoolmasters, compositors and even shop assistants, on the way back from their places of business after a hard day's toil, would cheerfully stop in his lecture hall in the evening and listen spellbound to Sasadhar for hours together. Soon the movement spread from the capital of Bengal to the district towns, and everywhere a new Hindu organization raised its head. Touring preachers completed the work, and one of them Srikrishna Prasanna Sen (1849-1902), added an emotional appeal and an eloquence which carried everything before them, while Pandit Shiva Chandra Vidyārnava made the deepest impression by his high Sanskrit scholarship, original thinking and refined oratory.

The same effect was produced among the richer and better educated classes of Hindus by Bankim Chandra's defence of the cult of Krishna as a praiseworthy and quite natural form of hero-worship and his reply to the Christian polemic literature of the Rev. Dr. W. Hastie and K. S. Macdonald.

New Hinduism Undertakes the Service of Man

At a still later stage, in the closing decade of the 19th century, even the service of mankind (regardless of caste or creed) ceased to be an exclusive distinction of the Christian and Brāhmo churches. At the trumpet call of Swāmi Vivekānanda (1863-1902), The wealth and manhood of Hindu India rose to the need of the day and absorbed this form of moral activity, as more than a thousand years earlier Vaishnavism had risen to absorb the socialistic features of Mahāyān Buddhism. The immense size of Hindu society and the newly acquired facility for forming organizations embracing the whole of India, took nearly all the wind out of the sails of the Christian and Brāhmo churches, whenever public calamities called for voluntary relief-workers. This neo-Hinduism is clearly a fruit of the English Renaissance, working in an unexpected direction. Miss Marguerite Noble, who entered Vivekānanda's order under the name of Sister Niveditā, (in 1900, dying in August 1911), most vigorously and eloquently carried on the intellectual propaganda of this "aggressive Hinduism" and succeeded in kindling among us a new sense of the aesthetic aspects of Hindu art, Hindu domestic life, Hindu folktales and Hindu ritual by her wonderful power of sympathy and delicate interpretation. Earlier than Vivekānanda, but in another part of India, Swāmi Dayānand (1827-1883) had started the Arya Samāj, which aimed at taking Hinduism back to what he understood to be the pristine purity of the Vedic age. Opinions will differ as to the spiritual value of his dogmatic creed, and the philological correctness of his translation of the *Riga Veda (Satyārth Prakās),* but there cannot be two opinions as to the energy, spirit of progress and philanthropy that he succeeded in infusing among his followers, who now number several hundred thousands and whose devotion to the service of suffering humanity extorts the admiration and emulation even of their opponents.

Rabindra Nāth Tāgore's "World Mission of India."

The latest form of the Hindu revival we owe to Rabindra Nāth Tāgore. It is a very close but unconscious copy of the movement which began in Russia in the 19th century,—the very language of the Slavonic leaders being repeated by the Indian poet. Its aim is exactly expressed if we replace the word *Russia* by *India* in the following descriptions of the movement in the former country:-

Peter J. Chaadaev (b. at Moscow, 1793), wrote, "What use is it to seek culture among the people of the West? Have we not the beginning of a social structure superior to that of the West?

Why should we envy the West, its religious wars, its feudal system, its chivalry, its inquisitions? Is the West, forsooth, the birth-place of Art and of all spiritual things? No, as you know, it is the East,—the East which we touch, from which we received our beliefs, laws and virtues, everything that has made us mighty.

"We belong to those nations which do not seem to form an integral part of humanity, but exist in order to give some great lesson to the world. The lesson which we are destined to give will assuredly not be lost.

"The East and West must no longer remain apart from one another. Their diverse cultures must be synthetized in a new culture. It is Russia's mission to bring about this millennial synthesis, not by force, but by means of a new social system or church, which will be the beginning of a universal Kingdom of Truth. In obedience to the will of God, Russia has to give the world new interpretations, a new message, a new example.

"Russia's gospel of resignation and humility, her asceticism, even her abstention from social activity, (seemed to him) notes of a Christianity purer than that of the West." (Quoted from C.H. Wright in the *Fortnightly review.)*

"Like the Slavophils, Chernyshevsky wished to preserve the primitive socialism of the village commune; but he looked forward to a Russia which, by a chance of history, should escape the capitalist stage of modern Europe and achieve its development in accordance with the theories of modern socialism." "To the struggle for existence, Mikhailovsky opposes the struggle for individual completeness, which he says, involves the fullest sense of the world around us." (Cambridge Modern History, xii. 296, 302.)

This latest form of Indian thought is based entirely on a new interpretation of our ancient Upanishads under the unconscious influence of Christianity. It is incorrect to call it a Hindu revival. It is really a cosmopolitan movement which aims at bringing all humanity together, and hence the Eastern poet's appeal has found a response in some of the noblest hearts of the West.

History of political agitation in modern India

The pioneers of political agitation in British India were the non-official Europeans who used to criticise the measures of Government rather virulently in their newspapers. The Press was placed under severe restraint by the E. I. C.* and four English editors were deported were deported from India by the Governors-General (1794,1803 and 1823) for their objectionable writings. There were restrictions also on "interlopers" or European outsiders living and owning property in British India. These Europeans began an agitation in Calcutta in 1832, on the eve of the renewal of the E. I. Co.'s charter, protesting against the Company's monopoly of trade and its autocratic government. But all this concerned the Europeans only, because the Indians, at that time, had no newspaper of their own in the English language, while their vernacular papers were merely literary journals without any tinge of politics.

But the example set by the Calcutta Europeans was not lost upon the rising generation of English-educated Bengalis, and their first appearance in the political field was under the wings of non-official English agitators. In 1842 Mr. George Thomson, M.P., came to Calcutta in the company of Dwārkānāth Tāgore, then returning from a visit to England. He discussed the political condition and problems of India with a number of well-to-do educated youths and delivered some inspiring speeches in public. The result was the foundation of the first political league of the Indians, *vis.*, the British Indian Association, in 1851.

But public agitation by the Indians first took a perceptible form in 1853 when the E. I. Co.'s charter was going to be renewed by Parliament. This opportunity was seized to press for political rights for the Indian people too. Our first political orator was Rām Gopāl Ghosli (1815-1868) and our first newspaper in English was the *Hindoo Patriot,* started in 1853 by Girish Chandra Ghosh

* Regulations of 1823 in Bengal and of 1825 and 1827 in Bombay. Sir Charles Metcalfe gave freedom to the Press in India in September, 1835.

(1829-1869)* who was later assisted and succeeded by Harish Chandra Mukherji (1824-1861).

But these newspapers were confined to Calcutta and had the most limited circle of readers. Their publication was irregular and their owners lost heavily on the ventures. Rām Gopāl Ghosh and his followers delivered academic speeches, painfully modelled on books like the *British Eloquence,* on a few set occasions. They reached only very small audiences—the only educated public of that day— and produced a little intellectual stir without the least influence on public opinion or the march of events.

Just after the Sepoy·Mutiny came the rising of the Bengal peasants against the European indigo planters (1860-62). Here European missionaries and officials (like the Rev. James Long and Ashley Eden) and Indian publicists (notably Harish Chandra Mudherji) joined hands and succeeded in putting an end to the oppression.

The next expansion of our political agitation was due to Krishna Dās Pāl (1838-1884) and M. G. Rānāde (1842-1901); but even their appeal did not go beyond the small educated upper middle class. At this stage its only method was the delivery of grave methodical speeches and the presentation of formal petitions to Government. Agitation became a living force for the first time during Lord Lytton's viceroyalty (1876-1879), thanks to the efforts of Sisir Kumār Ghosh (1842-1911) and his brothers, who founded the *Amrita Bāzar Patrikā,* as a democratic rival to the staid and aristocratic *Hindoo Patriot* of Krishna Dās Pāl.

The Ilbert Bill and the change it wrought

Then, during the viceroyalty of Lord Ripon, a revolution took place in the politics of the Indian people as the result of the violent agitation publicly conducted against the Ilbert Bill (1883) by the official Europeans who formed a pact with the non-official

* Girish and his brother had started the Bengal Recorder in 1851, but it ceased publication next year.

European trading community lawyers, planters, and journalists and even the Eurasians. They stood up in defence of their racial privileges, as against the claim of the Indians to equality under the law, and carried their point. The country was henceforth sharply divided into two hostile camps on purely racial lines. The Indians saw before their eyes an example of the strength and success of organized political agitation and of union among a community, in overawing the rulers. They had only to unite, organize themselves and follow the tactics and language of the European Defence Association, and they would gain the same success.

As the Viceroy wrote to Lord Kimberly (the Secretary of State for India),—"The great weakness of the Government for dealing with a European disturbance (in Calcutta) weighed with me, as it did with my colleagues. The Police force at the disposal of the Bengal Government was very small,—between 60 and 70 men; in any riot the least serious, we should have had at once to call out the troops, and I felt that to employ European soldiers against Europeans in this country would have been a step of the gravest kind." (20 Jan. 1884.) "Some members of Ripon's Council were completely demoralized." (Wolf's Marquess of Ripon, ii. 145, 144.)

"A monster indignation meeting (of the British community) took place in Calcutta, at which the speeches were of an intemperance beyond all limits of decency. The Volunteers (all non-Indians) were openly incited to resign in a mass, and certain persons even 'sounded opinions in the canteens'—in other words attempted to seduce the Army. On his return to Calcutta in the winter, the Viceroy was openly insulted in the streets by (British) planters brought down from the Mafussil for the occasion." (*Ibid.* ii. 128.)

"The Government was entirely committed to the passing of the Ilbert Bill, yet it gave way before the clamour of an insignificant section of the public, abetted by the sworn enemies of all reform in India—the Anglo-Indian bureaucracy. I am much mistaken if the natives did not also come to the conclusion that the justice of a course was insufficient for its triumph in politics, and that the only path of victory henceforth lay through agitation." (Blunt's *India Under Ripon,* 273.)

Sir John Tenniel in a cartoon published in the London *Punch* (15 Dec. 1883) warned the Anglo-Indians against setting "a bad example to the Elephant." The events of 1905 proved that the British example had *not* been lost upon the Elephant.

The immediate effect of the lesson thus learnt was the assembling of the Indian National Congress in 1885. Its organizers were the orderly upper class lawyers, to whom politics was a pleasant relaxation in the intervals of more lucrative business. Their aims and methods were far from democratic and it was almost inevitable that they should be devoured by their children,—the middle class democrats, at the Surat Congress of 1907. But even then politics was still far from having been brought to the doors of the common people. That consummation was left to the period following the First World War and to the initiative of Mahātmā Gāndhi. An appeal to the heart of the real *people* of India is no longer an impossibility, though their opinion cannot be made to crystallize on a purely political issue because of their total lack of political knowledge and experience, and dispersion among many provinces and castes.

The result estimated: the first faint beginnings of a nation in India

The question will be naturally asked—What has been the fruit of this long course of political agitation by the Indians and of the gradual liberalization of the constitution by Government? When the dust of contemporary controversy is laid, when the din of our daily papers has passed into silence, it will then be found that a nation has begun to be formed in India. The people have not gained liberty, but they are now on the way to attaining that equality or rather uniformity which is the indispensable preliminary to political liberty.

The French revolutionists fought and bled for liberty, equality, and fraternity. In the end, they gained neither the first nor the third, but only the second, and that enabled them to win liberty seventy years afterwards, under the Third Republic.

Liberty impossible without equality

The *sine qua non* of democracy is absolute social equality, equal rights not only before the law, but also in society, equal opportunities for all in life, and the equal reward of merit irrespective of birth, not only by the State but also by public opinion.

A people with water-tight class or caste distinctions, even when freed from foreign domination, cannot enjoy political liberty; it will be subject to the autocracy of a clique or a family.

How the Indians are being made uniform

We already see the faint dawning of such a sense of oneness among all the Indian people. The victory of a Bengali football team over a British regiment at Simlā now causes Panjābi spectators to rejoice. The sufferings of Tāmil emigrants in South Africa or Fiji are keenly resented in Calcutta and Punā. There is a monotonous sameness in the agenda paper and procedure of an orthodox Hindu caste conference and, say, an All-India Muslim Education Conference. Both have stolen their programme from the hated Europeans! Our nationalists denounce the West with the very arguments and methods borrowed from the West. The Muslim League has stolen its thunders (and tactics) from the Indian National Congress, which had stolen them from the Irish.

In addition to social equality, another factor of political liberty has already been introduced in our midst, though it has not yet leavened the mass. It is self-government. The test of self-government, the true requisite of nationhood,—is not the absence of foreign dominion, but the sharing by the people in the government of their own country through their representatives.

The political pre-requisites for conducting true self-government

There has been a great deal of loose thinking and writing, many political fallacies have gained currency in our midst, because the essence of representative government has not been clearly understood. The nation's capacity for representative government is not advanced by one inch when the members of a caste in a village raise funds from among themselves and dig a public well or build a temple, or when they settle a quarrel between two caste-brethren by the arbitration of five elders of the same caste Even when all the different castes of a village contribute to the cost of the well or temple, it is of no *political* value. The administration of the parish pump is no true education for the representative government of a country.

The management of parochial or sectarian business—however ably or honestly done—cannot qualify a people composed of many creeds races and provinces for conducting the State. A people have the capacity for self-government only when they can successfully administer the *central* government. Representative government, in its higher and only true sense, implies the power of taking a correct view of things not immediately before our eyes, nor familiar to us from our childhood, the power of judging promptly and using correctly men who do not belong to our own particular social circle but come from another province or caste, in short, the capacity of using the telescope and not merely the microscope of political vision. A true nation must have an entire population of standardized normal human "spare parts", who can be fitted into every normal vacancy in the legislature or the public service, without the possibility of any difference being caused in the result by differences of race caste province language or religion among them.

Wherein modern India is relatively weaker than medieval

This survey of India in the modern age would be incomplete and misleading if we do not notice two points of vital importance in which we have lost ground in comparison with the Mughal period. If we cannot modernize ourselves and become capable of competing with the outer world to the fullest extent in these two respects, we are a doomed race.

Ever since the middle of the 19th century, Europe has been so rapidly and steadily advancing by the application of science to arms and to the industrial arts, that India is today much less able to wage an economic or military contest with Europe than she was in the age of Akbar. Or, in other words, our relative position has actually grown worse in the course of the last three centuries. Today, in the face of European competition, we are helplessly weak in production and exchange, and the economic drain will dry this country to death if we do not modernize our industry, arts, transport and banking. In warfare, if India were to depend on her own indigenous resources without borrowing armament, leaders and trainers from Europe, she would not be able to stand against a modern army even for an hour. No nation can exist in the present-day world by merely cultivating its brain, without developing its economic resources and military power to the high pitch attained by its possible enemies.

The lesson of India's history

This study of our country's history leads irresistibly to the conclusion that we must embrace the spirit of progress with a full and unquestioning faith, we must face the unpopularity of resisting the seductive cry for going back to the undiluted wisdom of our ancestors, we must avoid eternally emphasizing the peculiar heritage of the Aryan India of the far-off past. We must recognize that in the course of her evolution India has absorbed many new elements later than the Vadic Aryan age and even than the Mughal age. We must not forget that the modern Indian civilization is a composite daily growing product and not a mummy preserved in dry sand for four thousand years.

The Europeans of South Africa warned the Indian settlers there, "Westernize or leave the country." Japān learnt this secret of national preservation sixty years ago. Turkey has recently taken the hint and the Father of the Turks, Atā Turk, Kamāl Pāshā, has made the State secular and modern. To India the unmistakable message of the Time-spirit is:

"Give up your dream of isolation, standardize and come into line with the moving world outside, or you will become extinct as a race through the operation of relentless economic competition in a world which has now become as one country."

(Thus far I wrote in 1928.)

—*J.N. Sarkar*

6. Swami Dayanand Saraswati and Indian Renaissance

A nation grows into what it shall be by the force of that which it was in the past and is in the present, and in this growth there come periods of conscious and subconscious stock-taking when the national soul selects, modifies, rejects, keeps out of all that it had or is acquiring whatever it needs as substance and capital for its growth and action in the future: in such a period of stock-taking we are still and Dayanand was one of its great and formative spirits.

Sri Aurobindo,
Bankim-Tilak-Dayanand, pp.36-37.

Swami Dayanand Saraswati was a typical fearless social and religious reformer in the 19th century. Through his life and career he preached Indians to imbibe courage, fortitude, moral soundness, power, strength of body and mind and such other virtues as would make them independent and possessors of sovereign imperial sway. He claimed India for Indians.

Dayanand stands out by himself, with peculiar and salutary distinctness, one unique in his type and he is unique in his work. He was Mystic and Yogi and could remain in *Samadhi* for 18 hours at a stretch. He would live on milk alone for days together. He remained hungry sometimes as it was not his custom to beg for food. He faced hardships and was stoned and poisoned many times.

Like a true saint he forgave them. Nobel-laureate Romain Rolland, Sri Aurobindo and Sir Syed Ahmed Khan paid him rich tributes for his character, wisdom, strong will and courage.

Dayanand's message was 'Back to the Vedas' and to lay the foundations of society on them. His interpretation of the Vedas was not only scientific and rational but also this was surely a master glance of practical intuition on his part, for in a real sense, the Vedas were the original source of religion, culture and civilization of India; they were the real foundations of Indian thought, philosophy and knowledge.

Born of a Brahmana family at Tankara in the State of Morvi, South Gujarat, Dayanand turned out to be a rebel and militant child of his family and the age in which he was born. His father Krashanji Laji Trivedi tried his best to prepare the child in the Shaiva traditional way. In the process Dayanand learnt certain lessons in Sanskrit grammar and some Vedic text by heart. He accompanied his father on his religious missions. He is said to have completed his formal education in 1838. His father had a banking house, a hereditary office, and he wanted Dayanand to help him in his business.

Like all other great men of the world Dayanand also passed through periods of conflict, suffering and an urge to seek the truth.

The conflict came his faith in the traditional religious practices was shaken at the sight of a mouse dancing on the idol of Lord Shiva for whom he was made to fast. He felt that it was impossible to reconcile to the idea of an omnipotent, living god, with the idol which allowed the mouse to run over his body and polluted his image without the slightest protest from him. All his father's arguments and persuasion could not end his conflict.

Soon after, notwithstanding the best possible care, his younger sister expired. It was his first bereavement, and the shock he received was very great. He said, 'Friends and relatives were sobbing and lamenting around me but I stood like one pertifield, plunged in revery.'[1] He realised that no one could escape death and he too could be snatched away any time. He asked himself: "What should I do to alleviate this human misery ? Where shall I find the assurance for and means of attaining salvation ? I came to a decision then and there that I would strive to find an answer to these questions, cost whatever it might, so that I could save myself from the untold miseries of the dying moments."[2]

His uncle who loved him dearly also passed away shortly afterwards. "His death left me in a state of utter dejection and with a still profounder conviction I settled in my mind that there was nothing stable, nothing worth living for in this world."[3]

Apprehending marital wedlock, he left home in 1846 in search of truth/*Moksha*. For more than 15 years he wandered through one part of the country to the other—on the banks of the rivers, thick jungles, in the hermits of various *yogis, sadhus, sanyasis;* on the peaks of the hills to learn the science of *yoga* and through *yoga,* the *Moksha* which was his ambition of life at that time. Ultimately he found a guru in Swami Virjananda at Mathura with whom he stayed for 3 years (1861-63). Swami Virjananda was a great grammarian. Dayanand had so far devoted himself to vedanta, *yoga* and some grammar. Perhaps it is quite possible that after his wanderings in the country and meetings with *sadhus, yogis, sanyasis* of various sects, he might have discovered that the deepest secret of religion and *moksha* lay hidden in the Hindu scriptures and as they are in Sanskrit, they could be opened only with the key of grammar. It was for this reason that he came to Virjananda, who was recognized as an established authority on grammar.[4]

During his stay with Swami Virjanand, besides mastering the *Ashtadhyayi, Mahabhashya, Nirukta. Nighantu,* which provided him with the key to unlock the treasury of the Vedas, Dayanand learnt to control his body and mind through yogic powers.

Having finished his, Dayanand made customary offerings of cloves, so dear to Swami Virjananda, as *dakshina* to his teacher, saying that he was a poor man and could not offer anything except that. Virjananda's reaction to it was indeed wonderful. He observed: "I demand from you something else as a *dakshina*. Take a vow before me that so long as you live you will work incessantly to spread true knowledge of the *Vedas* and the *Arsha-granthas* and condemn works which teach false doctrines and tenets; and that you will even give your life if necessary in re-establishing the Vedic religion. Dayanand bowed and vowed *"Tathastu*-so it be."[5]

"This is my *dakshina."* True to his world Dayanand fulfilled his vow to the last breath of his life.

After taking leave of his *guru,* Dayanand came to Agra in April 1863 and stayed here for two years passing most of his time in practising yoga and studying the *Vedas* and *shastras* thus preparing himself for the mission for which he had pledged himself before his *guru* Swami Virjananda.

Dayanand visited almost every part of India from Cape Comorin to the Himalayas and from Calcutta to Bombay. He was a man with a powerful intellect and social conscience. He challenged traditional beliefs and rituals. His personality and teachings affected the lives of million of people.[6] He denounced evils and vulgarities spread by the vested interests in the name of religion. Vedas in hand he challenged the Hindu orthodoxy to prove if they could justify on their basis polytheism, pantheonism, idol worship, casteism, untouchability, infant marriage, forced widowhood, *sati* infanticide and numerous other superstitions degenerating Hinduism. The whole front line and the reserve of orthodoxy came forward to silence him, but Dayanand brought them to their knees.[7]

After socio-religious work of reform in the Hindu society, Dayanand's next concern was to arouse national consciousness among his people. He was, undoubtedly, one of the major figures of India's national resurgence. Some of the writers strongly feel that the events of 1905 in Bengal was a direct impact of Dayanand's teachings.[8]

Throughout his life Dayanand endeavoured to purge the humanity of the prevalent social and religious evils. He was a visionary who looked far ahead of his times and visualized a society based on social justice, equality of opportunity and political freedom. He was of the view that character of the nation was the real foundation on which the superstructure of political uplift could be built.

He aimed at regeneration of the Indians and through Indians the whole humanity. He tried to expound Truth and to bring the followers of all religions together on one platform. He worked hard to make them free from malice. He generated the feelings of love and worked for their welfare and peaceful world existence.

Although charges are made against him that his attack on other religions had done more harm than good to the Indian society, but researchers in the field have absolved Dayanand of these charges because he never rejected that was good in other religions and never spared Hinduism of its social evils. Dayanand felt that there were learned men in all religions and if they could give up prejudices, accept all these broad principles on which all religions were unanimous, reject differences and behave affectionately towards each other, much good would be done to the world, the miseries of the people would decrease and usher an era of happiness.[9]

Dayanand is often blamed that he criticized the different religions and the different sects of Hindu society. However, his main aim was to criticise only those elements in different religions which led the masses to fight each other. He had no malice or hatred towards any religion; he simply criticized what he thought as untrue (in that religion), and wanted to bring different faiths under the banner of one universal religion. He was of the view that "all these things which are common to all religions obviously condemn false things, for they create difference in different faiths. It is my object to put clearly before public all the secrets and open things of all religions, so that all and sundry may be able to exchange their views and reach some unanimity."[10]

Dayanand strove hard to preach universal truth to bring all men under one religion so that they may, by ceasing to hate each other and firmly loving each other, live in peace and work for their common welfare.[11]

He could not be contented with mere theoretical propositions in this respect and embarked on practical ventures. He invited a conference of the representatives of almost all the religions in India on the occasion of the Delhi *Durbar,* 1877, in which Keshab Chandra Sen, Sir Sayyed Ahmad Khan, Munshi Alakhdhari and others participated Though the conference led at that time to no practical results, yet it served a big purpose; it paved the way for the later religious parliaments and conferences working for peace and happiness of mankind.[12]

It is a strange coincidence that Dayanand was poisoned by a Hindu but was treated by a Muslim doctor, Alimardan Khan. He passed away on October 30, 1883 and cremated at Malusar Cremation Grounds, Ajmer.

"In the matter of Vedic interpretation, I am convinced that whatever may be the final complete interpretation. Dayanand will be honoured as the first discoverer of the right clues. Amidst the chaos and obscurity of old ignorance and age-long misunderstanding his was the eye of direct vision that pierced to the truth and fastened on that which was essential. He has found the keys of the doors that time had closed and rent as under the seals of imprisoned fountains."

Sri Aurobindo,
Bankim-Tilak-Dayanand, p. 44.

Dayanand was a widely travelled and well read person. During his life-time he had held many discourses and held many *shastrathas* with the followers of other faiths such as Christians, Muslims, orthodox Hindus and many others; he wrote many books, pamphlets and tracts on religious rituals. His works included around 26 books, besides a number of minor unpublished works, a number of published lectures and reports, and his personal correspondence.

In 1863 he published his first work Sandhya (1) after completing his studies with Swami Virjananda. *Bhagavata-Khandanam* (2) was published in 1864 and distributed at the *Kumbha Mela,* Hardwar. It rejected the Bhagavata as *Unarsha* work. *Advaita-mat-Khandanam* (3) denounced the doctrine of non-duality of Shankaracharya's *Advaita.* It was followed by *Satyarth Prakash* (4) which was originally written in Hindi. It has been translated into many Indian and foreign languages. It is divided into two part, its first part gives rules for a positive life, while the second part analyses the falsities in various religions.

Describing the five *yajnas* to be performed daily, Dayanand published *Panchamahayajna vidhi.(5)*

Veda-Viruddha-mat-Khandnam (6) was originally written in Sanskrit. Shyamji Krishna Varma translated it in Gujarati and Bhimsen into Hindi. This work denounces idol-worship, belief in *avatars,* etc. It refutes the tenets of the Vallabhchari and other Vaishnava sects.

Vedanti-dhwanta-nivarana (7) is available in English also. It gives the meanings and expositions of the four principal aphorisms on which the neo-Vedantists rely to prove the oneness of God and Soul. This study refutes their contention and cites *Brahmans, Upanishads.*

Shikshapatri-dhwanta-nivarana (8) came as a reaction to *Shikshapatri* written by the founder of the Swami Narayan sect, *Aryabhivinaya (9) gives mantras* from all the four Vedas. It is a book of prayar and is translated in English.

Sanskaravidhi (10) was complied to help people to perform properly the sixteen rites from conception to death.

Rigvedadi-bhashya-bhumika (II) discusses the origin and subject matter of the Vedas. It was written in Sanskrit and Hindi and is also translated in English. *Bhranti-nivarana* (12) is a sample of *Rigveda* commentary.

Aryaddeshya Ratnamala (13) contains definitions and expositions of 100 such terms as one generally comes across in reading Hindu philosophy and Dayanand's works.

Vedabhashya (14) is a monumental work. This helps in understanding the method of Vedic interpretation adopted by Dayanand.

Autobiography (15) was written in Hindi and was published in an English translation in the *Theosophist* issues of October and December 1879 and November 1880. Dr. K.C. Yadav has in 1976 brought about a scholarly and scientific version of it, published by Manohar Book Service, New Delhi.

Ashtadhyayi-Bhashya (16) is a commentary on the famous grammarian Panini's *Ashtadhyayi*.

Gotama-Ahalya ki Katha (17) is a re-interpretation of the legend of Gotama-Ahalya, quite different from the versions available in the *Puranas*.

Sanskrit vakya Prabodh (18) is an aid to learn and talk in Sanskrit. *Vyavaharbhanu* (19) deals with various popular and everyday topics. These teaching are supported by interesting anecdotes and incidents.

Bhramochchhedan (20) is a reply to Raja Shivprasad *Sitar-e-Hind* of Benares's objections to Swamiji's *Rigvedadi-bhashya-bhumika*.

Anubhramochchedan (21) was published as a rebuttal, when Raja Shivaprasad published an answer to Swamiji's *Bhramochchhedan*.

Vedanga Prakash (22) published in 14 parts shows the different ways in which the grammar of the Vedic Sanskrit and that of classical Sanskrit deal with various grammatical matters.

Gokarunanidhi (23 pleads for the protection of cows in particular and other animals in general. It is available in English also.

Some of his important discourses and lectures published are *Shastrarha* (24), *Shastrartha Hugli* (25) published in Bengali; later a Hindi version was published under the title of *Pratima-Pujan-Vichar. Poona-Pravachana* (26) was first published in Marathi, later it was translated into Gujarati. Its Hindi version is known as *Upadesh Manjari. Shastrartha-Bareilly* (27) was first published under the title *Satya-satya-viveka* in Urdu. *Shastrartha-Ajmer* (28) was published both in Hindi and Urdu in *Aryadarpam* of Ajmer. *Shastrartha-Masuda* (29) was published in *Desh-Hitaishi* of Ajmer. *Shastrartha-UDAIPUR* was published by Pandit Lekhram in his biography of Dayanand.

There are also a number of letters and notices in printed form. Prominent among these are *Rishi Dayananda Ka Patravyavahar* (30), *Rishi Dayanand Saraswati ke Patra aur Vijnapan (31), Rishi Dayanand Saraswati Ke Patra aur Vijnapanan Ke Parishisht (32), Rishi Dayanand Ke Patra aur Vijnapan* (33). Vol. I, and *Rishi Dayanand Ke Patra aur Vijnapan* (34), Vol. II.

From the study of the life and works of Swami Dayanand Saraswati, it is found that his manner of working was very different. Here was one who did not infuse himself informally into the indeterminate soul of things, but stamped his figure indelibly as in bronze on men and things. Here was one whose formal works are the very children of his spiritual body, children, fair and robust and full of vitality, the image of their creator. Here was one who knew definitely and clearly the work he was sent to do, chose his materials, determined his conditions with a sovereign clairvoyance of the spirit and executed his conception with the puissant mastery of the born worker.

Dayanand seized on all that entered into him, held it in himself, masterfully shaped it there into the form that he saw right and threw it out again into the forms that he saw to be right. That which strikes us in him as militant and aggressive, was a part of his strength of self-definition. He was not only plastic to the great hand of Nature, but asserted his own right and power to use Life and Nature as plastic material.

On the basis of his deep study of the *Vedas, Upanishadas* he ridiculed the incompatible tradition that Vedas were merely the mythological and ritual books; he proved that these were the authoritative revelation and inspired Book of Knowledge, the source of all sanctions and standard of all truth.

Dayanand brought back an old Aryan element into the Indian national character.[13]

What Einstein has said about men of science is equally true about men of philosophy. I would say in similar words that many kinds of men devote themselves to philosophy, and not all for the sake of philosophy herself. There are some who come into her temple because it offers them the opportunity to display their particular talents. To this class of men, philosophy is a kind of sport in the practice of which they exult, just as an athlete exults in the exercise of his muscular prowess. There is another class of men who come into the temple to make an offering of their brain-pulp in the hope of securing a profitable return. These men are philosophers only by the chance of some circumstance which offered itself when making a choice of career. If the attending circumstance had been different, they might have become politicians or captains of business. Should an angel of God, as Einstein puts it, descend and drive from the Temple of Knowledge all those belonging to the above categories, it is feared, the temple would be nearly emptied. But still there are some who have found favour with the angel. What has led them to devote themselves to the pursuit of knowledge, is difficult to say. It may be, perhaps, that they felt an inner urge to flee from everyday life, with its drab and deadly dullness and thus to unshackle the chain of one's own transient desires. We cannot trace in their single span of life all the stages of human evolution through which they must have passed. There is something so unique and distinct in them and they are so much different from others that it is difficult to follow how the machinery of their brain works and how the clock of their heart moves. And when they go away, we realise what dynamic personalities they were; we then find that which they achieved for themselves was, in fact, the achievement for the humanity at large. Amongst these was Dayananda, the greatest of the personalities of the nineteenth century.

Dayananda was not an academic philosopher, unlike many of the philosophers of the present day whose philosophy remains untouched with their life and who have never translated their beliefs and doctrines into actions. A synthetic philosophy compatible with all aspects of life, a complete solution of the problems concerning visible and non-visible, and a perfect picture of the knowable and unknowable can only be given by one who has been sincere and truthful, who has placed himself above the worldly aspirations and who is free from the very many vices of an ordinary life. Philosophy does not believe in the finality of an answer to any of the problems howsoever simple they appear to be. The greatest of the thinkers are the least dogmatic for to be so is directly against the spirit of philosophy. But in spite of this modesty, a philosopher does not spare anybody from his drastic criticisms, for if he has found out a truth for himself, his sincerity demands that he should give it out with emphasis in face of all opposition. He moves undaunted in the world for he is confident that the truth that he has found would be his saviour. In matters of truth, a philosopher does not believe in compromises or pacts, truces and treaties and in this respect he differs from other worldly heroes whom we find struggling hard in the domain of politics and whose achievements, probably the human history glorifies the most. But a great philosopher lives through all times. He becomes a motive force behind all our national actions and aspirations, even when he is not bodily present with us. This lays a much heavier responsibility on the shoulders of a philosopher. This demands in him a crystal clear character free from blemishes and blasphemy. One who satisfies himself with the academical hair-splittings in his writings or sermons, but who is not prepared to live unto his ideas, whose life is contrary to his preachings, or one who believes that philosophy is simply a matter of brain exercise cannot be called a true philosopher. In fact, the truth once realised or attained does not admit duality in matters of life.

A BORN PHILOSOPHER

Dayananda was a born philosopher, not in the sense that he was moody or gloomy from his early life but on account of the fact that like a potential philosopher, his soul urged from the very beginning of his career to find out a solution for himself regarding some complex problems of life. He wanted not only an intellectual satisfaction on these matters, but he aspired for the realisation of truth concerning them. I would mention two incidents from his life which were responsible for the future turn of his activities.

The first concerns with the festival of Sivaratri. Mulji, a young lad of thirteen—as he was then known—was asked by his father to observe fast on the occasion of this festival and he was given assurance that at midnight, he would have the favour of seeing Siva, the great Lord with his famous bull and all the accompaniments; and in fact, he was made to believe that the idol was nothing more than the Siva Himself. Everybody was expected to wake up throughout the night to have a *darsana* of the Lord in flesh and bones, but to the disappointment of Mulji, everybody was laid deep into slumber, and what further happened, I shall quote in Dayananda's own words: When I was the only man awake, an important incident happened. Several rats came forth and began to dance at the idol of Siva and often usurped rice and offerings dedicated to the idol. I began to witness all this. An idea entered into my mind. Is this the same God Siva, about whose strength and valour and his bull which bears him. I had heard in the morning? I was thunderstruck. I thought, how could this idol be that all powerful, and a terror of enemies, who could not even check the tresspass of rats? Thus I became wild with thoughts, I began to question within myself,—this idol riding on a bull before me, is that of Siva, who makes tours, enjoys food, and drinks, sleep, bears the Trisula, rattles Damaru and shows divine wrath?'' This was the line of argument of a boy of thirteen. Perhaps, in a grown-up age, he would have satisfied himself with some matured arguments. Mulji with his childlike innocence said to his father, "Father, I have been told that Siva is all-powerful, but look how helpless. He is in driving these rats away." The only reply that could be given was, "My son, this is not the real Siva. This is an image only." Mulji was anxious to meet real Siva. How could he be satisfied with an image? This opened his eyes, a vision came into him and he once for all realised that the true Siva is somewhere else and something else. He must find Him out. Needless to say that he further discovered for himself that the idol in the temple could not even be the image of Siva, not to say Siva Himself, for He is without from and image. One this occasion of Sivaratri, Mulji achieved two things, firstly, a negative that the idols are neither God nor the image of God, and secondly, a positive aspect, a strong urge to meet true God. But Mulji throughout his life never questioned the existence of God. He axiomatically was confident of the existence.

Another incident revealed to Mulji a greater problem. I would put it also in his own words: "I was enjoying the festivities at a relative's place one night, when a servant came and communicated a dreadful news. He told me that my sister, who was of fourteen years, fell suddenly ill. In spite of all efforts made, she expired within two hours of my coming here. Sister's death was the first calamity in my life. The sorrow was appalling. At that sad demise, when the bewailing of the relations was tearing the sky asunder, I stood mute like a stone and began to ponder, "Oh, how short is our life. I shall also die some day. But is there no way by which I may be immune of death and may attain salvation? At the same place, I took a vow that I will make an effort to conquer death. At this juncture, I became sure, that outward demonstrations were all a humbug and nothing but the purification of the soul was the way to salvation." This happened when Mulji was eighteen years of age.

But soon after followed another incident, which he has described thus: "After some time, my uncle died. He was a learned man of divine virtues. He loved me from my very childhood and I was much moved by his separation. I thought that when all things in this world were perishable, why should I pass my day in their midst."

Mulji, the budding Buddha, had now clearly three problems before himself,— what life is, what death means, and how to overcome death. Sivaratri had already given him two problems, what true God is and how to meet Him. Dayananda's whole life is a dedication to these five problems. Buddha was also faced with similar problems. In fact, these problems are eternal, and perhaps, never a final answer will be given, but every great man will make an effort to find out a solution for himself. The solution which Buddha found out for himself may not necessarily be the same which Dayananda found out. But still the greatness of the two cannot be denied. Both approached truth, both obtained self-satisfaction, and through both of them humanity has been benefitted immensely, and yet the two personalities are different and incomparable.

RENOUNCEMENT

I have no idea of writing full biographical sketch of Dayananda, but still, I cannot resist myself in giving an account of how Mulji renounced the world. After all that had happened, it was difficult for Mulji to remain within the four walls of his house, and his people could realise, not before long, that the young boy was becoming uneasy to chalk out some plan for his future life. Mulji wanted to come to Benares for future study, but he was not allowed to do so. Hidden in his heart was kindling a fire for the search of truth. In spite of attempts, it could not be subdued. It is rather difficult to realise the nature of conflict that was raging in his heart-the dual conflict—on one side, love of home, affection of the mother, anger of the father and attachment of the nearest, and on the other hand, the passion for truth, the uncertainty of the future life and the disgust from the world. The one was an easy path of homely life, and the other the path of thorns. His parents were already apprehending, and finally, they thought out of a solutions. No fetters are supposed to be stronger than those of matrimony, and therefore, Mulji's parents decided to get him married. This presented a new difficulty to the young man, and finding no other way out, while preparations for marriage were brisk, he silently slipped out, bidding farewell to his home. We are told that he was once caught by his father but happily, he managed to escape again.

Mulji was first enunciated as Brahmachārī, and in course of it, he happened to be at *Chetan Matha, Baroda,* where he came in contact with a number of learned Sanyāsins. He writes, "Brahmananda and other Sanyāsins were successful in explaining to me the philosophy of Vedānta, that I am the almighty Brahman. Even before this, I had studied the books of Vedānta and understood them a little, but now my doubts were completely removed and I began to consider myself Brahman." Dayananda then moved to a place Chanaud Karuchi. He further says, "Here I met several Brahmachāris, Sanyāsins like Chidānanda and several other *yogis.* I had never before witnessed such people wellversed in *yoga.* After a conversation lasting for some days, one day I went to Paramānanda Paramahansa and requested him to instruct me. For a couple of months, I studied books known as *Vedāntasāra* and *Vedānta Paribhasa."*......" I was a Brahmachārī and as such I had to cook food with my own hands. This was a great hindrance in my studies. I had not given up my original name as yet and, as my father's popularity was well known, I had always a fear lest someone while conversing with me might recognise that I was the son of a particular man. So I was always anxious to have my name changed. By becoming a Sanyāsin, I could avoid the two difficulties mentioned above, and for this reason, I was anxious to take Sanyāsa." But there were difficulties in becoming Sanyāsin ordinarily, a young man is not enunciated as a Sanyāsin at a tender age. "After several months of this incident, two persons, who had given up worldly life came from south and stayed at a broken hut in the jungle. This place was about two miles from where I resided. One was a Sanyāsin and the other a Brahmachārī. The Daksini Paṇḍita, mentioned above became anxious to see them and he took me also there. We reached the place. My friend had specialised in Vedanta, and now he began to converse with those people on topics concerning Brahma. The discussion that ensued was an ample testimony to me of their being very learned. They told us that they were coming from Sārañgvera Matha established by Swāmi Sankarāchārya and were going to Dwārakā. One of them was known as Purnānand Saraswatī. I asked the Paṇḍita whether he could recommend me to him. The Paṇḍita agreed and he told the Sanyāsin that I was a young Brahmachārī and it was my desire to study Vedānta without any sort of hindrance. Further, the Paṇḍita told him that he could bear testimony to the fact that I was of good temperament and my character was excellent. With these arguments, inspite of my blooming youth, he pleaded for me to be admitted to Sanyāsa. He exhorted Swāmī Purṇānanda to enunciate me and further told him that in that way, I would be able to be completely free from worldly life and to study *Brahmavidyā* without any obstacle. On this, Swāmī Purṇānand raised two difficulties; firstly, that I was of young age, and nextly, that the Swāmī belonged to Mahārāṣtra while I was coming from Gujarāta. He wanted me to go to some Gujarāti Sanyāsin. However, my friend further convinced him and brought him round and he was pleased to admit me to Sanyāsa the third day. 'Dayānanda Saraswati was the name he gave to me." Dayānanda was already a Sanyāsin when he left home, so far as the spirit of Sanyāsa was concerned, but now after the due ceremonials, he became a full-fledged Sanyāsin. History has repeated itself, for Sankarācharya was also very young when he took Sanyāsa.

THE FURTHER SEARCH

It is easy for one to be admitted to Sanyāsa. In this country there is no dearth of formal Sanyāsins, but Dayānanda could not be satisfied with this much. He had yet to explore for himself the path, the goal of which had already been set up in the early part of his life. For the next many years, we find him enthusiastically and studiously devoting himself in acquiring knowledge, discussing philosophy with some, learning *yogic* practices from the other, and picking up the complexities of the Sanskrit Grammar from the third. He made an extensive tour, right from the Himālayas in the north to Narbadā in the south in the search of some good preceptor, who could lead him in matters of *yoga*. Once in the course of his search in Himalayan peaks, he writes, "I was anxious to cross these hilly regions which were either snow-clad or full of glaciers, for although I had not witnessed with my eyes, I had heard that some big souls live three in seclusion." Once while crossing Alakhananda, he had painful experiences. He writes, "I was plainly clad then and the cold was excessive and unbearable. Hunger and thirst had paralysed my body. I tried to swallow one small bit of ice in order to appease my hunger, but it gave no satisfaction. Now I waded through water. The river was deep at certain places and shallow at others, but nowhere less than two feet. The river was about twenty feet broad and its bed was full of small icy bits. These icy pieces were sharp-edged and they pierced through my feet. The blood began to flow profusely from the wounds. The excessive flow of blood on the hand and the excessive cold all round was taking possession of my heart. My legs were trembling and often I felt, I was falling down. It appeared to me as if I was going to lose my life in the bed of Alakhanandā. My limbs were so much benumbed, that had I once fallen on the ice, it would have been difficult for me to get up. Thus with great perseverance I could cross the river, and when I came out, I was almost dead." Dayānanda once thought of ending his life there on the spot, but immediately, Dayānanda writes, "The idea of death horrified me and I began to meditate. Why should I have a liking for death? Was it not worthy of me to end my life in search of knowledge?" Dayānanda had yet to fulfil his mission and he lived for it. Dayānanda went to explore the source of Narbadā river, and there too, he had similar experiences.

In the course of his wanderings, he acquired varied experiences of life. Once he had an opportunity of studying Tantrika philosophy too and in his disgust, he writes, "My astonishment knew no bounds, when I read with my own eyes in Tantrika books the sexual intercourse of mother and son, father and daughter, brother and sister or even with women of low castes, worshipping a naked woman, taking flesh, fish, and wine and expecting salvation through all this. I had a firm belief that rascals must have compiled these books to satisfy their own evil propensities and have termed them as religious scriptures."

Dayanānda finally meets a Guru who gave him full satisfaction. Swāmi Virajānanda of Mathura, the blind saint, was the greatest grammarian of his times and perhaps, he was the only man like Kumārilbhaṭṭa who was anxious to restore to India her Vedic ideals. Dayananda not only learnt from him the Vedic grammar, but it appears that most of his ideas were crystallised in his company, and by the time he leaves his preceptor, he finds himself full with the philosophy that he gave out to the world in his latter life. When Dayānanda takes final leave from his great teacher, Virajānanda speaks out, "Dayānanda, your education is complete. Now it is for me to demand a *Gurudaksinā* from you. But shall I demand money from you? No, that will not be. I will demand from you something that is more precious. I want your life. Just in my presence, take a vow that so long as you live, you will never flinch a little, even at the cost of your life, in dispelling darkness from the world and will establish supremacy of the Vedas." Needless to say that Dayānanda's answer was in affirmative. Uptil now he had been living for himself. The problems of life, death, salvation, and God were his personal but on initiation of his teacher, he now identifies himself with the humanity at large. The truth that he discovered for himself, he feels that the world should derive benefit out of it. He finds all around himself people bound up by superstitions and plunged into ignorance. He finds that India has lost her ancient heritage. For twenty years now, from 1863 to 1883, we find Dayānanda travelling over the country, holding in his hands the torch of Aryan wisdom, giving the message of one God and Vedic philosophy and regenerating the down-trodden race of the country.

THE SCOPE OF PHILOSOPHY

Dayānanda was essentially an Indian philosopher, and his method of treatment of the subject was also Indian. Without discrediting either an eastern or western philosopher, it can be easily seen that the two differ considerably in the mode of handling a common philosophical problem. No Indian philosopher thinks it worthwhile to discuss the scope of philosophy. Vyāsa, the great exponent of the Vedānta starts with the aphorism: "Then therefore the enquiry into Brahman." Kaṇāda of Vaiśeṣika says: "Then therefore Dharma we expound" and so the Pūrva-Mimāṁsākāra, Jaimini, says: "Then therefore the enquiry into Dharma." Pātañjali in his *Yoga* says: "Now the doctrine of *yoga* begins." Kapila in his Sāmkhya says: "Now the ultimate release from the three sorts of pains is the final *Puruṣārtha* (the goal of human life)." Gotama, who is no less an important philosopher, speaks out that salvation is attained by the thorough knowledge of the sixteen elements of logic: *Pramāna, Prameya, Saṁśaya, Prayojana, Dṛṣṭānta, Siddhānta, Avayava, Tarka, Nirṇaya, Vāda, Jalpa, Vitaṇḍā, Hetvābhāsa, Chhala, Jāti, and Nigrahasthāna."* The vedānta deals with such a Brahman, who is the first cause of the *Janma* etc. and who is the origin of divine knowledge. The Vaiśeṣika speaks of nine substances: earth, water, light, air, *Akāśa,* time, space, *Atman,* and mind and the seventeen qualities: colour, taste, smell, touch, number, size, individuality, conjunction, disjunction, priority, posteriority, knowledge, pleasure, pain, desire, aversion and effort. The Sāmkhya deals with twenty-four principles: *Prakṛti, Mahān* or intellect, *Ahamkāra* or self-sense, five *tanmātras,* sound, touch, smell, form and taste, *Manas,* five senses, five organs of action, five gross elements and lastly, *Puruṣa.* In the yoga, we find eight components of *yoga, Yama, Niyama, Āsana, Prāṇāyāma, Pratyāhāra, Dhāraṇā, Dhyāna* and *Samādhi.* The Purvamīmāmsā deals with rituals, formalities and observances.

These subjects enumerated here perhaps leave nothing which may not fall in the domain of philosophy. Then how does philosophy differ from other branches concerning knowledge? It is difficult to say. *Mukti, mokṣa or apavarga* is the final aspiration of a philosopher but it is difficult to reconcile how the subjects of investigation so different would carry one to the same goal. In some cases, I have found that a book on poetics or on physiology or even on astronomy is dedicated to the same cause. When the Sāmkhya says that there is no salvation without knowledge, what scope does it ascribe to knowledge? Is it the detailed knowledge of *puruṣa* and *prakṛti?* Does it mean the same thing as we understand of science today? Does it mean the study of those forces which can be profitably employed for running a big factory? Does it mean the study of evolution as an ordinary biologist does? Every time we hear that *avidyā* or ignorance is the cause of bondage, but which ignorance leads to bondage? Will a man who is not conversant with dynamics, calculus or trigonometry or one who has not attended a course of lectures on frog anatomy be debarred from the fruits of salvation? Some of the authors speak of *parā* and *aparā vidyā,* the one concerning knowledge of the world and the other concerning of Brahman. Is it only the Brahmanic knowledge that would lead one to the state of immortality, and does the knowledge of Brahman involve essentially the knowledge of all that is not Brahman?

A modern metaphysician makes a distinction between the *seeming* world and the *real* world, between substance and show. All of us know that things are not always what they seem to be; what appears to us is, sometimes at any rate, not real, and what really is does not appear. Perhaps philosophy is something which leads us from seeming to real, from apparent to invisible, but this is true with so many other sciences. An interesting argument runs like this: Metaphysics can have no place in the scheme of knowledge, because all intelligible questions which we can ask about reality must fall within the province of science. These are no facts with which some one or other of the sciences does not deal, and there is, therefore, no room for a series of 'metaphysical' enquiries over and above those enquiries which constitute the various sciences. Where there are facts to investigate and, intelligible questions to be put, we are, it is contended, in the domain of science; where there are none, there can be no knowledge. But perhaps, what the metaphysician asserts is not that there are *facts* with which the various special branches of experimental science cannot deal, but there are *questions* which can be and ought to be raised about the facts with which they do deal, other than those which experimental enquiry can solve.

Philosophy is always in search of reality or rather realities, beyond the sphere of appearances. Sometimes in the bewilderment one feels as if he does not find reality anywhere, because perhaps what *appears* to him is not real, and then the real becomes beyond approach. All our knowledge is strictly limited to appearances or as they are often called, *phenomena.* A phenomenalist will argue like this: What lies beyond phenomena is completely inaccessible to us and it is loss of time to speculate about its nature. We must, therefore, content ourselves with the discovery of general laws or uniformities of the inter-connection of phenomena, and dismiss the problem of their real ground as insoluble. But there is no strength in these arguments. The discovery of a general law of uniformity and to utilise it for some benefit does not take us far into the truth. The purpose behind the orderliness, the ultimate nature, the innumerable relationships between knower and the objects known and similar other subtle problems can be answered by a metaphysician only.

Dayānanda's philosophy is not restricted to a particular domain. He stands for complete knowledge. He agrees with Patañjali in defining ignorance and he explains knowledge in the following terms: "To look upon what is transient as transient, what is permanent as permanent, what is pure as pure, what is impure as impure, what is pain as pain., what is pleasure as pleasure, what is not-soul as not-soul and what is soul as soul is called *vidyā* or knowledge". He further says that by which the true nature of things is known is called *knowledge,* whilst that by which the true nature of things is not revealed and, instead, a false conception of things is formed is called *ignorance.*

Thus from Dayānanda's point of view, the following would be the domain of philosophy:

(i) The discussion of *ātma* and *anātma,* say metaphysics.

(ii) The discussion of transient and eternal or seeming and real. This is also metaphysics.

(iii) The discussion of pure and impure, that is ethical and non-ethical. This is ethics.

(iv) The discussion about pleasure and pain. This is psychology in the ordinary sense.

PHILOSOPHY AND RELIGION

It is true that without knowledge, there can be no freedom from bondage, but Dayānanda always impresses that knowledge, not transformed into actions, can bear no fruit. *Dharma,* the pseudo-synonym of religion, means the transcription of knowledge into actions, living life into one's beliefs. *Dharma* according to Kaṇāda is something that leads to the attainment of *abhyudaya* or the life of magnanimity and of *Niśreyasa* or the freedom from the worldly bondage. The Veda says[1]: "He who realises the nature of *Vidyā,* the true knowledge and of *Avidya,* the good moral life and divine contemplation, simultaneously conquers death by virtue of *avidyā* and attains immortality by virtue of *vidyā". Vidyā* here refers to philosophy and *avidyā* to religion in the ordinary sense. Virtuous life the worship of one true God and correct knowledge lead to emancipation, as Dayānanda puts it; whilst an immoral life, the worship of idols (or other things or persons in place of God), and false knowledge are the cause of the bondage of the soul. No man can ever, for a single moment, be free from actions, thoughts and knowledge. The doing of righteous acts as truthfulness in speech, and the denouncing of sinful acts as untruthfulness alone are means of salvation.

Gilbert Murray in his book on *"Greek Religion"* has given an anthropological exposition of religion. He says, "Religion essentially deals with the uncharted region of human experience. A large part of human life has been thoroughly surveyed and explored; we understand the causes at work and we are not bewildered by the problems. That is the domain of positive knowledge. But all round us on every side, there is an uncharted region, just fragments of the fringe of it explored, and those imperfectly; it is with this that religion deals." But this is merely an anthropological exposition of religion. One who has worked in the domain of science knows to what extent, almost to infinity, there extends the uncharted region in all matters of our knowledge. Compared to what has been not explored, the explored region is insignificant and a scientist, in most of the cases, only speculates and sometimes proceeds on hypotheses. Even then a vast region remains which does not admit of even speculations.

There are so many wrong notions prevalent in the West regarding religion. Perhaps, it has been due to the Church. Whitehead in his *"Science and the Modern World"* has exposed religion in the following terms: "Religion is the vision of something which stands beyond behind and within, the passing flux of immediate thing; something which is real, and yet waiting to be realised; something which is a remote possibility, and yet the greatest of the present facts; something that gives meaning to all that passes, and yet eludes apprehension; something whose possession is the final good, and yet is beyond all reach; something which is the ultimate ideal, and the hopeless quest." If this is the religion, certainly it is just an antithesis of *Dharma. Dharma* is not a thing of remote, it is not such an ideal whose quest would be hopeless, neither it is beyond all reach. *Dharma* is leading life unto knowledge. Prof. Taylor of the University of Edinburgh regards that if reality is a harmonious system, it must somehow make provision for the gratification of our ethical, religious and aesthetic interests. I would say that philosophy is not a mere intellectual satisfaction, the truths discovered by it must be verified or realised through life. Religious life is a verification of these truths. Of what avail metaphysics would be if it does not ascribe some purpose to life. If the world is unreal and illusion, metaphysics should also show some way of getting rid of it. If the world is real, then also, there must be some purpose of life in it, and metaphysics should bring it out. All philosophical findings should have a bearing on life. These truths when manifested through life become *Dharma.* Swami Dayānanda describes Dharma in the following words: "According to me, all that is beyond prejudice, reasonable, truthful, and in accordance to the divine tenets, the Veda is *Dharma." Dharma* does not admit of dogmas or superstitions. According to the Aryan discipline, only that person is entitled to be a seeker after knowledge who possesses a standard of character, whose sincerity and truthfulness are beyond doubt, who is free from prejudices and vices and who can be relied on for what he says. A man who does not follow *Dharma* has no right to study philosophy, for just as with an evil person, a weapon becomes an instrument of destruction, so with a man who has not attained a particular standard of character, the acquired knowledge would become a menace to humanity. And this is why, we find that Dayānanda's great teacher, Virajānanda, demanded from his disciple a high character, and we believe that Dayānanda proved to be one of the worthiest seekers after truth.

—*Raj Kumar*

REFERENCES

1. K.C. Yadav, *Autobiography of Dayanand Saraswati,* New Delhi, 1976, p. 17.
2. *Ibid.*
3. *Ibid.*
4. Ganga Ram Garg. *World Perspectives on Swami Dayanand Saraswati,* New Delhi, 1984, p.13.
5. K.C. Yadav. *op. cit.,* f.n. 100.
6. Tribute paid by Smt. Indira Gandhi, the then Prime Minister of India, in the occasion of the Nirvana Centenary Celebrations of Swami Dayanand Saraswati, *Ibid..* p. ix.
7. K.C. Yadav, *op. cit.,* p. 3.
8. A.D. Rein Court, *The Soul of India,* London, 1961, p. 236. Quoted in K.C. Yadav, *op. cit.,* p. 6, f.n.20.
9. *Satyartha Prakash,* Introduction, pp. I-X.
10. *Ibid.*
11. Haridas Bhattacharya (ed), *The Cultural Heritage of India,* Vol. IV, Calcutta, 1956, p. 635.
12. *Ibid.*
13. Sri Aurobindo, *Bankim-Tilak-Dayanand,* pp. 32-44.

7. *The Bengal Renaissance and Rabindranath Tagore*

(Andrews' first meeting with Tagore in London in June 1912 is described in the biographical sketch in this volume. During the remainder of the year while both remained in England, they met frequently. Andrews returned to India in November 1912, and paid his first visit to Santiniketan early in 1913, while Tagore was still absent in the west. In May of that year the Viceroy, Lord Hardinge, invited him to give a lecture at the Viceregal Lodge in Simla. The lecture, which was repeated in substance many times to audiences in India and South Africa, was published as the introduction to Tagore's *Letters to a Friend,* from which the following is taken.)

The course taken by the Bengal Renaissance a hundred years ago was strangely similar to that of Western Europe in the sixteenth century. The result in the history of mankind is likely to be in certain respects the same also. For just as Europe awoke to new life then, so Asia is awakening today.

In Europe it was the shock of the Arab civilization and the faith of Islam which started the west out of the intellectual torpor of the Dark Ages. Then followed the recovery of the Greek and Latin classics and a new interpretation of the Christian scriptures, both of which, acting together, brought the full Reformation and Renaissance. In Bengal it was the shock of the western civilisation which startled the east into new life and helped forward its wonderful rebirth. Then followed the revival of the Sanskrit classics and a reformation from within of the old religions. These two forces, acting together, made the Bengal Renaissance a living power in Asia. In Bengal itself the literary and artistic movement came into greatest prominence. Rabindranath Tagore has been its crown.

Early in the nineteenth century the burning question in Bengal was whether the spread of the English language should be encouraged or not. Between 1813 and 1833 a battle royal was being carried on in Calcutta between two schools of Anglo-Indian opinion. The Orientalists, as they were called, wished to confine education to the study of Sanskrit and Arabic literature, and to exclude the teaching of the west. Their opponents, the Anglicists, wished for many reasons, chiefly practical and commercial, to make English itself the educational basis.

Macaulay's famous minute, written in 1835, fixed the English tongue as the medium for higher education. 'Never on earth', writes Sir John Seeley, 'was a more momentous question discussed.' The phrase is an arresting one, and at first sight the words appear to be a gross exaggeration. But this impression is modified when we consider carefully all that lay behind the decision. It represented the first full inter-penetration of the two greatest civilisations that the world has even seen. Before this, at the beginning of the Nineteenth Century, eight hundred millions of mankind who lived East of the Persian Gulf were nearly as widely separated in thought, religion, and civilisation from the millions of Europe as they had been in the days of Alexander of Ashoka. Macaulay won the victory. Nevertheless, some of his premises were unsound and his conclusions inaccurate. He poured contempt of the Sanskrit Classics; he treated Bengali literature as useless. In expressing these opinions he committed egregious blunders. Yet, strangely enough, in spite of his narrow outlook, his practical insight was not immediately at fault. The hour for the indigenous revival had not yet come. A full shock from without was needed, and the study of English gave the shock required—but the new life which first appeared was not altogether healthy. It led immediately to a shaking of old customs and an unsettlement of religious convictions, carried often to a violent and unthinking extreme. The greatest disturbance of all was in the social sphere. A wholesale imitation of purely Western habits led to a painful confusion of ideas. It was a brilliant and precocious age, bubbling over with a new vitality; but wayward and unregulated, like a rudderless ship on a stormy sea.

The one outstanding personality, whose presence saved Bengal at this crisis, was the great Raja Ram Mohan Roy. Towering above his contemporaries, solitary and majestic, this extraordinary genius seems to have measured accurately the force of every new current as it flowed quickly past, and to have steered his own course with an almost unerring precision. As practical as Macaulay, he was no mere opportunist. He was a true prophet, and had the prophet's sacred fire of enthusiasm. On the literary side he was one of the most ardent promoters of the new Western learning, and eagerly helped forward Macaulay's programme. But the best energies of his marvellously full life were directed to recreate in the heart of the Bengali people that true reverence for the Indian past which should lead to a revival of their own Sanskrit Classics. Above all, he did not despite his Bengali mother-tongue, but brought it back into full literary use.

Debendranath Tagore, the father of Rabindranath, was the next outstanding figure in the Bengali literary revival. His work and influence lasted for more than half a century. If Raja Ram Mohan Roy may be likened to the root of this tree of literature, planted deep in the soil, Debendranath Tagore may be compared to its strong and vigorous stem, and Rabindranath, his son, to its flower and fruit. Rarely in the history of literature can such a direct succession be traced. Debendranath Tagore's religious character illuminated the age with a moral grandeur of it own. So impressive was his spiritual authority, that he received by universal consent the name of Maharshi, 'great saint.' During the flood-tide of English fashion he held fast to the ancient moorings and strengthened every bond which kept his country close to its own historical past. His autobiography, translated by his son, reveals the deep religious spirit of modern Bengal, along with its passion for intellectual truth. The Tagore family had already been attracted within the orbit of Raja Ram Mohan Roy, and the vivid memory of the great reformer was one of the strongest influences in moulding the life of Debendranath as he grew up from boyhood to youth.

By the middle of the nineteenth century, owing to these initial movements a creative period in Bengali literary history had set in. It represented not merely an awakening of Bengal, but the beginning of a new era for the whole of Asia.

This Bengal Renaissance bears on its surface the marks of conflict between the new Western learning and the revived Sanskrit Classics. Toru Dutt, the fairest and frailest flower among the writers, composed her songs only in English, but the fragrance of the Sanskrit past pervades all her works and makes them a national possession. Michael Dutt began by writing English verse; but he abandoned this, while his literary powers were still at their height, and composed his later poems in a wonderfully sonorous and majestic Bengali metre. He has been called the Milton of the Bengal revival Bankim's novels carry back the mind at every turn to the romance writers in the West. We can almost feel behind them the zest with which young Bengal explored their new-found treasures.

The strength of the period consisted in this, that the writers, amid all their passionate and devoted study of English, remained true to the ancient Indian ideal. They did not despise their own birthright. Not only the language, but also the subjects, of this new literature were brought more in touch with the people. The village life of Bengal, which had tended to fall into the background, gained a new appreciation. The mediaeval as well as the classical times were laid under contribution for subject-matter. The commanding ideal at last rose up before the minds of men, to build a truly national literature and art out of the living stones of indigenous poetry, music and song.

Into this rich heritage of the past the young poet Rabindranath entered, and he has done more than anyone else to make this ideal a living inspiration in Bengal. A friend of mine has described to me the scene that took place when the aged novelist Bankim was being honoured and garlanded. The old man took the garland from off his own neck and placed it on that of a young writer who was seated at his feet—Rabindranath Tagore. This act of Bankim has now been universally recognized as both generous and just. That which others were struggling to attain, in the midst of insuperable difficulties, Rabindranath has reached with the quick leap and joyful ease of supreme genius. The ideals of art, which were before only dimly discerned, he has seen with open vision.

Moreover, in his later works he has carried still further the spiritual mission of his father, and he has clothed his own deepest religious thoughts with a raiment of simplicity and beauty. His fame has come to the full in recent years, and his poetry has taken on a more prophetic tone. He has passed forward from the subjective period of unbounded delight to Nature, to enter into the mystery of the vast sorrow of the world; to share the heavy burden of the poor; to face death itself unmoved; to look for and attain the unclouded vision of God.

One dark, foggy morning in London, late in 1912, Rabindranath Tagore told me the story of his life. His first literary awakening, he said, came from reading the old Bengali poets, Chandidas and Vidyapati. He studied them in a recently published edition, when he was twelve or thirteen, and revelled in their beauty. He went still further, and, with the precocity of youth, imitated their style and published some poems under the name of Bhanu Sinha. Literary Bengal wondered for a time who this Bhanu Sinha could be. He laughed as he told me of this exploit of his boyhood, and went on to say that these and many other juvenile poems were merely conventional and imitative. They followed the old classical style.

When he wrote, however, the poems published later under the name of *Sandhya Sangit* (Evening Songs), he broke away from the classical style altogether and became purely romantic. At first he was described by the older generation for his new metres; but the younger generation was with him. He chose no English model; the early Vaishnava religious literature was the source of his inspiration. These religious poems ever afterwards remained intimately dear to him. Their influence is marked in his own lyrics, and especially in the *Gitanjali* series.

The time of his real birth as a poet he dated from a morning in Free School Lane, Calcutta. "It was morning", he said to me, "I was watching the sunrise from Free School Lane. A veil was suddenly withdrawn and everything became luminous. The whole scene was one perfect music—one marvellous rhythm. The houses in the street, the men moving below, the little children playing, all seemed parts of one luminous whole—inexpressibly glorious. The vision went on for seven or eight days. Everyone, even those who bored me, seemed to lose their outer barrier of personality; and I was full of gladness, full of love, for every person and every tiniest thing. Then I went to the Himalayas, and looked for it there, and I lost it... That morning in Free School Lane was one of the first things which gave me the inner vision and I have tried to explain it in my poems. I have felt, ever since, that this was my goal; to express the fullness of life, in its beauty, as perfection—if only the veil were withdrawn."

I copied this account down as the Poet told it on that dark, misty London morning; and I can remember distinctly even now the quiet laugh he gave as he said, 'and I lost it', and also the emphasis he laid upon the words 'fullness of life.'

His father, seeing his son's remarkable genius, very wisely insisted that he should leave Calcutta and go down to the banks of the Ganges in order to supervise there the family estate at Shileida. This work brought him into closest touch with the village life of Bengal. He had to deal each day with the practical affairs of men, and to understand and appreciate the elemental hopes and fears of mankind, stripped of all convention. To his own good fortune, also, as a poet, his joy in communing with Nature found at the same time its fullest and freest expression. During pauses in his active business life he would live all alone on the sand-flats of the Ganges, moving up and down from village to village in his boat. "Sometimes", he told me, "I would pass many months absolutely alone without speaking, till my own voice grew thin and weak through lack of use. I used to write from my boat the stories of the village life which I had witnessed in the course of my work, and put into written words the incidents and conversations which I had heard. This was my 'short-story' period; and some think these stories better than the lyrics which I had written before."

It was during this long residence at Shileida that the deepest love for Bengal, his motherland, developed. The national movement had not yet come into actual outward shape and form; but the forces which were to break forth later were already acting powerfully in the hearts of leading Bengali thinkers; and Rabindranath's soul caught the flame of patriotism, not in Calcutta itself, but among the villagers. His unshaken faith in the destiny of his country received its strongest confirmation from what he saw in the village life of his own people. He was not unaware of the dangers which threatened that life through its contact with the new social forces from the West. Indeed, this forms the theme of many of his short stories. But he believed, with all his heart, from what he had witnessed, that the stock from which the new national life was to spring forth was sound at the core. He spoke to me that morning with the greatest possible warmth and affection of the Bengali villagers, and of the many lessons he owed to them of patience and simplicity, of human kindliness and sympathy. It is not wonderful, therefore, that Bengal, from whose soil he seems to draw his deepest inspiration, should have been inspired in turn by his music and song with a high consciousness of its own destiny. He has given vital expression, at a supreme moment of history, to the rising hopes of his own people. Song and music are mighty instruments, when the spirit of a people is beating high with hope; and today men, women, and even little children, are seeing through the eyes of Rabindranath the vision of 'Golden Bengal'.

Slowly there came to him the clear call to give up his life more wholly for his country. He first went to Calcutta in order to found a school, and afterwards to Santiniketan with the same object. On his arrival at Santiniketan, to take up this new work, he was handicapped for want of funds. "I sold my books," he said to me pathetically. "I sold all my books, my copyrights, everything I had, in order to carry on the school. I cannot possibly tell you what a struggle it was, and what difficulties I had to go through. At first the object in view was purely patriotic, but later on it grew more spiritual. Then in the very midst of all these outer difficulties and trials, there came the greatest change of all, the true Varsha Sesha, the change in my own inner life."

He went on to tell me how, when he was forty years old, his wife had died, and almost immediately after, his daughter showed signs of consumption. He left the school and went away with his daughter to nurse her and tend her, but after six months of mingled hope and fear she passed away from his arms and left his heart still more desolate. Then came the third overwhelming wave of sorrow. His youngest son, to whom he had learnt to be father and mother in one, was taken suddenly ill with cholera and died in his presence—the child of his love.

As he spoke of these things that morning, the darkness of the London mists rolled away and the light shone through the clouds with a majestic radiance. This outward scene was but a faith symbol of the story that was being told me so quietly in that upper room. The Poet spoke of the days and hours wherein Death itself became a loved companion—no longer the king of terrors, but altogether transformed into a cherished friend.

"You know," he said to me, "this death was a great blessing to me. I had through it all, day after day, a sense of fulfilment, of completion, as if nothing were lost. I felt that if even an atom in the universe seemed lost, it could never actually perish. It was not mere resignation that came to me, but the sense of a fuller life. I knew then, at last, what Death was. It was perfection." Through what depth of suffering that peace and joy came out at last triumphant, the lines in his face told me as he spoke these words.

It was during this period that *Gitanjali* was written in his own mother tongue, Bengali. "I wrote," he said, "those poems for myself. I did not think of publishing them when I was writing." They mark the great transition in his life, when the Poet's social and national longings became wholly merged in the universal. He has attempted—to use his own words—"to express the fullness of human life, in its beauty, as perfection."

Since that period of sorrow he has fared forth as a voyager, a pilgrim. This is the last phase of all. It was his own health which first compelled him to set out to the West. But here again, as in the former period mentioned, the outward circumstance has brought with it a new spiritual development. "As I crossed the Atlantic", he wrote to me, "and spent on board ship the beginning of a new year, I realized that a new stage in my life had come, the stage of a voyager. To the open road! To the emancipation of self! To the realization in love!"

In another letter, which he wrote earlier to me, dealing with the meeting of the conflicting races of the world and the removal of colour prejudice, he uses these words: "This meeting of the races affords the greatest of all problems that men have ever been asked to solve. It is, I believe, the one question of the present age, and we must be prepared to go through the martyrdom of suffering and humiliation till the victory of God in man is achieved."

When Rabindranath Tagore first landed in London, in 1912, he had placed before his English friends some translations of his Bengali poems. He had offered them with singular diffidence, without at all realizing the value of his great achievement. "I found", he said, "that I had to strip my Bengali verses of all their gaudy ornaments and to clothe them in the simplest English dress." That English setting has since been acknowledge, by those who are best able to judge, to represent a beautiful and musical prose—a comparatively new form of English, which has enriched the literature of Great Britain. The triumph has been won—a triumph hardly ever before achieved in literary history—of an author translating his own poems into a wholly new language, thus giving his message to two peoples at once in a noble literary form.

This crowning success of Rabindnarath Tagore has already brought East and West closer together in a common fellowship and understanding. Where the forces of racial rivalry and religious division are so strong, it is indeed no small blessing to humanity when a generous voice can be clearly heard, above the discordant tumult of the times, which the whole world welcomes as a messenger and revealer of peace and good will to mankind.

8. *The Roots of Indian Nationalism*

(Andrews, as has been said, was a teacher of history. Like all true teachers he was also a student, and in his first years in India he gave a lot of time to the study of Indian history. In 1908 he wrote a very interesting article in the St. Stephen's College magazine, called *Indian History, its lessons for today.*[1] In that article, he quoted the saying that 'history is the best cordial for drooping spirits', and pointed out how the study of the history of Indian can increase our hope and confidence, and also raise numerous questions the answers to which may provide signposts for the future. Towards the end of the article are these words:

> "Go back to *your own history* for your picture of a free and spontaneous Indian life; do not be content to take your ideas of liberty at second-hand from the west.....You can never repeat the past, but you can learn from it noble lessons with regard to those great words, 'humanity, liberty, freedom'. You can learn these lessons, I repeat, from the history of your own Indian race.

The material in the passage which follows was used by Andrews repeatedly in a number of articles and books which appeared from time to time over a period of at least twentyfive years. The chief source is *The Rise and Growth of the Congress.*)

Introduction

Those who have sought to describe the history of India's political development have been used to take the year 1885, when the National Congress was founded, as their starting point; and in a sense they have been correct. But when they regard the years preceding that date as politically barren, they have surely failed to take account of one immensely important factor. They have not realized the very intimate connection in India between the political field and the sphere of religious development. For in India, more than anywhere else in the world, politics and religion have become mingled together in such a way that they can hardly be separated, however, much we may try to do so.

In Islam, as enunciated by the Prophet, religion actually rules the State. The Sikh Khalsa has shown us how the Indian mind works towards political and social freedom in and through a religious awakening. Swami Vivekananda and Mahatma Gandhi have, through their own religious inspiration, awakened a love for the Motherland such as no purely political leader has ever been able to evoke. Yet Swami Vivekananda remained a monk to the end and never entered the political sphere, and Mahatma Gandhi has often declared openly that he became a national and political leader only in order to carry out his faith in God in the midst of a political age.

Raja Ram Mohan Roy: Prophet of Nationalism

The most convenient period from which to trace the modern movement in the religious life of India, which led on to the Indian National Congress development, would be the very remarkable years, from 1828 to 1833, when Raja Ram Mohan Roy, the great religious and social reformer of Bengal, had reached the height of his spiritual powers. In every respect he towered head and shoulders above his contemporaries in the land of his birth, both European and Indian alike. By every modern historian of India he is rightly claimed as not only the clearest-sighted religious leader of his age, but also as its most advanced political thinker.

A fundamental faith in civil liberty characterized the whole life of Raja Ram Mohan Roy. Herein he was truly the prophet of Indian nationalism, for such a sovereign faith in liberal principles has been the most marked feature of Indian political life ever since. It has led not merely to a persistent struggle to be free from foreign control, but also to the initiation of internal reforms. The present movement towards the emancipation of the depressed and submerged classes owes its strongest incentive to the passion for liberty which Raja Ram Mohan Roy created.

This new spirit, awakening in Bengal at the beginning of the nineteenth century, extended in wider and wider circles till it reached every part of India. Later movements, such as the Arya Samaj and the Ramakrishna Mission, though quite independent in origin, were greatly helped in their progress owing to the pathway which had already been prepared by the Brahmo Samaj and its founder Raja Ram Mohan Roy.

The starting-point was Bengal; it was natural and almost inevitable because Bengal, as the focus and centre of British rule, was the first part of modern India to come into close contact with the west. Furthermore, the intellectual atmosphere of Bengal early in the nineteenth century encouraged the fullest freedom of thought. Bengal had peculiar gifts whereby the assimilation of western thought became comparatively simple. For such a process demands high imaginative power as well as intellectual capacity, and the cultured people of Bengal possessed both these qualities in full measure.

While the rest of India was still only slightly conscious of this new movement of human thought which had come from the west, Bengal was acutely awake. The hard mould of centuries had been broken and the new ideas of human progress found in Bengal their most congenial soil.

The Delhi Renaissance

The story has never yet been fully told of the remarkable revival of Islamic culture at Delhi, as it came into touch with western learning from 1835 to 1857. The renaissance in the north-west of India presented a remarkable parallel to the revival of learning in Bengal. The innate beauty and flexibility of the Urdu language, as it retained its near kinship with Persian literature on the one hand, and absorbed new ideas from the culture of the west on the other, afforded an admirable medium for this revival of learning in the north-west, just as the Bengali language was the true medium in Bengal. If Rabindranath Tagore has given the fullest expression in poetry to the Bengali revival, Muhammad Iqbal has done the same thing for the Punjab through his Urdu and Persian poetry.

All this remarkable revival of learning went on in Delhi right up to the outbreak of the mutiny of the sepoys at Meerut on may 11, 1857. These troops marched into Delhi in the course of a few hours, and from that time modern education and culture ceased. Those who had received the western learning were all suspected by the mutineers; many of them barely escaped with their lives. For many years after the siege and capture of Delhi every sign of the earlier education had vanished. Only very slowly did it return, and it never reached in later days the glory of its first efflorescence.

1857 and After

The events of that disastrous year changed the whole relationship between the Indian and the British races. As the revolt spread, the fiercest passions were aroused. A kind of hysteria of vengeance took hold of people who at other times acted and spoke in a normal and same manner. The massacres which had taken place at Kanpur and other places during the rebellion itself were followed, after the war was over, by reprisals from the side of the victorious armies no less horrible, and far more widespread. Life settled down to its ordinary routine, but the basis of sincere and friendly relationship was shattered for more than two generations. The brutal events of those terrible times set up a barrier between the two races; for though both people, the Indian and the British, are singularly free from the evil spirit of the vendetta, the aftermath of a war carried on with extreme desperation and violence could not easily be forgotten.

This untoward reaction did not occur merely in India. It was present in Britain also. Racial and religious equality before the law and in the administration had been pledged, in emphatic language, by the Queen's Proclamation (1858). It was therefore presumed by Indians that these two things would be carried out by the ministers who exercised her rule in India. But they were disillusioned; the smouldering forces of resentment, together with the increase of racial bitterness, prevented the pledge being carried out in practice. For a long time it was deliberately ignored by those in power, and the British Parliament connived at this. A confidential despatch of Lord Lytton, which became public property by some accident, has never been contradicted. It reads as follows: "Both the Governments of England and of India appear to me, up to the present moment, unable to answer satisfactorily the charge of having taken every means in their power of breaking to the heart the words of promise which they have uttered to the car."

A policy of 'divide and rule' has never been actually formulated; but what foreign Government could be safely entrusted with the power to play off one religious prejudice against another? This was done with brutal frankless after the Mutiny. The Muslims were deliberately repressed. The last vestige of the old Moghul Empire at Delhi was erased and the reprisals fell most heavily upon the followers of Islam. The rebellion was regarded, quite unjustly, as having had its origin among them. The truth seems to be that discontent was universal both among Hindus and Muslims alike, and the sepoy rebellion fainted the flame into open revolt.

But the theory somehow got abroad, and was very widely held by British administrators, that the whole outbreak had been a last bid for power on the part of Muslims, who had thus sought to restore at Delhi the throne of the Great Moghuls. Because they were so suspected even after the rebellion had been crushed, the Muslims steadily lost ground, both in education and in Government favour. Some of the noblest families were brought to the verge of ruin, and in Delhi itself even the direct descendants of the royal family lived in miserable destitution. As late as the early years of the twentieth century this state of things continued.

Syed Ahmad Khan: The Aligarh Movement

It is impossible to deal with the new life in India and not touch on the great Aligarh Movement, whose leader was Sir Syed Ahmad Khan. The Syed was born in one of the noble families in Delhi in 1817, and was brought up in the decaying Moghul court. But on entering Government service at the age of twenty, he threw himself heart and soul into the study of the west, as represented by the Englishmen he met and the books he read. When the Mutiny came, in 1857, he rendered invaluable help to many of the English men and women in his neighbourhood.

After the Mutiny, when the Mohammedans fell under suspicion, they were ready to resent this injustice and to grow bitter and bigoted in their turn. They regarded the new learning as *haram,* an unclean thing. Syed Ahmad set himself against this current of popular feeling with the utmost resolution. He gathered round him a body of young liberal Muslims who should help him to stem the current, and began with extraordinary patience and perseverance to organize education, and by that means to change the religious outlook of his fellow-countrymen. He was the founder of the Aligarh College and placed it under the guidance of the noblest English educationists he could find. The Aligarh Movement was one of the strongest educational forces in North India, and its effects have been felt in all parts of the Muhammadan world. Students from Java and the Malay Peninsula, from Kabul and Turkistan, from Mombasa and Zanzibar, have received their education at Aligarh and spread from thence the new Islamic thought.

No one but a giant in intellectual power and vigorous personality could have overcome the current prejudices so completely as to make the leading Muhammadans families, on whom success really depended, ready to send their sons to a College which their religious leaders condemned. Sir Theodore Morison, who knew Sir Syed intimately and had worked with him at Aligarh, writes: "Sir Syed was first and last a religious reformer;

he summoned his people to return to the sanity and simplicity of primitive Islam. He told them that the only instrument which could accomplish their regeneration was education, and that education must be on western lines. Had not the Prophet said: 'Go even to the Wall of China for the sake of learning'? Sir Syed suffered much social persecution, but no persecution could daunt his leonine courage; his great personality prevailed at length, and in the last years of his life he exercised a marvellous ascendancy over Muslim opinion. For myself I can say that I have never met another man so great as he."

Justice Ranade and the Social Reform Movement

The last, and in many ways the most enduring aspect of the new reformation in India has had its rise in the Bombay Presidency and is linked most closely with the name of Justice Ranade. Born in a district not far from Bombay, Ranade showed exceptional powers of scholarship and learning, and was appointed the first indigenous Fellow of Bombay University. Later on he rose by degrees to be judge of the High Court, but this was no the highest honour to which he attained. His name will be known to posterity rather as the founder of the Social Reform movement of modern India and as one of her profoundest religious thinkers.

Ranade comes near to Raja Ram Mohan Roy and Sir Syed Ahmad Khan in the largeness of his range of vision and the magnanimity of his character, but he was more advanced than either of them in the width of his constructive aim, his grasp of the principles underlying western civilization, and his application of them to Indian conditions. In his directly religious work he was one of the founders of the Prarthana Samaj, which corresponds somewhat closely with the Brahmo Samaj in its theistic principle and rejection of idolatry, though its organization is independent. This society has been in western India a main centre of social amelioration.

To Ranade, religion was as inseparable from social reform as love to man is inseparable from love to God. He taught incessantly that life could not be shut up into watertight compartments, but that religion must give unity to all spheres of activity. Thus his reforming faith was comprehensive. It inspired his careful economic studies as it did his social programme. His social programme led on to national aims. All human life was of one piece, and religion was the warp on which it was woven. He did not leave out the woman's side in the great advance, and his wife was a most noble helpmate to him in all his work; the Seva Sadan sisterhood was the outcome of some of his earliest labours.

Great and important as Ranade's activity was as an organizer of different movements, he was still greater as a thinker. His published works are a mine of sound, clear, accurate thinking on the problems of moral and social reconstruction. The great principle which runs through his teaching has already been hinted at. It was that the reformer must deal with the whole man and not carry out reform on one side only. "If a man is down, he has to get up with the whole of his strength; you may as well suppose that he can develop one element and neglect the others as try to separate the light from the heat of the sun, or the beauty from the fragrance of the rose. You cannot have a good social system when you find yourself low in the scale of political rights; nor can you be fit to exercise political rights unless your social system is based on reason and justice. You cannot have a good political system when economic arrangements are imperfect. If your religious ideas are low, you cannot succeed in social, economic or political spheres. This interdependence is not an accident, it is the law of our nature. No man can be said to realize his duty in one aspect who neglects his duty in other directions.

In summing up his great message to social reformers Ranade said: "Strength of numbers we cannot command, but we can command earnestness of conviction, singleness of devotion, readiness for self-sacrifice. In the words of the Prophet of Nazareth, we have to take up our cross, not because it is pleasant to be persecuted, but because the pain and injury are nothing by the side of the principle for which they are endured."

These words of the great Hindu reformer will sum up a very large part of the work which has been carried on during the last century in India. With the exception of Vivekananda's mission, it has been undertaken amid the bitterest opposition and often amid persecution of no ordinary kind. It has required commanding courage and abounding faith, and both of these have been in evidence.

REFERENCE

1. The article is reprinted in the Andrews Centenary number of *The Stephanion*, 1971.

9. *Delhi in the Nineteenth Century*

(The notes upon which this description is based were made by Andrews during his first years in India. At that time-1904-the present New Delhi did not exist; what we call 'Old' Delhi was an unimportant town in the Punjab, Lahore was the capital city, and the headquarters of the university. Very soon after his first arrival in Delhi, Andrews formed the habit of visiting a kind of informal, 'club' of elderly gentlemen which used to meet after sunset on the roof of the Old Library in Queen's Gardens. He made friends with the men who gathered there in the cool of the evenings, and persuaded them to talk with him about their memories of the past. Andrews' reminiscences of these talks were published in a series of articles in The Modern Review *in 1922, and after final revision appeared in book from in England in 1929, as* Munshi Zaka Ullah of Delhi.*)*

Introduction

From conversation with those whose lives scheduled far back into last century, I have tried to gather together some impressions of the condition of Old Delhi before the Moghul Court had entirely passed away. There are still a very few whose memories go back to those days, but the living records are rapidly being lost. When I first reached Delhi, nearly twentyfive ago, there were distinguished citizens who could actually describe the royal court.

Munshi Zaka Ullah Maulvi Nazir Ahmad were two of the oldest and most respected citizens of Delhi at the time when

I arrived there as a newcomer to India in March 1904. During the eight years that followed I was constantly in their company. Their deaths, each at the age of nearly ninety, rapidly succeeded one another in the years 1911-12.

The graciousness and dignity of the Moghul Age was made visible to me in my two Musalman friends. Munshi Zaka Ullah would talk for hours with me about the days of the Moghul court, about his own family history, his ancestors and traditions. It is a precious thing to me to have been able to obtain at first hand such a vivid picture of the past. Chiefly because of the friendship of these two old residents of Delhi, the city with its ancient memories and its glorious architecture has remained always my ideal vision of India and my first love. Delhi will always be Old Delhi to me. Nothing can take its place for me in the romance of Indian life.

Zaka Ullah's gentle courtesy, devotion and goodness embraced within its bounty all sorts and conditions of men. His acts of kindness were done in the true spirit of Islam, without any distinction of race, caste or creed. He would explain to me the central teaching of Islam concerning the compassion for suffering humanity, "which", said he, "is the supreme attribute of God in the Quran and in all the best Islamic thought."

Side by side with this love for all mankind he was a devoted lover of his own country. His family had come originally from beyond the Hindu Kush, but India was the birthplace of his parents and the home of his spiritual adoption. Voices are heard today declaring that India can never become one nation. Munshi Zaka Ullah, living in Delhi, knew better than most people what an amount of superstition, bigotry and ignorance had to be overcome before unity could be established. But he had a profound faith that Hindus and Musalmans should settle down at last in mutual tolerance and affection. That faith coloured all his actions.

In gathering together the material for the account of Old Delhi which follows, I have not gone to any printed records. What I have done is to relate things told me in conversation. In certain details my friends' recollection may be at fault, or my representation may be imperfect; but at least the record will have the colour and vivid character of personal eye-witness.

Bahadur Shah and the 'English Peace'

At the time when Munshi Zaka Ullah was a little child, the Moghul Emperor, Bahadur Shah, was already an aged monarch nearing his dotage. This Emperor could trace his lineage directly back to the House of Timur. His ancestors were Baber and Humayun, Akbar and Shah Jehan, He was the last of one of the most distinguished lines of kings that have ever ruled upon the earth.

No city had suffered more than Delhi during the anarchy of the eighteenth century, when the rule of the great Moghuls lost its grip upon the provinces. Towards the close of the eighteenth century the Maratha dominion from the South-west had reached forward as far as Delhi, the capital of the Moghul empire; but its hold upon the city was short-lived. In the year 1803 Sindhia was defeated by Wellesley at the battle of Assaye. This victory shook the Maratha supremacy, and brought with it, as one of its direct consequence, the British occupation of Delhi city.

Among the order inhabitants of Delhi whom I approached for information there was universal agreement that the brief Maratha rule had been oppressive, and that the people of Delhi and its neighbourhood had suffered grievously from looting and pillage while it had lasted. When the British troops took possession of the city without a struggle, leaving the Emperor in full, sovereign, independent command within the Fort, the general sympathy of the people was with them. Nevertheless, the Delhi people, Hindus and Musalmans alike, clung with faithful loyalty to their Moghul Emperors. For these Emperors were in no sense ordinary despots. Their chief virtue lay in a noble tradition of tolerance, especially towards their Hindu subjects. Their chief fault lay in the moral weakness of their personal administration. The corruption which they allowed brought its inevitable retribution and they succumbed without a blow to every form of more efficiently organized power.

The people of Delhi would undoubtedly have preferred their Moghul rulers to the English, if only the Emperors had been strong enough to project their city from violence. They were pleased that the semblance of power was left in the hands of the Moghul Emperors. The Fort, along with the palace, remained entirely free from the British jurisdiction and control. But outside the Fort, the real power passed more and more into the hands of the English, who were able to protect the city from external enemies and administer justice within the gates.

Delhi enjoyed a peace and calm such as it had not known before for many years. One of the old inhabitants whose memory went back to those times thus graphically described it to me: "The English Peace", he said, "became a phrase which passed into the everyday language of the common people. A man could go to pray to the tomb of Nizam-ud-din outside the city, and could ask for the intercession of the saint, without any fear of robbery or murder. In the city itself law and order were kept and great prosperity prevailed." Another who was the oldest survivor still retaining a vivid memory of those times, said to me: "The city did not know what order was still the 'English Peace' began. My own father used to tell me how before that time looking and robbery used to go on in the open streets within the city walls, and how none could go outside the city boundaries without having an armed escort of sometimes thirty or even forty men. Even these would turn and rob the persons who hired them, and there was no remedy."

Between 1830 and 1850, the 'English Peace' was firmly established. The city gates were shut each night and opened again every morning. By far the greater number of people lived within the walls, which were then intact. For the first time, because of the peaceful conditions, small number began to live outside the city walls; but there were only a few houses outside the Kashmir Gate, and none at all outside the Delhi Gate, where the ruins of the seven cities of Delhi covered the ground.

The road outside the city, leading from the different gates, were for the most part mere country tracks. There was no permanent bridge across the river Jumna, there was a thick jungle along the bed of the river. Inside the city the people were crowded together; where the present railway station stands was one of the most thickly populated parts of old Delhi. The large wide space between the Jama Masjid and the Fort, which is now kept without any building at all for military purposes, was at that time filled with houses of the middle class inhabitants of the city and the nobility of the Moghul court.

The majority of the residents had a comfortable and easy-going existence owing to the general level of the prosperity. For a long time prices remained extremely low. Wheat was about forty seers to the rupee, *ghee* four seers to the rupee. Articles of clothing were practically all made of homespun cotton cloth; wool was very rarely used. The padded cotton quilt was worn in the cold weather in order to keep out the winter cold. Anything that camp up country from Calcultta was usually brought by boat to Agra and thence on a pack-saddle, and therefore was very expensive. But every handicraft in Old Delhi was kept fully employed and a good price was obtained for durable handmade goods. The country made goods were fine in quality and not expensive and were remarkable for their rich dyes.

Down the middle of the central thoroughfare of Delhi, the world famous Chandni Chowk, ran a canal and shady trees grew on both sides. There was a universal opinion among those whose I questioned, that the Chandni Chowk had been spoilt by the modern 'improvements' that had widened the road, but covered over in doing so the water of the canal. "You cannot even imagine", said one old resident to me, "how stately the Chandni Chowk looked in the old days. It was the centre of the city filled with country-ware and country-produce. It was very bright with colour, because many awnings were put up in order to keep off the glare of the sun. All day long, except in the early afternoon in summer, when people retired to rest, it was crowded with those who were going shopping, or wanted to have a talk with their neighbours. They wore bright colour, and this added to the liveliness of the scene. Now, everyone looks dull, and there is no variety of colours. The beauty of the old Chandni Chowk is gone, never to return."

The gardens of the city were for the most part closed to the public. Some of these ancient Moghul gardens were used privately by the ladies of the Royal Court, and still bear the names of queens and princesses, such as the famous Roshanara Bagh. I was told that the Moghul Emperors were the first to introduce into North India these gardens with running water and roses and avenues of cypresses and other trees, which give a dream like beauty. Such gardens represented to them, amid the heat of Delhi, something of the coolness of the air of Central Asia which they had left behind. The rose especially was a favourite flower, because it reminded them of Hafiz and the Persian poets who often use it as a symbol in their own poems.

The water supply within the city during the earlier part of the nineteenth century was very inferior. There were not many public wells, and the water taken from them was supposed to produce a very painful kind of sin eruption for which Delhi had become notorious. Personally I can well remember the time when it was a serious danger, only second to malaria. I was told that malaria had always been prevalent in the late autumn, but the most serious epidemics had occurred after the Mutiny, when the jungle in the bed of the River Jumna grew very rank and was not cut down.

In the hot weather the poor people of Delhi used to suffer much from shortage of drinking water. Further supplies, in addition to the well water, used to be brought up in skins from the Jumna and sold in the streets. The great river, at that time, ran much nearer to the high wall of the palace within the fort. It has considerably shifted its course during the last hundred years.

Delhi in those days had little touch with the outside world. I could realize in the accounts I received, the interest which the varied pageantry of life created. The finest sight in the streets was the royal elephants, covered with cloth of gold, with huge gilded howdahs on their backs, as they were led in a stately, slow procession. These processions of the royal elephants on festival occasions through the Chandni Chowk, were not merely State functions; they were social occasions which broke the monotony of long days of toil at handicrafts and of hard labour in the fields; they gave a zest to life, and all the world looked on, arrayed in many-coloured dresses.

Not far from the Jama Masjid was an immense well called 'well of the elephants'. Here the royal elephants used to be brought, each morning and evening, to be bathed and to be given water. The children (those who related the story to me were themselves children in those days) would watch them with never-ending excitement.

Human intercourse was not hurried in those days. Men loved to stop and coverless with one another, seated by the side of the shop or in some portico. Life was lived in the open air. Food and work were both plentiful and there was no unemployment. The wheels of the active world did not go round too fast for average men and women to gain some pleasure out of human existence. There could enjoy life's panorama. There was a culture present imbibed from religion; an urbanity existed from close daily contact and kindly feeling which the modern rush and hurry have swept aside.

The aged Emperor, Bahadur Shah, was highly respected by the easy-going inhabitants of the royal city of Delhi. His very foibles and incompetences as a monarch were a part of his attraction. He was very peaceful unwarlike. His subjects would smile at his simplicity but they lived him all the same.

Bahadur Shah was tolerably skilled in those fine arts for which the ancient city of Delhi was famous. The four chief of these were music, manuscript illumination, miniature painting on ivory, and poetry. The highborn nobles round the Emperor joined in his artistic pursuits. Contests were held; the most highly-praised poems were recited; prizes were awarded. The whole city was interested in these recitals and the fame of the prizewinners went abroad. The Emperor himself would often take part for he prided himself more on being a poet than on being a king.

Meanwhile, however, in other directions the affairs of the administration went from bad to worse. The Emperor became the prey of greedy courtiers and sycophants, who used to flatter him to obtain his bounty. In this way large sums of money were extracted from him which ought to have been used for purposes of State. While the old Emperor sank in senility and dotage, the royal princes quarrelled among themselves. They were turbulent and violent-tempered, stirring up factions both in the palace and in the city. More than any other single cause, I was told, they brought about the final rain of the House of Timur.

One further fact deserves mentioning which is full of importance today. In Delhi city itself, the two communities, the Hindu and Musalman, had come to live peaceably side by side under the wise guidance of the Moghul Emperors, who had learnt to trust the Hindus, and were trusted by them in return. Those of my informants who were Hindus among the old inhabitants of Delhi told me without any reserve that their community was well treated under the last Moghuls and had no cause to complain. Even if, at times, there were outbreaks of mob violence among the ignorant masses over some insult to religion, these quarrels never reached beyond that substratum of society, and the animosity was easily allayed. The Moghuls knew how to make peace.

The intimate residence together side by side in the same city of Musalmans and Hindus had brought about a noticeable amalgamation of customs and usages among the common people. In Delhi—unlike further North in the central Punjab and on the Frontier—the Hindus had hold especially in commerce. The Musalmans had taken up the administration. Official posts were filled chiefly by them, with the exception of the revenue department. I have had more convincing and corroborative evidence about this friendly relationship between Hindus and Musalmans in old Delhi than I have had concerning any other factor. The information has come to me from both sides, and has been practically the same. It was evidently a feature of the city of which the inhabitants themselves were proud. These older residents whom I approached, whether Hindu or Musalman, spoke of this fact with enthusiasm, and contrasted it with the bitterness of modern times.

It was quite common, for instance, in those days, for the two communities to join together in different religious festivals. Hindus festival. This had become a natural local custom, and none but the zealots and puritans on either side raised any objection to such friendly proceedings.

The Musalmans had great respect for certain Hindu ascetics. There are famous Moghul paintings representing the Emperor and his Court visiting some such holy man. The Hindus, on their side, regularly flocked to pray for temporal benefits to the tomb of celebrated Muhammadan saint, whose grave was near the city. The tomb of Nizam-ud-din, outside the Delhi Gate, was also visited on special occasions by Hindus in order to obtain a blessing.

Again it was the custom of Hindu writers, who became famous in Urdu literature, and prided themselves on their knowledge of Persian to use the sacred world, *Bismillah* ('In the Name of God'), as an invocation, before they began to write. Hindu children went in large numbers to the schools attached to the mosques; there they learnt both Arabic and Persian. The Persian language was especially dear to them as the language of poetry, and the Parsian tradition still remain very strong in money of the leading Hindu houscholds in Delhi. Hindus would quote Hafiz and the other Persian poets both in their own Urdu writings and in their conversation. It was probably through this medium of the Persian language that the Hindus in Delhi became attracted to the Sufi doctrines in Islam, which were closely related to their own vedanta texts in spiritual ideals.

On Hindu feast days the children of Hindu households would always bring their offering of food to their teachers in the mosque schools. They would invite their teachers to their families to shares in their festivities, and such invitations were regularly accepted. Musalmans, on their side, spoke of the Hindu religious festivals with great courtesy and respect and were very particular to avoid any offence against Hindu customs. At their social functions, such as marriages and the like, parents were invariable sent to Hindu friends, and they were asked to grace the wedding by their company. They would come to pay their respects to the bride and bridegroom and offer their presents in return. On occasions of general rejoicing, such as the conclusion of the great Fast of Ramazan every year, congratulations would be sent by Hindus to their Musalman friends, and these would be graciously acknowledged. The art of living peaceably with neighbours of a different religion had reached a very high level.

The old Emperor, Bahadur Shah, was most punctilious in these matters right up to the end of his life. He would pass in procession with his royal elephants, decked in their cloth of gold, and would take his seat afterwards at a special tower in the fort, from which he could watch the crowd beneath at the chief Hindu festivals as well as Musalman feasts. The crowds would recognize him and make their obeisance, and thus much goodwill would be created. The Emperor, on these occasions, would give public recitations of his own verses and the people would loudly applaud.

The Delhi Renaissance

During the eighteenth century, Persian had been the court language all over the North of India, reaching as far down as Bengal. It was spoke in the presence of the king, and it was employed in the inscription of the royal edicts. But early in the nineteenth century a momentous change occurred. The Urdu language and script, which were both very near to the Persian in character, began to live, as it were, a separate life of their own, so that a kindred literature was produced which gradually diverged from the Persian forms and became adapted to India itself. Words of Sanskrit derivation, employed by the Hindus, found free access into this language, whose roots were firmly established in Islam.

During the reign of the last Moghul Emperors, Urdu literature made great progress. This was perhaps the most noticeable event in the history of the city at that time. Old Delhi had given birth to its youngest child, namely, the Urdu language, as a literary medium of the first historical importance.

In Delhi, the New Learning was ushered in by responsible and cultured men from the West, but in the first instance there was no outstanding genius, such as Raja Ram Mohan Roy in Bengal, to meet the West more than half-way and to acclimatise the actions taken by the British. Indeed, there was even stronger objection on the part of the orthodox, owing to the singularly vivid fear that religion itself would be undermined. This was told me on every hand by those whose fathers had themselves taken part in the great change.

As a simple matter of fact, the Delhi Renaissance, if it may so be called, was remarkably free from any direct tendency towards irreligion. It differed from the Bengal Renaissance in this respect. Practically all the teachers who came to the North of India, and most of the English servants of the East India Company, were religious men. Thus the New Learning, along with those who taught it, had never become associated with atheism in the young students' minds at Delhi. Certainly, all the elders, whom I met personally in later life, were markedly religious men. They possessed a sincere faith in God and strove to do what was right. A very tiny band of the most brilliant among them became Christians.

One interesting difference appears between Bengal and the Punjab. In Bengal, a sudden passion of literary enthusiasm for the newly-discovered English novelists and poets swept everything else before it. But the students in the North of India did not take very kindly to their new studies in English literature. By far the most popular side of the education offered in the old Delhi College was that which dealt with Science. Here, the interest was paramount, and it soon extended into the homes of the students within the city, where the new experiments would be repeated as far as possible in the presence of the parents.

Munshi Zaka Ullah, in his old age, used to tell me with kindling eyes how eagerly these scientific lectures were followed, and Low, after each lecture, the notes used to be studied, over and over again, and copied out by many hands. It was like entering into a wholly undiscovered hemisphere of the human mind. The young students were also caught by enthusiastic teachers. They were allowed to try astonishing experiments with unknown chemical gases. They were invited to dip into the mysteries of magnetism, which was just then coming to the front as a freshly discovered science. There was much yet to come, but these things formed actually for them a new world.

One further point of peculiar interest in the Delhi Renaissance was this, that the Oriental Department, which chiefly was concerned with Arabic and Persian literature, became very popular indeed. The classes, taught through the medium of Urdu, were not deserted for the new English studies. The standard reached in Persian and Arabic was often high. Maulvi Imam Baksh, the teacher of Oriental literature, must have been a very remarkable and gifted scholar. His reputation was as great with the Hindus as it was among the Musalmans.

What makes the Delhi Renaissance so profoundly interesting to the historian is the fact that these men, about whom I am writing, did things on their own initiative and thought things out for themselves. Just as, in Bengal, the New Learning brought with it an astonishing revival of Bengali literature and music and art, which found its culmination in Rabindranath Tagore, so also, at Delhi, Urdu literature has flourished along with modern science, and Muhammad Iqbal may be pointed to, in our own age, as the crown of its creative achievement.

The more one realizes the local situation of Delhi in those days, at a distance of one thousand miles from Calcutta, with no connecting railway at all, the more remarkable appears this sudden outburst of brilliant intellectual life, which came with the establishment of the old Delhi College. Professor Ramachandra's brilliant work as a mathematician was honourably recognized in

Europe. There was also Nazir Ahmad, who afterwards advanced to be the leading Urdu prose-writer and novelist of the nineteenth century, and world-famous on account of his profound Arabic learning. Shahmat Ali was made, in after-life, Prime Minister of Indore. Mukand Lal gained a high reputation as one of the first doctors, with a full western training, in North-west India. Ziauddin and Muhammad Husain were famous for their literary work. Altaf Husain, whose literary title was Hali, became the most renowned poet in Urdu literature, just as Nazir Ahmad was famous in prose. No such period ever arrived again in the history of the city during the nineteenth century. For many years, at a much later date, it was my daily task to teach in St. Stephen's College in Delhi. My own experience of the intellectual life of the city of Delhi was utterly unlike that which I have related about these early days. The commercial atmosphere of the whose district today lies with a heavy weight upon Delhi. The old culture and refinement and intellectual alertness now appear to be rapidly passing away. We have had no brilliant array of students in modern times such as existed in Zaka Ullah's days.

The contrast was so great that I used to ask him about this very point. He would tell me that what I said was correct. There had never been anything like it again. He put down a great dead of the earlier efflorescence to the newness of the subjects which were taught as part of the English learning. It was, he told me, like entering some magic and enchanted land. No one could tell what might be revealed next. The scientific experiments, above all held the students' imaginations. The vivid anticipation of fresh discovery was always with them. They felt themselves to be pioneers in their own country, and therefore dreamt dreams and saw visions.

Among his own contemporaries, Zaka Ullah had a great reputation for being able to solve all the mathematical problems that were set before him. Even while he was still a student, at the early age of seventeen, he had brought out his first mathematical work in Urdu. The Delhi people were greatly surprised and delighted at a mere lad undertaking such a difficult task, and the first edition was sold out in four days. Zaka Ullah took the whole of the profits, amounting to thirtytwo rupees, the first sum of money he ever earned by his own writings and purchased some gold ear-rings for his sister.

One of the uncles of Sir Syed Ahmad, a Nawab of Delhi, whose house was looked upon as a strange place of mathematical and astronomical learning, full of scientific instruments, with pulleys hanging from the roof, and astral globes and charts and astronomical tables scattered about sent for the lad who had dared to bring out a book on mathematics at the age of seventeen. "Well young man," he said to him, "I hear that you are a second Euclid. I will give you three days to solve a mathematical problem for me." At the end of the three days Zaka Ullah came back to him and said that the problem was insoluble, because at the final stage it was necessary to do something geometrically which was impossible. The Nawab was greatly surprised and pleased, "My dear lad," he said, "you have really solved the problem, because you have arrived at the final stage beyond which there is no solution."

Yet we can only with difficulty realize today what a struggle it must have been, both for Zaka Ullah's grandfather and for his father, to give up their child unreservedly and wholeheartedly to the new English education. For this strange learning from the West was already being called *Kafir,* or infidel; it was openly said to produce atheists. No doubt the parents were helped in their decision by the famous worlds of the Prophet, which are one of the supreme distinctions of Islam: "Get knowledge, wherever it is to be found, even as far as China". That great sentence has been the means, in every age, of breaking down the barriers which have separated Islam from alien cultures. This principle, underlying Islam, accounts for the fact that assimilation of fresh knowledge has been one of its distinguishing marks throughout all Islamic history.

The Delhi Renaissance came later in time than the Bengal movement, and it was less enduring in character. No horrors of bloodshed and upheaval overtook Calcutta, such as those which happened in Delhi in 1857. It is not difficult to trace the fatal havoc to building spiritual life which one year of the Mutiny wrought. Delhi never recovered its supremacy as a centre of intellectual advance. It is not merely the physical side of man's nature that is injured by the dread arbitrament of War; the soul of man is injured also.

The Mutiny

It is a strange and moving contrast when we come to place side by side Old Delhi before the Mutiny and New Delhi in its sudden rise to power. The Imperial Court had its aged dotard king, its recalcitrant princes, its nobles and its Court ceremonies. The decaying splendour of the palace, with its literacy after-glow of poetry and art, illuminated for one brief moment the ruined past before the end came in utter overthrow.

If the question be asked, why the 'English Peace' was immediately overthrown by the first earthquake shock of the Mutiny, the answer is complex. There were elements of revolt always present within the Delhi Fort itself, and underlying the acquiescence in British rule, the subjection to the foreigners was keenly felt. The foreigner remained a foreigner; and the humiliation of falling from the high position of the capital of a mighty empire to the low level of an insignificant local town could not but be galling in the extreme. I have witnessed the sense of this humiliation, still intensely felt, even in a gentle and forgiving old man like Munshi Zaka Ullah himself.

I can remember very vividly a scene in Delhi when I called upon one of my oldest friends at his house, just after a Durban which had been held by the Lieutenant-Governor of the Punjab, within the Diwan-i-Am, or Hall of Audience, inside the Fort. He had only a few moments before returned from the official ceremony and laid aside his Durbar dress. Suddenly there came upon him the memory of that Hall of Audience in Moghul times. He said to me openly: "Oh to think how I have degraded myself in that royal hall today by stooping to the stranger!" He did not seek to hide from me the anguish of humiliation he had been through.

In Delhi, the orthodox Muhammadan leaders had led the opposition to the New Learning. They were convinced that the foremost reason in the minds of the British authorities for the opening of the classes in English was to covert their children to Christianity. A suspicion grew up that every influence would be used in other to change the religious customs of the country. This fear lay directly behind the outbreak among the Indian troops, in 1857, when they were compelled, entirely against their religious sentiments, to bite off the ends of cartridges that had been greased. The fact that this compulsion about the cartridges was universally believed in Upper India to be an attack upon the Hindu and Musalman faiths, reveals the strength of the suspicion in the national mind at that time. It also discloses a lack of imagination on the part of the British rulers, that they should seek to deal forcibly with such a truly conscientious objection.

The Munity of the troops at Meerut came with a shock of vast surprise to the citizens of Delhi. The Punjab, which lay to the north of Delhi, appeared to be quite unprepared for a revolt so far-reaching and profound. It was in the lower provinces and among the troops enlisted further east than the Punjab and Delhi that the discontent with the British rule had reached its culminating point of open revolt. But it is not improbable that the natural dislike of the foreigner would have smouldered on in the same manner in the Punjab and Delhi if the British occupation there also had lasted longer. However, as far as I have been able to ascertain, there was no deep-rooted hatred of the foreigner in Delhi before the Mutiny began. There was simply the natural and intelligible dislike of being a conquered, instead of a ruling people. The average citizen was unwilling on his own account to revolt. It was when the soldiers, who had been recruited in the more eastern provinces, began the revolt at Meerut and marched suddenly on the city, that the people were carried away in the passionate excitement of the moment; and the princes of the royal palace, who had been most bitterly humiliated of all by the British occupation, headed the revolt.

To the young student of the Delhi College, who had imbibed the New Learning, the Mutiny came as a terrible shock. Their own Principal, Mr. F. Taylor, whom they loved and admired, was killed. For some weeks, no news whatever was heard of Professor Ramchandra; and the report was spread about that he was killed also. Their minds were in a tumult. They did not know which way to turn, or what to do. To go against their own countrymen, who had revolted, seemed to them impossible; to side with them in the revolt seemed even more unthinkable. Not a single student took that latter course. During the time that the city was in the hands of the mutineers, they were all of them under suspicion.

The final assault from the Ridge under Nicholson upon the Kashmir Gate was at last made. The city was recaptured by the British. Nicholson himself fell in the breach and died in the hour of victory. His death was a grave calamity, not only for the English, but also for the city. He was a strong character, famed throughout the North for his courage. Being a man of iron will, with a stern sense of duty, he might have been able to keep discipline among the British troops, after the victory, when no one else could keep it.

For days after the capture of Delhi nobody's life was safe. Murders were common, violence was almost universal. Zaka Ullah, with his delicate, sensitive nature, saw these things and heard about them. He was forced to be an eye-witness; and the sight could never be blotted out from his mind. The murder of the Professor whom he loved and revered most in the world, Maulvi Iman Baksh, a saintly man who had helped forward to the almost of his power the Delhi renaissance, was the culminating point in the whole tragedy. His former revulsion against the mutineers, who had killed. Mr Taylor and others, including women and children, now turned back again upon this conquering army, which in the hour of victory committed such unspeakable atrocities. The news of the slaughter of the royal princes near Humayun's tomb added to the misery of those days. These horrors were soon to invade Zaka Ullah's own family circle. For the order went forth that every house within the area between the Delhi Fort and the Great Mosque was to be rased to the ground, as an act of punishment, and also for military reasons. No compensation at all was to be given. Innocent and guilty were to suffer, both alike.

The old house and property of the family of Zaka Ullah came within this area. Therefore, along with many hundreds of other innocent people, his aged father and mother and the whole family were truthlessly driven out. They found themselves homeless and outcast, starving and destitute, at a time when multitudes of others were in the same condition.

Then followed a terrible journey The whole family went out together towards Nizam-ud-din's tomb, which lies about three miles from Delhi outside Delhi Gate. They slept at night on the open ground; and in the day time they took refuge inside a ruined tomb, every hour anticipating that the end had come. Only once did Munshi Zaka Ullah speak to me about those days of torture and hunger, of dread and horror. It was evident to him, especially in after years, that the faith of his father had been above all their protecting shield.

During one whole night, he said to me, he could not sieep on account of his anxiety for those he loved. The whole night through, his father Sana Ullah remained silent and wakeful, keeping a vigil of prayer to God. His face was filled with light in the darkness, a light which seemed to come from within. In the morning, Zaka Ullah learnt that a band of plunderers, bent on looting and murdering, had passed close by the very place and had looked in; but they had turned aside, when they saw the old saint engaged in prayer. Some hidden power had restrained them; thus the family had been preserved.

Zaka Ullah's Educational Ideas

Munshi Zaka Ullah's great work in life is rather to be found in his writing than in his active teaching career. It is true that he had great influence with his pupils, and that they loved him and revered him with a deep personal devotion. But his special ability was revealed in the manner in which he wrestled with an entirely new educational problem. For he endeavoured to prove, when nearly everyone was against him, that higher western education could be carried on in the Indian vernacular books, without insistence upon the English language and English text-books as the only medium of instruction. He believed that the teaching of young children through the medium of a foreign language, imperfectly understood, ruined all true education. He fought, at the time, a losing battle, but he fought bravely to the end. It now seems that history will prove his solution to be the right one after all.

Munshi Zaka Ullah had himself learnt science and mathematics through the medium of Urdu, as Professor Ramchandra had taught them, and he did not see why his children should not do the same. He had learnt chiefly from lectures, given by word of mouth in the vernacular; he had not studied from text-books at all. But he was quite certain that text-books could be written, and he was prepared to write them. His offer was accepted. It would have been difficult to have discovered anyone more fitted for the task.

He soon abandoned the mere verbal translation of English books, and launched out into writings that were either wholly, or in part, original. I have still with me many of his chief works which he presented to me. They are full of original information, written in a simple and fluent Urdu style. They cover a great variety of subjects. Their publication and their use in schools have done not a little to a set a standard for Urdu literature; to make it lucid and clear and easy to follow for the ordinary reader, and to free it from an overgrowth of Persian and Arabic words, which none but the learned understand.

Munshi Zaka Ullah was one of the few men who accepted whole heartedly the need for a modern outlook. He recognized to the full, owing to his own educational experience at the old Delhi College that without a full accetpance of the results of modern science and a full knowledge of them also, the East must inevitably tall behind the West, and the door of all future progress be closed. But at the same time he insisted that the medium of instruction should be the child's own vernacular language, not English. He was true to his own ideal, teaching his own students through the medium of Urdu. His life had a greatness of its own which different in tone and quality on the one hand from the English-educated Musalman and on the other hand from the Muslim who had stood entirely aloof from the modern world of the new learning. He possessed the liberality of the former and the old-world refinement of the latter. Every one who met him could feel that he had kept his own soul. He had not lost it in an artificial attempt to master another culture before he had been fully grounded in his own.

What he had accomplished in his own life and had worked out in his own experience he was anxious to impart to others; but he had not the gift that is needed in a pioneer, namely, the force of vital, dynamic personality that could drive his conviction home to the minds of others. If he had possessed the volcanic personality of Sir Syed Ahmad Khan, or even of his life-long friend and companion, Maulvi Nair Ahmad, he might perhaps have won the victory for what he knew, in his heart of hearts, to be the truth of modern education.

Islam in India

Munzhi Zaka Ullah's opinions on one point were very strong indeed. He objected vehemently to Musalmans, whose forefathers had been in India for many generations, regarding themselves as foreigners, or making a line of separation between their own interests, as Musalmans, and the interests of India itself. No subject roused him to indignant protest more than this.

"India", he said to me, with impassioned accents that I can still recall "India is our own mother country, the country which gave us birth. We have made our homes here, married here, begotten children; and here on this soil of India we have buried our sacred dead. For a thousand years, our own religion of Islam has been intimately bound up with India; and in India, Islam has won some of the greatest triumphs for its own peculiar form of civilization. I cannot bear to hear Indian Musalmans speaking without reverence and affection for India. It is a new fashion, unfortunately springing up, which did not exist in my younger days. The fashion is a bad one, and should not be encouraged. By all means let us love our Musalman brethren in other countries, and feel their joys and sorrows; but let us love with all our hearts our own country, and have nothing to do with those who tell us that we Musalmans must always be looking outside India for our religious hopes and their fulfilment."

There were few subjects on which Munshi Zaka Ullah in his old age became more eloquent than this. His heart was bound up with India, and his nature was rooted like a tree in India soil. When I asked him one day what he regarded as the one thing of greatest importance in India at the present time, he replied without any hesitation, "Religious Toleration." The answer was unexpected, and it struck me very much indeed. I had fully expected him to say 'Education', but his answer was more striking than that.

Naturally, I often spoke with the old man about his own Musalman community, and here I touched on a subject that was specially dear to him. For his intense love for India made him not less but more devoted to his own religion. Night and day he worked and studied, planned and thought for the good of Islam. For over fifty years he tried to set forth, in the Urdu vernacular, the new learning upon which he believed the progress of his own Islamic community to depend.

I have heard constantly in Delhi that report, disparagingly repeated, that he was a 'free-thinker'. If the phrase 'free-thinker' means that he thought freely and sincerely and with an open mind about religion, and regarded the spirit of his Islamic faith to be more important than the letter, then the phrase is nobly true concerning Zaka Ullah, and he well deserves the title. For it would have been hard to find a man more free from formalism and bigotry, more open-minded and tolerant. This made him a close friend and associate of earnest Hindus all through his long life.

But if the phrase 'free-thinker' is meant to imply a scoffer at religion, or one who thinks or speaks slightingly about religious belief in others, then the charge is wholly and entirely false. His attitude was always one of reverence and respect, and he was himself a deeply and sincerely religious man.

I repeat, he was not a formalist. He believed at all times in the spirit rather than the letter. He venerated those, like his father and grandfather, with whom the formal side of religion was a living reality. With his hard-earned money he sent his parents to perform the pilgrimage to Mecca and Medina, prescribed by Islam in its formal code.

But his own nature, in this respect, was different. He lived a life of simplicity and comparative poverty with the consciousness of God's presence ever about him and he left off during the greater part of his life many of the outward observances which were connected with his Islamic faith. Every word that he said to me implied that he was a true Muslim and, as I have already said, he made the respect Islam and understand its true inward greatness in a way that I had never done before.

10. The English Positivists and India

The "New Imperialism", the term used to define the expansion of the British Empire in the last quarter of the nineteenth century, was new in that support for it was conspicuously ardent among all segments of the public. Anti-imperialist sentiments diminished in importance as faith in Britain's mission to save the world increased. Conscious of their economic decline in relation to German and American expansion, British patriots looked increasingly to imperialism to avert economic distress and loss of international prestige. Some critics did remain and they denied that expansion could prevent decline, Colonies, they argued, were an unnecessary expense, a source of military weakness and poor trading partners. Yet, many of these critics defended retention of India. India had been part of the Empire since the eighteenth century and there was general agreement that it was Britain's "trusteeship" and would lapse into chaos if abandoned.[1]

Among the earliest anti-imperialists who included domination of India in their criticism were the English followers of Auguste Comte.[2] Opposition to imperialism came natural to Positivists, for Comte had insisted that the regeneration of the Western world, and eventually the whole world, depended on the termination of colonial relationships. Regeneration was contingent on the reinstitution of morality in politics and a 'Concert of Europe' to bring peace to the world, Imperialism promoted discord between European countries and thus prevented them from concentrating on their own affairs. The English Positivists went beyond an immediate concern for the welfare of Great Britain and western Europe and expressed a deep interest in the quality of Indian life under Imperial rule. Since 1857 they had used the Indian connection as a striking example of the exploitation of the weak by the strong.

The London Positivist Society[3] had been formally organized under the Presidency of Richard Congreve (1818-1899) in 1867. When the Positivist Society was formed there was no competition among the members for the position of leader—Congreve had been designated leader by Auguste Comte and had been preparing himself by studying medicine, a course which Comte declared essential for Priests of Humanity. Congreve's Positivism, never highly intellectual, was characterized by dogmatism and evangelical fervour—an approach that eventually alienated some of his earliest followers.[4] Congreve believed the organization's primary concern should be religion; other Positivists thought it should be political and social action.[5] In 1878 the split came; Congerve dissolved the London Positivist Society and with his loyal followers formed the English Church of Humanity.

Congreve's group remained interested in the Empire and questions of British foreign policy and wrote numerous pamphlets expressing their views. Following the Indian Mutiny of 1857 Congreve had published the pamphlet "India", which attracted Comte's favourable notice, contributed to the anti-imperialist theory of the Positivists, and became the principal document of Positivist thinking on India. Congreve admitted that there may have been reasonable justification for the conquest of India in the eighteenth century, but maintained that these arguments, along with British policy, needed to be completely re-evaluated. The usual arguments advanced for retaining India were that it contributed to English prosperity and international status, and that Britain was civilizing the "natives" by converting them to Christianity. Congreve denied the truth of these arguments: there was little commercial gain. India was a source of political weakness rather than strength, and the dearth of converts proved that Christianity could not adapt to the Hindu social system. The members of the industrial and ruling class were benefiting from this connection, Gongreve wrote, while the women and working class were losing. These people, exploited yet morally superior, were the only ones capable of seeing the disadvantages attached to the Indian policy. Addressing these two groups, Congreve wrote: "Let it be clear that you wish England to lay aside her aggressive and bullying attitude and adopt a policy which shall manifest to all here desire for peace, and her determination to respect the rights of others".[6] Congreve optimistically believed that a revolution would not be necessary to get the British out of India. He predicted that they would leave as a result of "an improved moral judgment—the outcome of a new religious impulse".[7]

While Congreve was concerned that Englishmen recognize the problems of the Indian connection and work to sever this connection, he was also devoted to the spread of Auguste Comte's Religion of Humanity. Positivism, he wrote, was "Catholicism plus science" and he predicted that it would be successful where Christianity had failed.[8] However, the Positivists generally preferred to support local groups that were familiar with local issues and problems than send "missionaries" as the Christian churches had done.

Despite this, there were three Positivist "missionaries" in India—Samuel Lobb, James Cruickshank Geddes and Henry J.S. Cotton. These men had gone to India first and declared their commitment to Positivism later. Employed as members of the Indian Civil Service they also propagated Positivist ideas. Faced with this situation, Congreve developed a theory of Positivist missionary work in India. If Positivists were to choose an Indian career, Congreve wrote, they would have to do so with a "missionary" spirit, break all ties with England and devote all their energies to their adopted country.[9] But the situation was complicated in the cases of these three individuals because they were employed by the British and because they had family ties in

England. Modifying his advice for Lobb, Geddes and Cotton, Congreve urged them to devote their energies to the formation of an Indian Positivist Society attached to the London organization. This group could suggest sound policies to the British rulers and help speed the termination of the imperial connection.[10]

The Positivist "missionaries" accepted what had become the English Positivist theory on India, but their intimate knowledge of this country caused them to go beyond these writings to analyze the disintegration of Indian social institutions. Each man looked at the problem and the solution from a particular angle: Lobb through the eyes of an educationist, Geddes as an economist, and Cotton as an administrator. And each could find Positivist arguments to fit his theory. Although Comte had been opposed to commentaries simplifying his theory, this did not deter the "missionaries" from adapting this doctrine to fit the Indian situation.

Samuel Lobb (1833-1876) had received his education at St. Paul's School and Trinity College, Cambridge, where he passed his M.A. in 1855. He joined the Indian Educational Service in 1861and the following year was appointed Professor of History at Presidency College. In 1868 he left India because of ill health; spent the winter on the Mediterranean and returned to take over the principalship of Krishnagar College, one of the leading district colleges. Lobb was a quiet and introspective person with few close friends. His widowed sister, Mrs. Peachy, lived with him in India and acted as the mistress of his household. Lobb was to remain at Krishnagar until his health forced him to resign; he spent the next two years in great physical pain and died on May 20, 1876.[11]

True to his cautious nature, Lobb had not made any sudden decision about Positivism. He had been interested in this philosophy before he first went to India but waited until 1865 to begin sending subscriptions to the Positivist fund and 1872 to request formal membership in the London Positivist Society. Although he had been hesitant to declare his commitment to this philosophy, he had begun writing books and articles on Positivism in 1867.[12] In his writings published in Bengal he attempted to simplify this complicated foreign doctrine so that it could be understood by the typical educated Bengali.[13]

Lobb concentrated on solving what he considered the major problem of Indian society: social and moral anarchy. He argued that the English-language schools had spread disruptive doctrines but had been unable to break down the strong fabric of Hindu polytheism. The unsystematic and careless teaching of science, philosophy and English had resulted in a society plagued by dissatisfaction, social experimentation, skepticism, the breakdown of old traditions, dissension between "modernizers" and "traditionalists", obvious economic problems and even epidemics and plagues. Of the Hindu mind he wrote, "scientific modes of thought are not in consonance with its most marked characteristics".

It was in the polytheistic stage, Lobb insisted, not the positive stage, and was unequipped to deal with the new ideas that had so thoroughly upset the basis of traditional morality and institutions.[14]

Althought Lobb's picture of the confusion caused by English education was grim, he admitted a remedy. What India needed, he wrote, was "a system adopted to the peculiar needs and special idiosyncracy of the Hindoo, which dispensing with the old Vedic idea of revelation, shall rest upon a logical basis, and yet be such as to satisfy the moral requirements of man's nature".[15] Positivism could, he wrote, give to men "emancipated from old beliefs a resting place'. The Hindu mind could never be 'depolytheized" through the efforts of an alien and unsympathetic government but this could be accomplished by voluntary missionaries, partly indigenous and partly foreign, propagating a Western doctrine that had been moulded into appropriate forms by Eastern intellectuals[16] Lobb saw him self as one of the pioneers in this great task and hoped to find Indian intellectuals who would carry on the work.

Lobb's first concern was to reclaim those minds that had been "emancipated from old beliefs" and felt lost without a philosophy or religion to guide their actions. In his articles for the *Bengalee* he simplified and reinterpreted Positivism for Indian needs.

Believing that the Hindu mind was not yet ready to grasp scientific principles, Lobb emphasized the religious aspects of this philosophy. Some understanding of science was necessary but Lobb assured his readers that this could be easily accomplished by becoming "acquainted with" arithmetic, astronomy, mechanics, chemistry, physiology, and history. To read on treatise on each of these subjects was deemed sufficient. This slight acquaintance with science could not be expected to "depolytheize" minds but Lobb hoped it would enable individuals to at least stop their theological speculations and concentrate on scientific studies designed to serve Humanity.[17]

As an educator Lobb regarded careless and haphazard teaching of science to unprepared minds dangerous to the individual and to the community. Science was a powerful force, Lobb warned; if handled correctly it could be the vehicle to emancipate Hindu minds, if mishandled it would mean their doom. Evaluating the teaching of science in India, Lobb observed that there was little or no experimentation, a lack of current textbooks, poor and unprepared, students who lacked the necessary background, and an emphasis on memorization. Students graduated from these classes not with a firm grasp of the scientific method but what a large body of memorized facts.[18] This reckless teaching of science would lead a division between feeling and intellect, whereas science, taught according to Comte's hierarchy, would lead to higher morality.[19]

Lobb believed that if he were even partially successful in Positivizing the Hindu mind, the gains for social stability would be tremendous. It would help Western-educated young men realize, he wrote, the destructiveness of their efforts to change the caste system, introduce women's education, and encourage widow remarriage. Caste was an ancient and functional institution with a firm hold on the society. Instead of working to abolish caste, Lobb thought reformers should spend their energy trying to find a social base to replace its theological base. The education of women was dangerous proposition because unplanned education could produce chaotic results in a group still largely untouched by the disruptive influences of the West. Widow remarriage he opposed, because Comte had developed the idea of religious marriage which sanctioned perpetual widowhood for both men and women.[20] Positivism would promote social harmony through its regulation of individual emotional instincts and communal-social relationships. Once a few "select minds" learned about this doctrine and its potential value, Lobb predicted they would be prepared to reorganize society.[21]

The doctrine which Lobb expounded appealed to a number of Bengali intellectuals, two of whom became deeply interested in the Positive Philosophy One of these men, Grish Chunder Ghosh (1829-1869) became friendly with Lobb as early as 1867. The two exchanged a number of letters in which Lobb attempted to explain the advantages of Positivism in calming the unsettled feeling of the times. Lobb's letters and conversations were convincing: Girish became deeply affected by Positivism, defended it publicly, and put the *Bengalee,* the newspaper he edited, at Lobb's disposal.[22] Of the Indian Positivists associated with Samuel Lobb, Dwarkanath Mitter (1833-1874), the second Indian appointed High Court justice, was the most prestigious. When Lobb wrote to Congreve about Dwarkanath's adherence, the leader of the English Positivists imagined that all educated Indians would soon convert. Towards Dwarkanath Lobb expressed a warmth of feeling unusual for one so reticent; on one occasion he wrote to him. "you are the only Positivist friend I have in India and I can assure you that it is cheering now and then to inter-change a few thoughts with one who has so much in common with my own sentiments as yourself".[23]

Lobb's association with these men was well-known; however, Christian missionaries accused him of surreptitiously propagating Positivism in the classroom. He denied this charge: Positivism "appeals only to those already emancipated", Lobb wrote, "who feel a want and are willing to undergo the conditions laid down by it for satisfying that want". Positivism was a difficult doctrine to master, he repeated, and the Positivists were unwilling to welcome into their fold immature minds.[24] In fact, Lobb was as hesitant to introduce Positivism as he was to introduce science to an unprepared mind. That Positivism had penetrated a few select minds was salutary, but Lobb ruled out the possibility of attracting a large following.

James Geddes (1837-1880), the second Positivist "missionary" to appear in Indian, had joined the Indian Civil Service after attending the University of Aberdeen, He went to Indian as a very young man with hopes of a great career but without any concern with or knowledge of Indian problems. In India, he became deeply distressed by the poverty he wintnessed and began to read books and articles on this subject. When he read Congreve's pamphlet "Indian" he agreed with this assessment and became determined to learn more about Positivism.[25] Finally, it was the ideas in Congreve's Positivist Manifesto of 1859 that he adopted as the basis of his own view of India: that the British had weakened their moral image as a world power by continuing to support an unjust position in India; that the poor of England suffered because of the connection; and that it was the duty of the English working class to loudly proclaim their dissatisfaction with British imperialism.[26]

Geddes first went to India as a member of the Judical branch of the I.C.S. He was appointed magistrate and was frequently transferred, occasionally serving in some other capacity. While on furlough in England, 1870-1871, he met Congreve, married Congreve's sister-in-law and joined the London Positivist Society. His association with the Positivists led him to deliver a lecture to the positivist organization on May 21, 1871, to commemorate "Modern Industry". Published as *The Month Gutemberg,* this lecture became the most controversial pamphlet associated with the London Positivists. In the same year Geddes published *The Logic of Indian Deficit,* which in combination with *The Month Gutemberg* outlined a revolutionary theory of Indian and, by extension, world problems. He blamed the poverty of both the Indian peasant and the British working class on the manufacturers and traders, the only people who gained from imperialism and wars.

When the finances of India were reviewed by the House of Commons in 1870 it was found that there was a large deficit; the Committee appointed to untangle the financial confusion invited Geddes to give evidence Geddes came before the Committee in July, 1871 and when asked about the Orissa famine, bluntly answered that it was the direct result of government taxation and public works projects. His gloomy predictions about the future of the British in India provoked one of the Committee members to Question Geddes' loyalty to the government he served.[27]

In his pamphlets and articles Geddes developed a theory of Indian economic problems that many Englishmen found shocking and many Indians attractive. While the governing class in England benefited, the Indian peasantry was being crushed under an unfair system of taxation, an administrative system too expensive for a poor country, absentee plantation owners, and expensive irrigation and railway projects. The Government believed that India was becoming more prosperous. Geddes argued that the only gains were on paper: peasants were forced to turn to cash crops so that they could pay their taxes: cash crops meant less area devoted to food crops so the peasants had less to eat; and taxation was spend on public works projects such as railways which only helped the British more systematically exploit the people. Economic decline affected the social institutions, Geddes believed, blaming the British for the deterioration of Indian social and religious life.

Geddes' predicted that the spending policies of the British Government in India would eventually bring bankruptcy. This financial burden would then fall on the British working class who already supplied the military manpower to control India for the wealthy ruling class. Putting Indian problems into a world context, Geddes urged the workers of the world to unite in trade unions to repudiate nationalism and imperialism and demand that profits be put to social use. The Indian connection, Geddes suggested, might eventually cause a social revolution in England. But there was a solution. The universal adoption of the Religion of Humanity, Geddes optimistically concluded, would solve all problems by inspiring morality in politics.[28]

Geddes' remarks and publications, 1871-1873, were more radical and attracted more attention then anything Congreve had written. Official displeasure, manifested in order constantly shifting Geddes from one location to another, combined with Congreve's mild but firm rebukes, were sufficient to restrain Geddes from any further attacks on government policy. Following his return to India in 1871 he had written three articles on "Our Commercial Exploitation of the Indian Populations" for the *Calcutta Review* but his plans for a series of articles on "Our Religious Embarrassments in India" were abandoned.[29]

While Geddes' opinions on the economic situation had made the Government doubt his loyality, they earned him the praise of the Indian educated class, who recognized him as a man willing to risk official displeasure to help the Indian people. They were most familiar with the *Culcutta Review* articles, which accused the British of exploiting the Indian peasants for British gain. What particularly attracted these budding nationalists was Geddes' assumption that Indian self government would be infinitely fairer and more sympathetic. They had gained a nationalist argument from Geddes' internationalist message.[30]

Serving as a magistrate in the outlying areas had prevented Geddes from establishing intimate contact with the Western-educated class in Calcutta and developing a "circle" of Indian friends as had the other two Postivist "missionaries'. Although he made no converts he was deeply admired by the Indian Positivists. "And if our little body lives and grows", wrote Jogendro Chandra Ghosh, the leader of the Indian Positivists, "it shall always be our pride to recall his name side by side with that of Lobb and Dwarkanath Mitter as the pioneers of Positivism in India".[31]

—*Geraldine Hancock Forbes*

REFERENCES

1. Herman Ausubel, *The Late Victorianbs,* (New York, 1955), pp. 81-85; A.P. Thornton, *The Imperial Idea and Its Enemies; A Study in British Power,* (New York, 1959), pp. ix-xiv; David Thomson *England in the Nineteenth Century, (1815-1914)*, (Harmondsworth Middlesex, 1950), pp. 203-212.

2. Positivism, the philosophical system elaborated by Auguste Comte (1798-1857), was a highly complex scheme for the organization of human society according to scientific principles. Central to Compte's theory was the law of three stages, developed in his first major work, *Cours de philosophie positive,* which explained the relationship betwcen the evolution of the human mind and the progress of human civilization. According to Comte, all minds, all sciences and all societies passed through three stages of intellectual development: the theological stage (further subdivided into the festishtic, polytheistic and monotheistic stages); the metaphysical stage and finally the positive stage. In his *Systeme de politique positive,* Comte, outlined his plans for a Positive sociocray and religion. The Religion of Humanity, the culmination of the whole scheme was designed to unify and organize society so that individuals could live together without conflict and devote their lives to improving the human condition.

3. The major collections of documents on the English Positivists are the Positivist Papers in the British Museum (hereafter *P.P.*) and the Richard Congreve Papers in the Bodleian Library (hereafter *M.E.L.*). Among published works are Walter M. Simon's *European Positivism in the Nineteenth Century: An Essay in Intellectual History,* (Ithica, 1963) and "Auguste Comte's English Disciples", *Victorian Studies, VIII* (1964); Edwin McGee's *A Crusade for Humanity: The History of Organized Positivism in England,* (London, 1931); and Thomas Nyland's *The English Postivists;* (M.A. Thesis, University of London, 1937).

4. Nyland, *The English Positivists,* pp. 69-72.

5. Simon, European Positivism, p. 163.
6. Richard Congreve, "India", *Essays: Political, Social and Religious,* II, (London, 1892), pp. 74-104. Quote taken from p. 104.
7. Richard Congreve to Jogendro Chandra Ghosh, 19 August 1881, *P.P.* Ms., 45262.
8. Congreve, "Propagation of the Religion of Humanity", *Essays,* I p. 311; Simon, "Auguste Comte's English Disciples", p. 162.
9. Congreve, "Moral and Social Questions Connected With Our Empire", *Essays,* I, p. 437.
10. Congreve, "Circulars 91, 100, 104", *Essays,* II.
11. "Samuel Lobb" *M.E.L.* 183; Congreve to Dwarkanath Mitter, 7 September 1872, n Dinabandhu Sanyal, *Life of the Hon'ble Justice Dwarkanath Mitter; One of the Judges of Her Majesty's High Court of Calcutta,* (Calcutta, 1883), p. 109; "Samuel Lobb", *P.P.*, Ms. 45246.
12. His writings include articles in the *Calcutta Review* (1868-1871), a highly respected and well-known English Language monthly published in Calcutta; the *Bengalee* (1867-1871), a popular anti-government weekly; *Thoughts on the War by a Positivist* (1870), on the Franco-Prussian War; *A Brief View of Positivism* (1871); and a translation, with others of *the Eight Circulars of Auguste Comte* (1881).
13. "Sacerdotal Fund", *P.P.,* Ms. 45257; Congreve to Samuel Lobb, 20 March, 1877, *M.E.L.,* e. 70; "The Late Mr, Samuel Lobb", *Bengalee,* supplement, 27 May 1876.
14. "Influence of the West on the East", *Indian Observer,* 6 January 1872, pp. 1-2, *M.E.L.,* 487.
15. "Miss Carpenter's Six Months in India", *Calcutta Review,* XLVII, (1868) p. 22.
16. "Letter to the Editor", *Indian Observer,* 6 January 1872, pp. 11-121.
17. The Aim of Positivism", *Bengalee,* nd; "Importance of Positivism and the Preparation Necessary for the Study of It",

Bengalee, 3 August 1867, 2 October 1867; "Dr. Siircar on Scientific Education", *Bengalee,* nd; "Positivism Something More than a Systematization of Science", *Bengalee,* nd; in Positivist *Articles from the Bengalee,* (Calcutta, 1870), hereafter *PAFB.*

18. A Graduate, "Mr. Lobb on Calcutta University", *Mookerjee's Magazine,* I (1872), p. 47.

19. As a member of the Calcutta University Syndicate Committee, formed in 1871 to considered changes in the scientific curriculum, Lobb argued that increasing the number of science courses would neither bring about social change nor sharpen the critical faculties of students. He recommended that the required science courses include those designated by Comte as the first sciences to study. S. Lobb, "Physical Sciences in the Calcutta University", *Calcutta Review,* LIII, (1871), pp. 321-341.

20. "Caste", *Bengalee,* nd.; "Divorce", Bengalee nd., in PAFB.

21. Positive Religion", *Bengalee,* 19 November 1870, 3 December, 1870, 10 December 1870, in *PAFB.*

22. S. Lobb to Girish Chunder Ghosh, 24 July 1868, 5 June 1867, 10 October 1868, in Manmotha Nath Ghosh, *The Life of Girish Chunder Ghosh* (Calcutta, 1911).

23. Lobb to Dwarkanath Mitter, 1 February 1870, in Sanyal, *Life,* p. 118.

24. Positivism Aid Moral Teaching", *Bengalee,* 5 April 1873, p. 108; Lobb to Mitter, 16 January 1871, Sanyal, *Life,* p. 122; "A Positivist Professor", *Friend of India,* 16 March 1871 p. 303.

25. Congreve, "James Cruickshank Geddes", *M.E.L.,* 183.

26. Congreve, "Positivist Manifesto, 1859", in J. Geddes, *The Logic of Indian Deficit,* London, 1870), p. 10.

27. Great Britain, *Parliamentary Debates,* House of Commons, Series 3, CCIII, cc. 1600-1630; Great Britain, *House of Commons Sessional Papers,* "Report for the Selcct Committee of East Indian Finance", 1871, VIII,1.

28. For Geddes' ideas on Indian and English problems, see J.C. Geddes, *The Logic of Indian Deficit; The Month Gutemberg: On Modern Industry,* (London, 1871); "Our Commercial Exploitation of the Indian People—I, II, and III", *Calcutta Review,* LV (1872), pp., 340-381, LVI (1873), pp. 139-170 and LVI (1873), pp. 352-382.
29. Congreve to Geddes, 17 April 1874, 4 October 1874, *PP,* Ms. 45231; "Mr. Geddes on India', *Friend of India,* 17 October 1872, p. 1196; "Mr. Eastwood and Mr. Geddes", *Bengalee,* 10 May 1873, pp. 148-149; Geddes, "Our Commercial Exploitation—III", p. 352.
30. "The Late Mr. Geddes", *Indian Mirror, 2 April 1881;* Hindoo Patriot, 15 March 1880, p. 128.
31. Congreve, "The Sacrement of Incorporation", *Essays,* II, p. 752.

11. Social and Cultural Reconstruction

Progress of Christianity in India

Christianity was a force in the social and cultural history of India during the first half of the nineteenth century. Its progress in India during the first half of the nineteenth century is traced here. In 1793, William Carey, a Baptist missionary, arrived at Calcutta, without a licence from the Directors, with the desire of preaching Christianity in India in Indian languages. The foundation of the Serampore Baptist Mission in 1799 was a turning point in the 'modern era of Missions'[1] in India. Within a few years, Christian missionary stations were established in Calcutta, Madras, Bombay and at other places. 'One Society, then another, one missionary, then another, landed on the coast of India'[2] for preaching Christianity. The London Missionary Society sent missionaries to Chinsurah, to Travancore, to Madras, Vizagapatam and Bellary. The Church Missionary Society started a mission centre at Agra and used the agency which Corrie had employed at Chunar. An Indian Christian began to work at Meerut and two missionaries were stationed in Calcutta. The Baptist Society soon began to work at Jessore, Chittagong, Dinajpur and some other places. The Bible Society helped the missionaries in translating the Bible and it was soon circulated in the various missionary centres in India in different languages.

From their safe refuge at the Danish settlement of Serampore, sixteen miles north of Calcutta, the Baptist missionaries, like Carey,

Thomas Marshman and Ward, made earnest efforts for the conversion and education of Indians, in spite of the Despatch of the Court of Directors, dated 7 September 1808, 'declaring their policy of strict neutrality in all matters of religions, and in spite of the contempt thrown on their efforts at home'.[3] But the Company's Government soon gave up this policy and the Charter Act of 1813 laid down: 'It is the duty of this country to promote the introduction of useful knowledge and of religion and moral improvement in India and that facilities be offered by law to persons desirous of going to and remaining in India to accomplish this benevolent design'. This facilitated Christian missionary work in India. In 1820, an Anglican Bishop was appointed for the first time in the East India Company's dominions in India and Bishop Middleton came to Calcutta as the first Metropolitan of India. Most of the Protestant Missions were started in India between 1815 and 1830 and the Bishopries of Madras and Bombay were established in 1833. A large number of high caste, educated Hindus in Bengal, Madras and Bombay were converted to Christianity. In Bengal, conversion work was carried on by Christian missionaries like William Carey, Joshua Marshman, William Ward, Daniel Brahmdon, William Grant and Rev. Alexander Duff. Such work was done in Bombay by Dr. John Wilson, in Madras by Robert Noble and in the Punjab by Dr. Forman.

By the end of 1850 the stations from which the Christian gospel was preached in India and Ceylon numbered two hundred and sixty and these engaged the services of two hundred and three missionaries belonging to twenty-two missionary societies. Of these missionaries two were 'ordained natives'.[4] With the assistance of five hundred and fifty one native preachers, they carried on the work of conversion vigorously. They founded three hundred and nine native churches.[5] The missionaries also maintained twenty-five printing establishments.[6]

In the period after the Indian Movement of 1857-59, the Christian missionaries directed their attention to the conversion of low castes and hill tribes like the Santhals, Oraons, Mundas, Nagas, Khasias and Garos.

Sati and Its Abolition

Sati, or the practice of Hindu women burning themselves on the funeral pyres of their husbands, though rarely being buried, has been referred to in Vedic literature[7] and mentioned in the Puranic tradition.[8] The continuance of this practice, with more or less emphasis, is attested to by a number of references in the literature and relics of subsequent historical times (e.g., *sati* memorials). It gained a new lease of life during the medieval period of Indian history, so that on the eve of the modern age instances of *sati* were quite common. It was also prevalent in the Vijaynagar Empire. The Italian traveller, Niccolo Conti, who visited Vijayanagar about the year A.D. 1420, notes that 'the inhabitants of this region marry as many wives as they please, who are burnt with their dead husbands'. Another traveller, Fernao Nuniz, also remarks: 'The women have the custom of burning themselves when their husbands die and hold it an honour to do so... When a captain dies, however many wives he has they all burn themselves when their husbands die and hold it an honour to do so... When a captain dies, however many wives he has they all burn themselves and when the king dies they do the same. This is the custom throughout all the country of the heathens, except with that caste of people called Telugas (Telugus) amongst whom the wives are buried alive with their husbands when they die.'[9]

In the sixteenth century, Ralph Fith, who visited India during 1583-91, refers to the *sati* practice in his description of Ahmednagar, Burhanpur and Benaras.[10] Some of the Mughal rulers attempted to suppress or regulate it. Akbar, for example, tried to prevent the burning of a woman against her free will.[11] William Hawkins (1608-13) writes: 'I have seen many poor women brought before the king (Jahangir) whom (by his commandment) none may burn without his leave or sight at them; I mean those of Agra. When any of these cometh, he doeth persuade them with many promises of gifts and living if they will live, but in my time no persuasion could prevail, but burn they would.'[12] Other travellers like Nicholas Withington (1612-16)[13] and Edward Terry (1616-19) have referred to it.[14] Francois Bernier,[15] who travelled in the Mughal Empire during A.D. 1656-68 and saw several *sati* cases, writes:

The accounts given of it (women burning) have been certainly exaggerated, and the number of victims is less now then formerly; the Mohammedans, by whom the country is governed, are doing all in their power to suppress the barbarous custom. They do not, indeed, forbid it by a positive law, because it is a part of their policy to leave the idolatrous population, which is so much more than their own in the free exercise of its religion; but the practice is checked by indirect means.[16] No woman can sacrifice herself without permission from the Governor of the province in which she resides, and he never grants it until he shall have ascertained that she is not to be turned aside from her purpose; to accomplish this desirable end the Governor reasons with the widow and makes her enticing promises; after which, if these methods fail, he sometimes sends her among his women, that the effect of their remonstrances may be tried. Notwithstanding these obstacles, the number of self-immolations is still very considerable, particularly in the territories of the Rajas, where no Mohammedan governors are appointed.

Jean Baptiste Tavernier (1670-89) thus describes this practice.[17]

A woman cannot burn herself with the body of her husband without having received permission from the Governor of the place where she dwells, and those Governors who are Mohammedans hold this dreadful custom of self-destruction in horror and do not readily give permission. On the other hand it is only the women who become widows without children who can be reproached for not having loved their husbands if they have not courage to burn themselves after their death, and to whom this want of courage will be for the remainder of their lives a cause of reproach. For, as for the widows who have children, they are not permitted under any circumstances to burn themselves with the bodies of their husbands; and very far from custom obliging them, it is ordained that they shall live in order to watch over the education of their children. Those whom the Governors peremptorily refuse to grant permission to burn themselves pass the remainder of their lives in severe penances and in doing charitable deeds.

But these efforts of the Mughals did not effectively check the practice. We find several references to it in contemporary literature[18] as also in the accounts of some European writers of the eighteenth century. Bolts remarks: 'Even those very women who live sequestered from the world and of course are inexperienced in such difficulties and misfortunes as served to fortify the mind and heart, or such distress as will render life irksome or impel to desperation, often manifest such fortitude as amazes Europeans but to hear of the horried deaths which they voluntarily brave, of burning alive with the dead bodies of their husbands in funeral pyres.'[19] Craufurd has given a thrilling description of the manner in which the women burnt themselves:

> A funeral pile being erected on a piece of ground that was consecrated to the purpose, the body of the Raja was brought from the fort, accompanied by many Brahmins and others and followed by the widow attended by relations of both sexes. Being arrived at the funeral pile, the body was placed on it, and certain ceremonies being performed the widow took leave of her relations. But she was perfectly composed, smiled and endeavoured to comfort them. She then advanced to the pile, and in a solemn manner walked round it. She stopped; and after contemplating the corpse, touched the feet with her hand and raised it to her forehead, inclining her body forwards. She then saluted the spectators in the same manner, and with the assistance of the Brahmins mounted the pile and seated herself by the side of the corpse. Some who stood near her with torches in their hands set fire to it and as it was composed of dry wood, straw and other combustible materials it was instantly in a flame.[20]

'Such a devoted woman', when about to burn herself as a *sati,* was not allowed to be touched and thus defiled by a non-Hindu. The Dutch Director (in Bengal), Sichterman (1744) 'was obliged to pay twenty-five thousand rupees for an imprudence of this kind, which he had been guilty of.'[21]

The courage and fortitude with which the widows, unperturbed in the least by considerations of worldly enjoyments, offered themselves up in such ghastly sacrifices, were extraordinary. 'Such is the influence of customs and the sense of shame', writes Craufurd, 'that women of the highest birth will undergo this awful sacrifice with as much fortitude and composure as ever were exhibited by any philosopher of antiquity.[22] Scrafton remarks: 'Many authors ascribe this (*sati*) to have been instituted to prevent their wives poisoning them; but I am well persuaded that often they submit to it by a nice sense of honour and conjugal affection.'[23] The Dutch traveller, Stavorinus, who witnessed a *sati* case at Chinsura on 25 November 1770, writes that the woman 'underwent everything with the greatest intrepidity and her countenance seemed at times to be animated with pleasure, even at the moment when she was ascending the fatal pile'.[24] He paid particular 'attention to her in order to discover whether any convulsive motions agitated her feet, but they remained immovable in the midst of conflagration'. Compulsion might have been sometimes used but that was, remarks the same writer, 'seldom necessary as they possess sufficient enthusiasm willing to devote themselves to this horrible death'.[25] He also refers to the case of the wife of a rich Bengali broker of the Dutch East India Company gladly offering herself as a *sati,* though her husband had been a veritable debauchee and had left her company; she refused to obey the instructions of her friends and relatives who tried to dissuade her from the act on the ground that her husband 'had used her so ill in his lifetime'. Holwell and Craufurd refer to the case of the wife of one Ram Chand Pandit, a Maratha settler at Cassimbazar, who died on 4 February 1743. The woman was of about seventeen years and belonged to a rich family. All the merchants of Cassimbazar and her relatives 'left no arguments unessayed to dissuade her from it. But she listened to none, and her friends finding her thus peremptory and resolved, were obliged at last to assent.'[26] She only waited till the Faujdar's permission for her burning had been received. Malcolm has mentioned, on the authority of some eye witnesses, the case of another Maratha lady showing equal resolution and strength of purpose.[27] She was Muchta Bai, the only daughter of the celebrated Sri Devi Ahalya Bai of Indore. After the death of her, only son and of her husband, Muchta Bai expressed her resolution to burn herself with the dead body of her husband. 'No efforts (short of coercion) that a mother and a sovereign could use were untried by the virtuous Ahalya Bai to dissuade her daughter from the fatal resolution. She humbled herself to the dust before her and entreated her as she revered her God, not to leave her desolate and alone upon earth.'[28] Muchta Bai remained calm and did not forsake her resolution. 'You are old, mother', said she, 'and a few years will end your pious life. My only child and husband are gone, and when you follow, life, I feel, will be insupportable; but the opportunity of terminating it with honour will then have passed.'[29] The daughter remained unmoved and the old mother had to witness the awful scene. Baji Rao II, almost a contemporary of Ahalya Bai, discouraged this practice in the dominion of the Marathas[30] amongst whom, the position of women being comparatively securer, this practice was not so general as in some other parts of India. But it was very much in evidence among the Rajputs,[31] with whom the allied practice of *jauhar,* or mass *sati,* was also common.

Sometimes, a temple was erected on the spot where a *sati* sacrifice had occurred.[32] Craufurd notes that he saw one of those places 'where the spot on which the funeral pile had been erected was enclosed and covered with bamboos, formed into a kind of bower planted with flowering creepers. The inside was set round with flowers, and at one end there was an image.' Ahalya Bai built a monument on the spot where her daughter had burnt herself.[33] Hamilton Buchanan writes that the custom of widow burning was very common in the district of Shahabad and that 'in almost every manor are three or four places, marked by a coated cone of clay, where the horrid sacrifice has been performed. At these places, *Sat Chauras* or *Siras,* women of all ranks continue to make little offerings, and the relations of the victims keep the monument in repairs.'[34] W.H. Sleeman saw at Bahrol,[35] on 3 December 1835, 'a very unusual number of tombs built over the ashes of women, who have burnt themselves with the remains of their husbands. Upon each tomb stands erect a tablet of freestone, with the sun, the new moon, and a rose,[36] engraved upon it in bas relief in one field, and the man and woman, hand in hand, in the other.'[37] General G. Hervey has noted the existence of many *sati* shrines at Bikaner.[38]

The abolition of the *sati* rite in 1829, like other social reforms of the period, was possible owing to the combination of three forces. The measures adopted, on the ground of administrative necessity, by the Company's Government in India, the attempts of the Christian missionaries, and the growth of an enlightened Indian opinion—all worked together for this important reform in Indian social life.

In 1772 the Company declared its intention to 'stand forth as the Diwan' so far as administration was concerned; but it still followed a policy of non-interference with regard to social and educational matters of the Indians. The Company's Government in Bengal then promised to 'preserve the laws of the Shastra and the Coran, and to protect the natives of india in the free exercise of their religion'. The manual of Hindu Law prepared by a body of learned Brahmins under the orders of Warren Hastings encouraged the *Sati* rite.[39] The following emphatic expression was noted in Colebrooke's translation of the *Digest of Hindu Law,*[40] compiled under the superintendence of Sir William Jones: 'No other effectual duty is known for virtuous women at any time after the deaths of their lords, except casting themselves into the same fire. If a woman in her successive transmigration declines doing so, she should not be exempt from shrinking again to life in the body of some animal.'

But the Supreme Court in Calcutta tried to restrict the rite within the limits of its immediate jurisdiction, and the inhabitants of Calcutta had to perform *sati* in the suburbs.[41] The Danes at Serampore, the Dutch at Chinsura and the French at Chandernagore prohibited it within their jurisdictions and the inhabitants of those places could act as they liked outside the boundaries of the settlements of those Companies.[42] The English Company's Government at Madras tolerated the practice but between the years 1770 ad 1780, at any rate, it was not allowed within the scattered territories then under the control of the Government of Bombay.[43]

Some officers of the Company's Government suggested to their superiors the need for taking effective steps against such a horrible practice in spite of the continuance of the policy of non-interference in relation to Indian social matters. But the company still shrank from issuing definite official orders forbidding it fully. On 28, January 1789, Mr. M.H. Brooke, Collector of Shahabad, wrote to Lord Cornwallis.

Cases sometimes occur in which a Collector, having no specific orders for the guidance of his conduct, is necessitated to act from his own sense of what is right. This assertion has this day been verified in an application from the relations and friends of a Hindu woman for my sanction for the horrid ceremony of burning her with her deceased husband. Being impressed with the belief that this savage custom has been prohibited in and about Calcutta and considering the same reasons for its discontinuance would probably be valid throughout the whole extent of the Company's authority, I positively refused my assent. The rites and superstitions of the Hindu religion should be allowed with the most qualified tolerance, but a practice at which human nature shudders I cannot permit without particular instructions. I beg, therefore, My Lord, to be informed whether my conduct in this instance meets with your approbation.[44]

Brooke was of the opinion that, in spite of its policy of non-interference in religious matters, the 'Government could prohibit a practice at which 'humanity shudders'. But he was instructed only to use dissuasion and not coercive measures or official powers to prevent *sati* sacrifice.[45] Sir John Shore's Government also followed the policy of Lord Cornwallis in this matter. On 17 May 1797, James Battray, Magistrate of Midnapur, wrote to the Government in Calcutta that he had been able to prohibit the *sati* of a widow aged only nine; but even then he apprehended that she would soon sacrifice herself. The Government asked him 'to do his best to dissuade her'. Thus, apart from some isolated efforts on the part of individual British officers, the *sati* practice was not definitely forbidden by the Company's Government in the eighteenth century.

The Serampore missionaries, working for conversion to their faith in certain districts of Bengal, had the opportunity of observing Indian social customs and religious practices. William Carey witnessed a *sati* in the Hugli district in the year 1798.[46] In the year 1804 the Serampore missionaries, taking a census of *sati* cases within a radius of thirty miles from Calcutta, found that more than 300 *sati* cases had taken place within six months.[47] William Carey consulted some Pandits, who opined that 'the practice was encouraged rather than enjoined' by the *Shastras*.[48] He disclosed the results of his investigation to his friend, Mr. Udny, who was then a member of Lord Wellesley's council.

On 4 January 1805, J.R. Elphinstone, Magistrate of the old Bihar district, informed the Government that he had prevented the *sati* of a girl of *bania* caste at the request of her friends. Having no definite orders for the prevention of this practice, he solicited further instructions from the Government. Lord Wellesley caused his views to be forwarded to the Court of *Nizamat Adalat,* which was responsible for the detection and prevention of crimes within the Presidency, and requested that body, on 5 February 1805, to ascertain if the *sati* practice could be abolished.[49] The Judges of the *Nizamat Adalat* consulted some pandits and forwarded their views to the Governor-General. In the opinion of the pandits, girls belonging to the four higher castes might burn themselves except under certain circumstances, such as when they were in a state of pregnancy, or menstruation, when they were under the age of puberty and when they had infant children whom there was no one else to support. In forwarding these opinions, the Judges 'advised that while the custom could not be abolished generally without greatly offending "religious prejudices", it might be abolished immediately in some districts, where it had fallen into disuse, and checked or prevented in others on lines indicated by the replies of the pandits.' They recommended 'a policy of mingled abolition and compromise'.[50] Lord Wellesley could not introduce any decisive measure against the practice as he had to leave his office on 31 July 1805. In the year 1799, twenty-two wives of a Kulin Brahmin were burnt alive with his dead body at Nadia.[51] About the same time a rich Kulin Brahmin died at Sukchara, three miles east of Serampore. Of the forty wives he had married, only eighteen survived till his death and on that occasion they burnt themselves leaving behind more than forty children.[52] We have already noted that the number of women burnt alive with the corpse of their husbands within thirty miles around Calcutta during the year 1804 was about three hundred. Lord Minto stated that *sati* was rampant, especially near Calcutta.[53] In 1812 nine women burnt themselves on the funeral pyre of the Raja of Kanika, in Orissa.[54] We may compare and figures for *sati* cases that took place in Cassimbazar and places situated at the mouth of the Hugli river in May and June 1812 in Table 2.[55]

On 3 August 1812, Wauchope, Magistrate of Bundelkhand, solicited instructions from the *Nizamat Adalat* about the policy to be pursued in *sati* cases.[1] The *Nizamat Adalat* forwarded his letter to the Governor-General, who replied in the month of December that the *sati* practice, having behind it the sanction of Hindu doctrines, 'must be allowed in those cases in which it was countenanced by religion, and prevented wherever it was not'.[57] The original suggestion of the *Nizamat Adalat* that the sacrifice might be checked immediately in certain districts was not considered by the Governor-General. Certain rules framed in 1813 empowered the Magistrates and other officers to prevent the use of force or drugging in *sati* cases and the sacrifice of women in pregnancy or of girls under puberty. The police being enjoined to act on these rules were to take notice of every case as early as possible. Some supplementary instructions were published in 1815 directing the magistrates to submit annual reports and returns of *Satis* within their respective jurisdictions. Some other rules were circulated in 1817 prohibiting the burning of widows, who had infants at the breast or children under four or seven years of age, there being no responsible persons to take care of them. Relatives of a *sati* were to inform the police of her resolution to burn herself failing which they were to be fined or imprisoned.

Table 1

Places	*Female's Name*	*Age*	*Children Left*	*Husband's caste*
1	*2*	*3*	*4*	*5*
Kalleka-poora	Hera	18	1	Brahmin
Do	Radha	22	2	Oilman
Do	Sukhee	33	2	Blacksmith
Do	Sarutee	25	2	Brahmin
Do	Koomare	40	4	Carpenter
Baloochuru	Kaminee	32	3	Brahmin
Bamaniya	Rajee	25	3	Kaistha
Do	Roopee	25	2	Brahmin
Shree-nugura	Bimala	31	3	Carpenter
Juyu-para	Koushulya	45	5	Gardener
Juyu-para	Koushulya		5	Gardener
Do	5 Women		4	Merchant
Kashimbazar	Soonduree	35	3	Goldsmith
Do	Dassee	34	3	Brazier
Calcutta	Shyamee	32	2	Brahmin
Do	Tara	19	1	Goldsmith
Do	Soonduree	31	3	Blacksmith
Do	Jeera	25	3	Kivartta
Billiya	Rummunee	27	2	Brahmin
Kumula-poora	Rutuna	16	0	Husbandman
Do	Munee	33	3	Oilman
Do	Dassee	25	2	Goldsmith
Do	Bhuguvutee	38	4	Rajpoota

(Table Contd...)

1	2	3	4	5
Kamula-poora	Lukshimee	60	5	Washerman
Do	Shyamee	30	3	Gardener
Do	Mutee	38	4	Oilman
Manasinghapoora	Daminee	40	3	Kaistha
Do	Pudma	33	2	Do
Do	Suleeta	45	6	Do
Do	Somee	30	3	Carpenter
Burdhman	Koomaree	23	3	Rajpoota
Do	Dropudee	31	3	Carpenter
Do	Tripoora	38	4	Blacksmith
Kochu-nugura	Duya	35	4	Do
Brahmun-poora	Nuyanee	21	3	Weaver
Nuya-serai	Sidhoo	25	3	Potter
Inkoo-serai	Kumunee	19	1	Brahmin
Do	Sukhee	32	3	Do
Do	Shyamee	30	3	Barber
Rampoora	Shyamee	38	3	Brahmin
Gopal-nugura	Sona	39	3	Kivartta
Anur-poora	Kince	16	1	Bagdee
Manik-poora	Bhuwanee	29	3	Kivartta
Do	Bhabinee	38	2	Gardener
Do	Suruswutee	19	1	Oilman
Do	Viskkna	40	4	Weaver
Pareshwura	Shyamee	37	4	Brahmin
Ichanugurya	Priya	17	1	Do
Do	Chitra	52	4	Do
Do	Kulindee	25	4	Oilman
Katulya	Mohinee	33	4	Barber
Teguriya	Soonduree	38	3	Kivartta
Do	Sushee	38	3	Barber
Do	Nuyanee	25	3	Brahmin
Chunakuli	12 women	..	30	Brahmin-Kuj

The rules of 1812, 1815, 1817, being mere 'Circular orders' without any legal sanction behind them were not very effective in checking cases of *sati*. The *Nizamat Adalat* remarked in 1819 that it was doubtful whether 'the measures publicly adopted with the humane view of diminishing the number of these sacrifices by pointing out the cases in which the Hindu law is considered to permit them have not been attended with a contrary effect to the one intended'.[58]

In considering the *sati* reports for the year 1821 from the magistrates of Cuttack, Balasore and Khoordah, the *Sadar Nizamat Adalat* passed the following remarks and orders:

> The Court observe that Eighteen Suttees are reported to have occurred in the immediate jurisdiction of the magistrate of Cuttack during the past year, and that only one within the jurisdiction of the Joint Magistrate stationed at Balasore is reported, but within that of the Joint Magistrate of Khoordah nine are reported to have occurred; with respect to those cases which occurred within the places immediately subordinate to the Magistrate of Cuttack only two explanations have been afforded one of which exhibits illegality on the score of non-age. In the case of Musammat Kumlah, No. 18 of the statement, it was clearly competent to the magistrate to have punished as for a misdemeanour, the washerman Rajib who pushed the woman into the flery pit as assisting at a sacrifice not wholly voluntary and that it would have been preferable to have committed entirely into an investigation rather than to have released the offender without punishment, after he had been convicted of the offence. The Court expect a brief remarks to accompany each case in future to be abstracted from the report of his Police Officers. The same observation is applicable to the statement furnished by the Joint Magistrate of Khoordah.[59]

It is not reasonable to argue merely on the strength of the returns obtained for several years after 1815 that *sati* cases increased in Bengal after the promulgation of the above-mentioned Regulations. We have no such returns for all the preceding years to enable us to make any comparative statement and then to say that the cases were more numerous after 1815 than before; all that we can say is that there were so many cases in the years for which we have definite returns. Referring to *The Government Returns of Sati Cases* we find that in the six divisions of Calcutta, Dacca, Murshidabad, Patna, Banaras and Bareilly, there occurred 380 cases in the year 1815, 442 cases in 1816 and 700 in 1817.[60] From 1818 to 1828 the number varied from 839 in 1818, 650 in 1819, 597 in 1820, 654 in 1821, 583 in 1822, 557 in 1823, 572 in 1824, 639 in 1825, 511 in 1826, 517 in 1827 and 463 in 1828.[61] It should be noted that *sati* cases were then more numerous in Bengal than in other parts of India; and within Bengal the districts under the jurisdiction of the *Sadar Nizamat Adalat* in Calcutta and especially the Hugli district had the largest number of cases.[62] In 1815, 252 cases out of 380 occurred in the Calcutta Division; in 1816, 289 cases out of 442 and in 1817, 441 cases out of 706 occurred in the same area.[63] In the years 1815-1817, there were 864 *sati* cases in the five Bengal districts of Burdwan, Hugli, the Jungle Mahals, (a district consisting of dissections from Burdwan, Midnapur, Rangpur, etc., with Bankura as the headquarters of the public functionaries), Nadia and the suburbs of Calcutta, while during the same period 663 cases were reported from the rest of British India including the city of Banaras.[64]

In the Patna district, widow burning was a common practice though not so frequent as in Bengal proper.[65] This was the case in the district of Shahabad about which Hamilton Buchanan has noted: 'The annual number of victims may be about 25. The contagion of example has even extended to the Muhammadans, and I heard of the widow of a weaver, who had buried herself alive in her husband's grave'.[66] In some parts of the Bhagalpur district widows burnt themselves 'pretty frequently', especially among the Bhojpuri tribes settled in Monghyr.[67] In the Gorakhpur district, situated to the north of the Ghaghara river, certain irregularities attended *sati* sacrifices. Referring to this place Martin writes: 'Widows of the highest castes may burn at any period after their husband's death that they please, even if they have been present when their husbands died; nor is this here admitted to be an irregularity, as it would be considered in Bhagalpore.'[68] Buchanan remarks in his account of Purneah that 'the widows of the Hindus of Mithila are admitted to the same privileges in burning themselves with the bodies of their husbands as in Bengal; but the custom is very rate. In many parts no one remembered ever having seen such a sacrifice; and perhaps in the whole district such an event does not usually happen more than once in a year. It seems to be most prevalent towards the north-east, where the customs of Mithila are less prevalent, and on the borders of Batrishazari (modern Jalpaiguri) where the customs is frequent.'[69] The widows of Kamrupies or Assamese settled in the district of Rungpur were permitted to burn themselves with the bodies of their husbands or even to throw themselves into a pit filled with fire; but neither practice was at all common, and in the course of a year not more than three or four widows sacrificed themselves in the whole district excluding Batrishazari (Jalpaiguri).[70] The practice of *sati* was prevalent amongst all classes. In 1818 there were 141 cases of *sati* in the Hugli district. Among them were only 40 Brahmins, 26 Kayastha and 4 Vaidyas, while the remaining 71 belonged to the lower castes, such as Sadgope, Bagdi, Dhoba, Tanti, Kaloo, Tamil, Goala, Maira, Teli, Jelia and Chootar, Chandal, Muchi and the like. In 1819 the number of *satis* in the 24 Parganas was 52; of them 20 were Brahmins, 10 Kayasthas and 2 Vaidyas and the rest were from the lower classes of the society. In 1823, the total number of *satis* in the Bengal Presidency was 576. Among them 235 were Brahmins 34 Khetris, 14 Vaisyas and 292 Sudras.[71]

In that year the list gave 839 Suttees, and, of this number, considerably more than one-half, or 544 occurred in the Division of Calcutta....In 1819, there was a sensible decrease in the number of Suttees but even in this year they were reported at 650. The Calcutta Division, as usual, headed the list with 421 and in it, Hooghly only gave 115. In the same year the province of Banaras gave 92 to the flames, Bareilly 17, and the whole of the Behar districts 40....In 1820 there was a still further decrease but even then the numbers were 597.

,.... As regards statistics from Madras, in the three years before 1816, for which the officials reported in a lump, 45 widows burnt themselves in Ganjan. Within the same period six widows were sacrificed in Vizagapatam, and 17 in the three years after 1816, at a time when the police duties had been transferred to the Collector. In Rajahmundry, the widows of 2 Brahmins, of 1 Rajah and of six Soodras burnt themselves also in the three years after 1816. But 42 were returned for the period from Masulipatam; 14 from Guntoor, 12 from Nellore, none from bellary, 13 from Chittoor, 4 from Chingleput, and 18 from Combaconum. Towards the south of the Peninsula the custom was rare and in some places unknown. Then we have a remarkable letter, dated 1 April 1820, from Mr. Thomas Newnham, Judge of Cuddapah. This gentleman reported that four instances of Suttee had taken palce since 1816; that such cases were generally rare and in the neighbourhood of Cuddapah unknown.... The Judge of Trichinopoly reported about the same time, that he could trace no instance of Suttee for ten years in his district, except the case of a widow of a pleader in his own Court.....In some Zillahs, as Cuddalore for instance, no Suttees took place, and only in Tanjore towards the south, did the immolations, for one year and a half, amount to 24. The Judge of South Malabar mentioned the singular and encouraging fact, that the custom was unknown in that part of the country....We may sum up Madras statistics by saying, that Suttee prevailed in the northern zillahs, existed in a less degree in the centre, and was unknown in the west and south, except in Tanjore and one State in Canara.[72]

In Bombay the instances were more rare than in Madras. Only one instance had occurred in the district of Ahmedabad....On the whole, the Bombay returns are slight in comparison with those from Madras and sink into nothing when compared with Bengal.[73]

In 1823, the total number of *satis* in the Bengal Presidency was 576. Of them, 235 were Brahmins, 34 Khetris, 14 Vaisyas and 292 Sudras.

The police tried to enforce the regulations already referred to, though they were not always successful. In the year 1819, a young wife of a Brahmin of Calcutta could offer herself as a *sati* on the funeral pyre of her husband on the third day after his death because she had to wait for two days for it to be ascertained that she was neither under sixteen or pregnant.[74] In 1821. five widows were saved from death through the intervention of the police and four were persuaded to draw back at the last moment, whereof only one 'was not affected by the instrumentality or assistance of the police'.[75] In the year 1823, a beautiful woman, aged eighteen years, of Santipur in the Nadia district arrived at the bank of the Ganges with a determination to burn herself on the funeral pyre of her husband. on hearing this the *Thanadar* of Santipur, along with many others, tried to deter her from the act by various arguments and temptations. But she did not forsake her resolution and burnt herself with all formalities.[76] In 1827, only one girl of sixteen years could be rescued from *sati* sacrifice through police intervention.[77]

Some executive as well as judicial officers of the Company tried during this period to prevent *sati* or expressed their opinions against it. In 1806 Charles Harding, of the Bengal Civil Service, as Magistrate of Banaras, tactfully prevented the widow of a Brahmin from burning herself.[78] On 14 September 1813, Mr. Lushington, a Madras magistrate wrote to his superior in the Government that the prohibition of *sati* would give 'universal satisfaction' with the exception of a few Brahmins who 'received a nefarious reward for presiding at this infernal rite'.[79] Walter Ewer, Superintendent of Police, Lower provinces, expressed his views against the practice through a letter, dated 18 November 1818, to the Judicial Secretary to the Government. In the first place he argued that the *sati* sacrifices were seldom voluntary, a widow being 'distracted with grief at the event (of her husband's death), without one friend to advise or protect her', was 'little prepared to oppose the surrounding crowd of hungry Brahmins and interested relatives either by argument or force'.[80] Secondly, he held that such sacrifices were very often meant for temporal happiness of the surviving relatives of the dead than for the spiritual bliss of the dead or his wife. The relatives of the dead thus became free from maintaining a widow and could control her property. He was opposed to the standing orders of the Government relating to *sati*, and, referring to these, he remarked: 'it appears to me that if the practice is allowed to exist at all, the less notice we take of it the better, because the apparent object of the interference of the police is to compel the people to observe the rules of their own Shastras (which of themselves they will not obey) by ascertaining particular circumstances of the condition of the widow.'[81] He was of the opinion that the practice could be abolished without exciting any general opposition or dissatisfaction. Ewer's views were vigorously supported by Courtney Smith, second Judge of the *Nizamat Adalat*, who noted in 1821 his disapprobation of the circular orders of the Government relating to *sati* sacrifices.[82] While forwarding to the Government the returns of 1819-20, Smith pointed out 'that the toleration of *Sati* was a reproach to British rule and that its abolition would be attended by no danger'.[83] He demanded its 'entire and immediate abolition'. J.H. Harrington, a distinguished Judge of the *Sudder Court* in those days, after a thorough scrutiny of the *sati* returns, recorded a Minute of 43 paragraphs in which he agreed with the views of C. Smith and admitted that, while 'the toleration of Suttees was a reproach to our Government', 'the entire and immediate abolition of it would be attended with no sort of danger'.[84] The Chief Judge, Leycester, advised its suppression 'by proclamation' in those divisions where it was not so frequent, viz., Dacca, Murshidabad, and Bareilly in Allahabad, Bundelkhand and Calpee.[85] The other Judges declared that the abolition of *sati* was likely to disturb public peace, but one of them, named Mr. Dorin, suggested that the rite could be abolished in one district, for example, the Hugli district, 'by way of experiment and example'.[86] The Governor-General-in-Council was of the opinion that 'the authoritative interposition of Government with a view to abolish the rite of Suttee either in the manner recommended by Smith or by the adoption of the partial measures respectively suggested by Leycester and Dorin, would not only fail of success but would tend to excite a spirit of fanaticism, and eventually to produce very injurious consequences'.[87] Lord Hastings stated in his reply on 17 July 1821, that he could not approve of any of those plans and he expressed the hope that the more educated Indians would 'gradually become disposed to abandon the practice'.

The Company's Government in India informed the Court of Directors of its own measures and sent to them the reports of its officers working in different parts of India for the prevention of *sati*. On 7 June 1823, the Court wrote as following to the Governor-General in India:

> You are aware that the attention of Parliament and the public has lately been called to the subject. It appears that the practice varies much in different parts of India both as to the extent to which it prevails and the enthusiasm by which it is upheld.... It is upon intelligible grounds that you have adopted the rules which permit the sacrifice when clearly voluntary and conformable to the Hindu religion. But to us it appears very doubtful (and we are confirmed in this doubt by responsible authorities) whether the measures which have been taken in pursuance of this principle have not tended rather to increase than no diminish the practice. It is moreover with much reluctance that we can consent to make the British Government, by specific permission of the Suttee, an ostensible party to the sacrifice; we are averse also to the practice of making British Courts expounders and vindicators of the Hindu religion when it leads to acts which not less as legislators than as Christians we abominate.[88]

They did not send any explicit orders for the prohibition of *sati* but expressed their willingness to co-operate in any measures which the Calcutta Government's superior means of estimating consequences may suggest'.[89]

One of the Judges of the *Nizamat Adalat*, named Mr. Haringay, who personally advocated the abolition of *sati*, proposed in a Minute, dated 28 June 1823, that additional regulations might be issued to enable the police to prevent *satis* until full investigations had been made.[90] But the other judges were opposed to fresh regulations which, in their opinion, would serve to 'deepen in the native mind the impression of the rite being legalised and countenanced by the Government'.[91]

Lord Amherst, who joined the office of the Governor-General on 1 August 1823, also paid attention to this matter. But he, like the Marquis of Hastings, was afraid that the abolition of the rite would disturb the allegiance of the Bengal native army. This is clear from what he wrote to the Court of Directors on 3 December 1824: 'Nothing but the apprehension of evils infinitely greater than those arising from the existence of the practice should induce us to tolerate it for a day.'[92] The letter concluded 'with an expression unfavourable to the adoption of new measures of importance; with a reference to the introduction of a system of general education, which would render interference with a religious rite injudicious and with a promise that the subject should always receive full attention but without any "pledge" for the future or the announcement or sketch of any specific plan'. Lord Amherst's Government also considered the probable effect of any prohibitory measures on the feelings of the native army. The majority of the *Nizamat Adalat* declared on 23 July 1824, that rather than adding new regulations it would be better to pass an enactment prohibiting *satis* in future throughout the country.[93] This *Adalat* considered the matter again in November 1826. Two judges, Mr. Courtney Smith and Mr. Alexander Ross, urged immediate and absolute prohibition of the rite. Their Minutes were put before the Governor-General's Council, on 13 January 1827.[94] Its Vice-President, Mr. Bayley, could not advocate such a peremptory policy but recommended that the rite should be abolished in areas like the districts of Delhi, Saugor, Nerbudda, Kumaon and Rungpur, which being lately brought under the sway of the Company had not come under the influence of the earlier regulations.[95] On 18 February 1827, Harrington, with his experience of local affairs of a quarter of a century, opined that the rite could be abolished only by an improvement of the people affected through the diffusion of knowledge and moral instruction.[96]

On 1 March 1827, Vice-President Mr. Combermere strongly pleaded for the adoption of Mr. Bayley's proposals.[97] Lord Amherst, however, did not approve of this step. The judges repeated their views at the end of 1827. But Lord Amherst remarked on 4 January 1828: 'I cannot believe that the burning or burying alive of widows will long survive the advancement which every year brings with it useful and rational learning. Except on the occurrence of some very general sickness, the progress of general instruction and the unostentatious exertion of our local officers will produce the happy effect of a gradual diminution and in no very distant period the final extinction of the barbarous rite of Suttee.' The Court of Directors then committed the matter to the wisdom of the Bengal Government and pointed out at the same time 'that one of the difficulties attendant on the consideration of the subject arose out of the difference of opinion which prevailed among the ablest public functionaries, as to the safety and expediency of any interference on the part of Government for the suppression of Suttee'.[98]

The acting Magistrate of Cuttack wrote to G. Stock-well, Commissioner of the 19th Division, Cuttack, on 1 August 1829:

Beyond an annual statement of Suttees which may have taken place, it has hitherto not been customary, in this District at least, to make any special report on this casual occurrence, but as Government is at present engaged in taking the sense of the community at large on the expediency of suppressing them, I trust, I may be excused from making a few remarks on the subject.

2nd. It was my misfortune to be called on in the capacity of Magistrate to sanction the performance of one of these revolting scences but a few days ago. Painful as must be the feelings of every Christian to be an eye-witness even of such degrading sights, still harder is the lot of those who are in some degree made the passive instruments of their performance. Sooner therefore than tactly submit to such an outrage of decency I resolved to see what effect words would have towards dissuading the infatuated creature from so wretched a purpose.

3rd. Accordingly I, in company with several other Gentlemen, went to the house where we found the poor woman seated, perfectly composed, but quite deaf to our united entreaties. Finding therefore all remonstrance vain I was compelled to allow the procession to advance hoping to the last that pain would accomplish what persuasion could not. But no, with eager delight she approached the flames and after distributing a few things to her friends leapt in.

4th. It may be here remarked that instead of Piles a Pit is commonly dug for the performance of these ceremonies which practice has obtained in this District.

5th. Prior, however, to the completion of her rash act, I planted a ladder with my own hands, and stood by with the Police in attendance to rescue the unfortunate creature, had she signified even by a motion her wish to return to Earth. But very far must have been her thought from such a contemplation; on the contrary, she courted the flames with a kind of frantic joy and in less than 3 minutes she was lifeless.

6th. From what I saw on this occasion I am perfectly convinced that the order of Government alone is wanted making the penalty of such offences death, and we should then hear that suttees like the Saugor sacrifices had ceased to exist. So satisfied was I of this, and a subsequent occurrence proves that my supposition was not erroneous, that I resolved not only to discountenance but to disallow their performance whilst I was in this Magistracy.

7th. Accordingly when the day before yesterday another Suttee was announced to be about to take place, I positively put my veto on it, and without allowing time for the performance of certain preliminary steps, such as decking themselves with garlands, oiling, etc., I hastened to the spot, dispersed the mob, ordered the dead body to be burned immediately, and the widow to be given into the custody of her father.

8th. As I expected, resolution carried the day, not the slightest disapprobation has since been evinced, and this circumstance may I trust tend towards convincing Government that if the order of a

Magistrate acting on his own responsibility can suppress such proceedings, with what satisfaction and with what happy results might not their orders be attended for the entire abolition of such degrading cruelties.[99]

On taking civil charge of the district of Jabalpore in March 1828, W.H. Sleeman 'issued a proclamation prohibiting any one from aiding or assiting in Suttee and distinctly stating that to bring one ounce of wood for the purpose would be considered as so doing'.[100] But even then he could not refuse his assent to the burning of the widow of one Umed Singh Upadhyaya on 29 November 1829, because it was strongly demanded by the Brahmins of that district and the lady also showed a strong determination to die on her husband's pyre. Thus some of the predecessors of Lord William Bentink were sensible of the inhumanity of the *sati* rite but they shrank from its total abolition for fear of offending orthodox Indian opinions and disturbing the Indian army.[101]

At the same time the spirit of Indian Renaissance had been generating, in various ways, anti-*sati* feelings throughout Bengal. Reforms to be effective should be supported by a demand from within, and it was thus a happy coincidence of events that an enlightened Indian opinion had grown up in the first half of the nineteenth century to cooperate with the Company's Government in the work of introducing salutary changes in different spheres of life. Rammohan Roy 'devoted all the energies of his noble soul' to save women 'from a cruel death'.[102] 'Never since the days of Chaitanya', remarks Mr. R.C. Dutt, 'has Bengal witnessed such an intensive agitation as during the first quarter of this (nineteeth) century. Never has one man attempted and achieved more for his countrymen than Rammohan Roy.'[103] It was during Rammohan's stay at Rungpur that the burning alive of one of the widowed wives of his brother Jagamohan on 8 April 1810, gave a rude shock to his feelings and sine then he took a secret vow to work wholeheartedly for the abolition of this custom.[104]

After the circular orders, already referred to, had been issued, orthodox society in Calcutta sent a petition to the Government soliciting their repeal. Rammohan and his friends then submitted a counter-petition in August 1818 wherein it was stated:

> Your petitioners are fully aware from their own knowledge and from the authority of credible eye-witnesses, that cases have frequently occurred where women have been induced by the persuasion of their next heirs, interested in their destruction, to burn themselves on the funeral pile of their husbands; that others were induced by fear to retract a resolution rashly expressed in the first moments of grief, of burning with their deceased husbands, have been forced upon the pile and then bound down with ropes and pressed with green bamboos until consumed with the flames; that some, after flying from the flame, have been carried back by their relations and burnt to death. All these instances, your petitioners humbly submit, are murders according to every Shastra as well as to the common sense of all nations.[105]

In conclusion, the petitioners expressed that they looked 'with the most lively hope to such further measures relative to the custom of burning widows as may justly be expected from the known wisdom, decision, and humanity which have ever distinguished your Lordship's administration'.[106]

It was from the year 1818 that Rammohan threw himself vigorously into the campaign against this custom. By going down to the Calcutta burning-ghats he tried to 'avert the Suttee sacrifices by earnest persuation'.[107]

On 30 November 1818, Rammohan issued an English translation of his first work on the subject of *sati* entitled 'A Conference between an Advocate for, and an Opponent of the Practice of Burning Widows Alive'.[108] It was noted in its brief preface that this brochure was a literal translation of one originally written in Bengali, which 'has been for several weeks past in extensive circulation in those parts of the country where the practice of widows burning themselves on the pyre of their husbands is most prevalent'. His second tract, known as 'A Second Conference between an Advocate for an Opponent of the Practice of Burning

Widows Alive' was dedicated to the Marchioness of Hastings on 26 February 1820, in the following style.[109] "The following tract being a translation of a Bengalee Essay, published sometime ago, an appeal to reason in behalf of humanity, I take the liberty to dedicate to your Ladyship; for to whose protection can any attempt to promote a benevolent purpose he with so much propriety committed?' Rammohan concluded it with the following passionate appeal on behalf of women in general and Indian women in particular:

Women are in general inferior to men in bodily strength and energy; consequently, the male part of the community, taking advantage of their corporal weakness, have denied to them those excellent merits and they are apt to say that women are naturally incapable of acquiring those merits. But if we give the subject considerations, we may easily ascertain whether or not your accusation against them is consistent with justice. As to their inferiority in point of understanding, when did you ever afford them a fair opportunity of exhibiting their natural capacity? How then can you accuse them of want of understanding? if, after instruction in knowledge and wisdom, a person cannot comprehend or retain what has been taught him, we may consider him as deficient; but as you keep women generally void of education and acquirements, you cannot, therefore, in justice, pronounce on their inferiority. On the contrary, Lilavati, Bhanumati, the wife of the prince of Karnat, and that of Kalidas, are celebrated for their thorough knowledge of all the Shastras: moreover, in the Vrihadaranyak Upănishad of the Yjur Veda it is clearly stated that Yagnavalkya imparted divine knowledge of the most difficult nature to his wife Maitreyi, who was able to follow and completely attain it!

Secondly, you charge them with want of resolution, at which I feel exceedingly surprised; for we constantly perceive, in a country where the name of death makes the male shudder, that the female, from her firmness of mind, offers to burn with the corpse of her deceased husband; and yet you accuse those women of deficiency in point of resolution.

Thirdly, with regard to their trustworthiness, let us look minutely into the conduct of both sexes, and we may be equally enabled to ascertain which of them is the most frequently guilty of betraying. If we enumerate such women in each village or town as have been deceived by men, and such men as have been betrayed by women, I presume that the number of the deceived women would be found ten times greater than that of the betrayed men. Men are, in general, able to read and write and manage public affairs, by which means they easily promulgate such faults as women occasionally commit, but never consider as criminal the misconduct of men towards women. One fault they have, it must be acknowledged, which is, by considering others equally void of duplicity as themselves, to give their confidence too readily, from which they suffer much misery, even so far that some of them are misled to suffer themselves to be burnt to death.

In the fourth place, with respect to their subjection to the passions, this may be judged of by the custom of marriage as the respective sexes; for one man may marry two or three, sometimes even ten wives and upwards; while a woman who marries but one husband, desires at his death to follow him, forsaking all worldly enjoyments or to remain leading the austere life of an ascetic...

Rammohan continued his campaign against *sati* with the profound seal of a true national reformer. He used his journal *Sambad Kaumudi,* which began to appear from December 1821,[110] 'as a regular weapon in this agitation'. In 1822 he published his 'brief Remarks Regarding Modern Encroachments on the Ancient Rights of Females. According to the Hindoo Law of Inheritance', wherein he noted: 'It is not from religious prejudices and early impressions only, that Hindoo widows burn themselves on the piles of their deceased husbands but also from their witnessing the distress in which the widows of the same rank in life are involved, and the insults and slights to which they are daily subjected, that they become in a great measure regardless of their existence after the death of their husbands; and this indifference, accompanied with the hope of a future reward held out to them, leads them to the horrible act of suicide.'[111]

It seems that Lord Hastings' Government recognized the importance of Rammohan's campaign. It was noted in their despatch of 15 August 1822, written a few months before the Governor-General's departure from India: 'His Lordship in Council does not despair of the best efforts resulting from the free discussion of the matter by the people themselves, independently of European influence and interposition; and it only remains for him to watch carefully the indications of a change of sentiment amongst the people...and to encourage to the utmost every favourable disposition.'[112] The potency of Rammohan's anti-*sati* agitation is further attested to by what Bishop Heber observed in his journal. In the course of his conversation with Dr. Marshman on 15 January 1824, the latter is said to have remarked: 'The Brahmins have no longer the power and popularity which they had when he first remembers India, and among the laity many powerful and wealthy persons agree and publicly express their agreement with Rammohan Roy in reprobating the custom which is well known to be not commanded by any of the Hindu sacred books, though some of them speak of it as a meritorious sacrifice.'[113] Nothing daunted, Rammohan continued his anti-*sati* agitation in the teeth of a vigorous opposition from the orthodox party with its leader Raja Radhakanta Deb.[114] R.C. Dutt has noted that 'for a time Rammohan's life was in danger'.[115] But Rammohan being inspired with the fiery zeal of a hero dedicating himself to a righteous cause could not rest satisfied till his cause had triumphed.

By the year 1828 the Company's Government also came to hold definite opinions for the abolition of the *sati* rite. Lord William Bentinck, a 'reformer by temprament,'[116] succeeded Lord Amherst in July 1828. He resolved to deal with the question without delay, and 'come to as early a determination, as mature consideration would allow' and 'having made that determination, to stand by it, yes or no, and set his conscience at rest'. He took the preliminary step of ascertaining the views of the army, the judiciary and the executive officers of the Government. He addressed a confidential letter to fortynine officers in the military department 'as being from their judgement and experience the best enabled to appreciate the effect of the proposed measure upon the native army'. Of these officers, twenty-four supported total and immediate suppression of the rite, eight were in favour of indirect abolition through magistrates and other public officers, two advocated abolition but were opposed to absolute and direct prohibition by the government; only five were opposed to interference of any kind with the practice.,[117] Thus the Governor-General gathered the information that the prohibition of the practice would not affect the army in the least.[118] The two superintendents of police for the Lower Provinces, Mr. Walter Ewer and Mr. Barwells, expressed the opinion that this might be effected without the least danger. All the five judges of the *Nizamat Adalat* advocated the abolition of the rite.[119] and they submitted returns of *satis* in 1827-28 showing a decline in number.[120] 'If this diminution', wrote Lord William Bentinck, 'could be ascriebd to any change of opinion upon the question, or the progress of education or civilisation, the fact would be most satisfactory, and to disturb this sure though slow progress of self-correction would be most impolitic and unwise. But I think it may be safely affirmed that though in Calcutta truth may be said to have made a considerable advance amongst high orders, yet in respect to the population at large no change whatever has taken place, and from these causes at least no hope of abandonment of the rite can be rationally entertained'.[121] As a matter of fact, the *Samachar Chandrika,* a leading journal of the time advocating orthodox ideas, expressed the view, through articles published on 8 August and 3 December 1829, that *sati* was an old and honoured rite and that as such the Government of Lord William Bentinck should not abolish it.[122] But Gouri Shankar Tarkabagis, editor of the *Samachar Chandrika,* undoubtedly supported Rammohan Roy for the abolition of *sati*.

Lord William Bentinck considered it advisable to consult Raja Rammohan Roy, the great Indian champion of the anti-*sati* movement. The *India Gazettee* of 27 July 1829 noted: 'An eminent philanthrophist who has long taken the lead of his countrymen on this great question has been encouraged to submit his views of it in a written form, and has been subsequently honoured with an audience by the Governor-General, who, we learn, has expressed his anxious desire to put an end to a custom constituting so foul a blot.' The *Gazette* suggested three courses which the Government could adopt: rigidly enforcing the existing regulations, or suppressing *sati* in Bengal and Bihar, or abolishing it throughout the Presidency.[123] Rammohan tried to dissuade Lord William Bentinck from a direct suppression of the rite by Government measures which might create a formidable popular opposition. His opinion was that the 'practice might be suppressed quietly and unobservedly by increasing the difficulties and by the indirect agency of the police.'[124]

It is rather surprisingly that Rammohan could give such advice. But this was due to his belief in the efficacy of constitutional advance by steady and persuasive means in preference to any sudden innovation effected by legislation. Blessed with sober judgment and a deep insight into the human mind, Rammohan, in the opinion of Collet, had a 'constitutional aversion to coercion'.[125] Horace Hayman Wilson, a leading Orientalist of the time, was also against any public legislative enactment for the suppression of the rite.[126] He considered it to be a 'dangerous evasion of the real difficulties to attempt to prove that *satis* are not essentially a part of the Hindu religion', and that 'the attempt to put down the practice will inspire extensive dissatisfaction...that the principle of a purer morality, as well as of a more virtuous and exalted rule of action, now actively inculcated by European education and knowledge, will receive a fatal check'.

But Lord William Bentinck laid before his Council a long Minute on 8 November 1829, wherein he remarked thus about Dr. Wilson's and Raja Rammohan Roy's opinions: 'I must acknowledge that a similar opinion as to the probable excitation of a deep distrust of our future intentions was mentioned to me in conversation by that enlightened native Rammohan Roy, a warm advocate for the abolition of *sati* and of all other superstitions and corruptions engrafted on the Hindu religion, which he considers originally to have been a pure deism. It was his opinion that any public enactment would give rise to general apprehension...[127] He mentioned that, 'of the 463 *satis* occurring in the whole of the Presidency of Fort William, 420 took place in Bengal, Bihar and Orissa, or what is termed the Lower provinces, and to these 287 in the Calcutta Division alone.' The people of these districts, he pointed out, had been reduced to such a 'habitual submission of centuries, that insurrection or hostile opposition to the will of the ruling power may be affirmed to be an impossible danger... Were the scene of this sad destruction of human life laid in the Upper instead of the lower Provinces in the midst of a bold and manly people I might speak with less confidence upon the question of safety.' Judging from the reports of the civilians and missionaries and the opinions of the judges of the *Nizamat Adalat,* he ventured 'to think it completely, proved that from the native population nothing of extensive combination, or even of partial opposition may be expected from the abolition'. About the army he had satisfied himself by receiving reports from the prominent military officers that it would not be upset. He then expressed the hope before the members of his Council that 'they will partake in the perfect confidence which it has given me of the expediency and safety of the abolition. Charles Metcalfe, the most prominent member in the Governor-General's Council was apprehensive that the measure 'might possibly be used by the disaffected and the designing to inflame the passions of the multitude and produce a religious excitement', but he noted his concurrence.[128] The Council as a whole held: 'We are decidedly in favour of an open, avowed and general prohibition, resting altogether upon the goodness of the act and our power to enforce it.'[129]

On 4 December 1829, *sati* was declared by Regualtion XVII 'illegal and punishable by the Criminal Courts'. Persons helping a voluntary sacrifice were to be held guilty of culpable homicide; but sentences of death could be inflicted, at the discretion of the court, on those who were convicted of using violence or compulsion, or impeding the free will of the victim by administering drugs or by other means. The Regulation stated:

> The practice of *Suttee,* or of burning or burying alive the widows of Hindoos is revolting to the feelings of human nature; it is nowhere enjoined by the religion of the Hindoos as an imperative duty. On the contrary, a life of purity and retirement on the part of the widow is more especially and preferably inculcated, and by a vast majority of the people throughout India the practice is not kept up nor observed; in some extensive districts it does not exist; in those which it has been most frequent it is notorious that in many instances acts of atrocity have been perpetrated which have been shocking to the Hindoos themselves, and in their eyes unlawful and wicked...[130]

The Regulation applied in the first place directly to the Presidency of Bengal. A similar enactment was passed in Madras on 2 February 1830. In Bombay the Government of Sir John Malcolm repealed that clause which declared 'assistance at the rites of self-immolation not to be murder'.[131]

The promulgation of the Regulation did not produce universal opposition or cause a widespread resentment in the army or in the country. J.A. Dalzell of the Madras Civil Service wrote to T. Hyde Villiers on 1 March 1832: 'It may not be improper to notice here as bearing upon the point of enquiry, that in the province which was committed to my charge, the circulation of the peremptory orders for the suppression of the rite of *Suttee* did not occasion the slightest indication of dissatisfaction; and it did not come to my knowledge that a different impression was produced in my district of the Madras settlement.'[132]

In Bengal, according to Marshman, twenty-five attempts at *sati* were made after the passing of the Regulation, but they were prevented by the simple interposition of the police.'[133] One such case, when the wife of an old Brahmin named Trilochana Tarkalankara of Krishnagar was about to die on the funeral pyre of her husband, prevented by the police was in January 1831.[134]

But a vigorous opposition against the anti-*sati* Regualtion was organised in Calcutta by the large orthodox section of society. Many of them were influential persons and they had as their leaders some prominent magnates of Bengal such as Raja Radhakanta Deb, Maharaja Kalikrishna Bahadur, Babus Gopimohan Deb, Nilmony De, Gokulnath Malik, Ramgopal Mallik and Bhabani Charan Mitra.[135] The *Samachar Chandrika,* the powerful organ of orthodox Hinduism, 'sounded the alarm'.[136] The *India Gazette* of 30 November announced that a petition against the abolition of *sati* had been already in preparation, but it expressed the hope that the *Sambad Kaumudi* and the *Bangadut,* organs of the liberal sections of Indian society, would try to remove popular misconceptions about the measures of the Government.[137] This *Gazette* and the *Asiatic Journal* of June 1830 wrongly state that the petition against the Regulation found little support and that signatures to it were extorted by threats and tauntis.[138]

As a matter of fact, on 19 December 1829[139] a petition of 'a numerous and respectable body of petitioners', as Lord William Bentinck described them, consisting of 800 inhabitants of Calcutta,[140] was presented to the Governor-General praying for the abandonment of the Regulation. The petitioners denounced the opinion of Rammohan that the practice of *sati* was not enjoined by the laws of Hindu religion as a 'doctrine derived from a number of Hindoos who have a postatized from the religion of their forefathers, who have defiled themselves by eating and drinking forbidden things in the society of Euroepans and are endeavouring to deceive your Lordship in Council'. They submitted that 'in a question so delicate as the interpretation of our sacred books and the authority of our religious usages none but pundits and Brahmins and teachers of holy lives and known learning and authority ought to be consulted' and not 'men who have neither any faith nor care for the memory of their ancestores'. They requested his, 'Lordship in Council', to assume 'the difficult and delicate task of regulating the conscience of a whole people... on the authority of its own sacred writers' by consulting orthodox experts. To help him in this matter they 'appended a paper of citations from legal authorities', signed by 120 pandits.[141] Another petition of a similar nature, signed by 346 'respectable persons' of Belgharia, Ariadaha (near Calcutta) and some other neighbouring places, was submitted at the same time.

According to the desire of the Governor-General, Raja Radhakanta Deb, Maharaja Kalikrishna Bahadur, babus Nimaichand Siromani, Haranath Tarkabhusan, Bhavanicharan Bandopadhyay, Gopimohan Deb, Nilmony De, Gokulnath Malik, Bhabani Charan Mitra and Ramgopal Malik appeared before him on 14 January 1830, to get his reply to their petitions against the anti-*sati* Regulation.[142] He received them respectfully and after much discussion about *sati* handed over to them a paper containing his reply to their petitions.[143] The reply was to the effect that the authorities which they had cited 'only confirmed the supposition that widows are not by the religious writing of the Hindoos commanded to destroy themselves...No attack on Hindu religion was committed or intended. If they disputed his interpretation of Hindu or British laws they might appeal to the King-in-Council.[144] On 16 January a congratulatory petition signed by 300 Indian inhabitants of Calcutta and 800 Christians, thanking the Governor-General for his humane measure, was forwarded to him[145] by Raja Rammohan Roy and a few other respectable inhabitants of Calcutta.[146]

The address of the native inhabitants, of which Rammohan was the 'reputed and probable author',[148] attributed 'the introduction of *Suttee* to jealousy and selfishness, acting under the cloak of religion, but in defiance of the most sacred authorities'. It rejoiced at the prospect of 'the most ancient and purest system of Hindu religion being no longer set at naught by the Hindus themselves' and expressed the 'deepest gratitude'[148] and the 'utmost reverence' to the Governor-General. A meeting was held in the Government House in Calcutta to discuss the *sati* question, where pandit Gourishankar Tarkabagis (popularly known as Gurgure Bhattacharya) spoke on behalf of Raja Rammohan Roy against the practice of *sati* before 500 or 600 persons who advocated it.[149]

The orthodox party also tried to organise itself in order to counteract the influence of Rammohan's movement and in an effort to get the anti-*sati* Regulation repealed. On 17 January 1830, the prominent Bengali and Hindustani members of this group convened a meeting in the premises of the Sanskrit College to decide their policy against the Regulation. Babu Bhavanicharan Bandopadhyay asked the members to consider the remarks of the Governor-General in reply to their petitions relating to *sati*, and with the permission of all Raja Radhakanta Deb read out its purport. All agreed to make an appeal to the King-in-Council against the anti-*sati* Regulation and they formed themselves into a permanent organisation known as the *Dharma Sabha*. Many rich and influential men of Calcutta became its members. The Sabha realized on the spot subscritpions amounting to Rs. 11,260 and decided to erect a building for their meetings.[150] The object of this association, as its organisers declared, was to enable 'the excellent and noble to unite and continually devise means for protecting our religion and our excellent customs and usages'.

The efforts of the orthodox party could not, however, repress Rammohan's zeal. Undaunted, he issued in the same year a brochure[151], entitled 'The Abstract of the Arguments Regarding the Burning of Widows Considered as a Religious Rite'. In it he analysed the *Smriti* texts from Manu to Raghunandan and pointed out that the practice of *sati* had not been advocated by all. Neither the *Vedas,* nor Manu, nor Yajnavalkya, argued Rammohan, supported it. Angira, Vishnu, Harita and some other later writers recommended either concremation or a virtuous life. But Rammohan pointed out that they recommended concremation on the part of widows as a means to obtain future 'carnal fruition', that it was forbidden by the *Bhagwad Gita,* Manu and Raghunanda, and that Vijanesvra, the author of *Mitakshara,* considered it inferior to 'eternal beatitude or virtuous life'. He argued further that even Harita and other advocates of *sati* did not support it if it was not voluntary. Thus he held that *sati* was 'both suicide and female murders' and remarked in conclusion: 'We should not omit the present opportunity of offering up thanks to Heaven, whose protecting arms have rescued our weaker sex from cruel murder, under the cloak of religion, and our character as a people, from the contempt and pity with which it has been regarded on account of this custom by all the civilised nations on the surface of the globe.'

When the orthodox Hindu leaders of Calcutta sent their appeal to the King-in-Council against Lord William Bentinck's Regulation abolishing the practice of *sati* Rammohan drafted and carried with him a counter-petition[152] and presented it to the House of Commons.[153] The Raja was presented when the appeal against the abolition of *sati* was rejected by the Privy Council and the decision announced on 11 July 1832. The Privy Councillors who heard the appeal at the Council Chamber, Whitehall, were the Lord President of the Council, the Lord Chancellor, the Master of the Rolls, the first Lord of the Admiralty, the Paymaster of the Forces, the Marquis of Wellesley, the Marquis of Landsdowne, Lord Amherst, Lord John Russell, Sir James Graham, Sir L. Shadwell and E.H. East.[154] To express their feelings of joy at this decision of the Privy Council, a meeting of some members of the reform party and of some Europeans was held in the evening of 10 November 1832 in the public hall of the sadharan Brahma Samaj. Srijut Dwarkanath Tagore presided over this meeting and it was decided to forward letters conveying congratulations and thanks to the King and the Privy Council and to the Court of Directors through Raja Rammohan Roy. It was also resolved to convey thanks to Raja Rammohan Roy for his efforts towards the abolition of *sati.*[155]

In spite of the anti-*sati* measures of 1829 and the growing strength of the reform movement, stray cases of attempted or successful *sati* were reported occasionally during the last century from some Indian states and also from certain parts of British India.[156] In June 1839, after the death of Ranjit Singh, four ladies were burnt with him.[157] In November 1840, after the death of Kharak Singh, one lady died a *sati*; two wives of Nao Nehal Singh; grandson of Ranjit Singh, became *satis;* 310 women (10 wives and 300 unmarried ladies of his *zanana*) died at the obsequies of Raja Suchet Singh; four wives of Jawahir Singh were burnt on the funeral pyre of their husband on 4 September 1845; and after the death of Sardar Shyam Singh at the battle of Sobraon, his wife voluntarily burnt herself.[158] In the month of August 1839, the *sati* sacrifice of the widow of Chytun Singh Thakur of Khursawan in Singhbhum was prevented through the efforts of Lieutenant S.R. Tickell, Assistant Political Agent, Singhbhum, and I.R. Ouseley, Governor-General's Agent, Chota Nagpur.[159] But Thakur Chytun Singh's young daughter, married to Chote Rai, younger brother of the Mayurbhanj Raja, had burnt herself as a *sati* at Baree Podda (Baripada) with her dead husband, a day or two before Chytun Singh died, and a day or two later Koour Chukerdur Singh's sister married to the Keonjore Raja was also burnt with the dead Raja.[160] In 1841, orders were passed by the Government prohibiting the practice of *sati* in the Tributary Mahals of Orissa.[161] Lord Ellenborough was not very serious about the prohibition of this rite. He 'expressly declined to sanction an offer made by the charge d'affaris at Hyderabad, to procure from its Mahomedan Ruler a prohibition of the rite'.[162] A 'dreadful instance of *Suttee* is said to have taken place in Jodhpur when Raja Man Singh died on 4 September 1843, and his queens were burnt with him.'[163] His Highness the Nizam of Hyderabad, 'who had proclaimed that the performance of *sati* within his dominions would be accounted a crime', could not succeed in 'entirely suppressing the custom among his people'. The *Bombay Standard* of 20 March 1858 stated that just before that date the Indian authorities had permitted the burning of a widow in the city of Aurangabad where His Highness the Nizam's soldiers were located and within two miles of which a contingent of British troops were stationed. The *Bombay Standard* of 5 August 1859 also noted 'a recent *Suttee* at Koonjhoor near Hansi'; but those who had taken part in it were heavily punished and the *thanodar* and the whole police force were dismissed.

The Government of India took various steps for the abolition of this practice and earnest efforts were made by some British officers like Lord Hardinge, Lord Dalhousie, Major General Ludlow, the Political Agent at Jaipur[164], and others. many of the leading nobles in the different states declared for the abolition of the practice and 'small tributary provinces issued enactments against it'.[165] In November 1853, the Governor-General-in Council ordered that 'no further delay should occur in admitting the Young Raja (of Ahmadnagar) to his dignities, under the district understanding however that he is to be responsible for the prevention of *Suttee* by whosoever's act or instigation it may be committed'.[166] In October 1839, the Raja of Satara was considered by the Governor-in-Council, Bombay, to be 'entitled to great praise for the laudable measures adopted by him for the abolition of the rite of *Suttee,* etc., in his territory'.[167] The State of Jaipur declared it a penal offence in August 1846, and Lord Hardinge caused it to be notified in the Government *Gazette.*[168] before Christmas of that year, the Governor-General could announce the prohibition of *sati* by eleven out of the eighteen Rajput States and by five out of the 'remaining sixteen free States of India'.[169] Lord Dalhousie furthered the work of his predecessors. He not only repeated their 'remonstrances in general terms and in particular to the rulers of Alwar, Bikanir and Udaipur, but also gave signal proof of his determination to punish as well as to condemn'.[170] In the State of Dungarpur in Rajputana, a Thakur's son, who had taken part in a case of *sati*, was imprisoned along with two Brahmins 'who had abetted the crime, the Thakur himself being heavily fined for connivance of the act.'[171]

The practice of *sati* continued for many years particularly in the States of Central India and of Rajputana, where instances have been mentioned by Tod[172] and the *Rajputana Administration Reports* for some years. It was reported by the officiating agent in Marwar on 8 October 1859, that a widow aged eleven had immolated herself on the funeral pyre of her dead husband. The orders of the Secretary of State for India and the efforts made by the Government of India through their agents in the States did not at first prove to be very effective in abolishing this practice. Most of the chiefs of the States, with the exception of a young chief of Alwar, did not co-operate properly with the British Government in this matter but were rather lukewarm and sensitive about it. With the growth of education and enlightenment and also the adoption of stronger steps by the Government of India and their officers in the States of Rajputana and Central india, the practice of *sati* gradually disappeared after 1870.

It may be noted here that about this time there were quit a few debates regarding the sanction of *sati* by the Hindu Shastras. In 1856, H.H. Wilson wrote in his article entitled 'On the Supposed Vaidik Authority for the Burning of Hindu Widows and on the Funeral Ceremonies of the Hindus',[173] that 'the text of the *Rig Veda* cited as authority for the burning of widows enjoins the very contrary and directs them to remain in the world'. In giving a reply to this article, Raja Radhakanta Deb tried to prove that the Shastras sanctioned the burning of widows.[174]

Stray cases have been reported in more recent times from certain parts of British India. Two such cases took place in Gaya District in 1901 and 1903.[175] At Barh in the Patna District of Bihar there was an abetted *sati* case in November, 1927; in 1930 again a widow in the Hazaribagh district of the same Province 'attempted to commit *sati*'.[176]

ABOLITION OF INFANTICIDE, SLAVERY AND HUMAN SACRIFICE

Humanitarian considerations by the East india Company's Government and by some Indian reformers of advanced views led to the abolition of some cruel and obnoxious social customs and practices. One such practice was that of infanticide. One form of infanticide was widely prevalent among the Rajputs, the Jats and Mewats in Western and Central India and U.P. and among the Jharija (Jadeja) Rajputs. Because of difficulties in marrying girls they were killed, when infants, by not being given proper nourishment or sometimes even by rubbing poison on the nipples of the mother's breasts. Another longstanding practice among the Hindus was that of throwing children into the mouth of the Ganges to fulfil certain religious vows. For example, a woman having no children used to take a vow that if she had more than one child, one would be offered to mother Ganges.

Shocked by such inhuman practices, some enlightened British officers tried to stop these but without any effect. So laws had to be passed by the Company's Government against both these forms of infanticide, which were declared murders by the Bengal Regualtion XXI of 1795 and Regulation VI of 1802. But even the Bengal Regulation XXI of 1795 extended by Regulation III of 1804 could not check these practices completely as detection was not an easy task. But these practices gradually disappeared throughout the country with the growth of education and thanks to the energetic efforts of some 'military political officers such as Wilkinson, Willoughley, Erskine, Jacob, Pottinger and Melville'.[177] Alexander Duff wrote in 1844: 'If ever political agents, members of Council, Governors, Governors-General and Courts of Directors shall be arraigned at the bar of an impartial, posterity, they may rest assured that their best exculpatory evidence will be found, not in the brilliant records of their civil diplomacy or military exploits, but in such humble, noiseless, and unpretending volumes which, like the parliamentary papers on infanticide, portray their strenuous and unwearied exertions in the sacred cause of humanity.'[178]

Contemporary documents collected from different parts of the country and some other records show that various types of slavery were prevalent here.[179] A poor man of a locality sold himself in perpetual bondage to a rich man there, and one sold his children or servants to another in lieu of a certain amount. Slaves could be sold or transferred by one to another, or one slave of a person could be bound to serve his master's descendants for all generations to come. Besides Indian slaves, Abyssinian salves were occasionally employed by some rich men.

The treatment meted out to the slaves was not very harsh but was somewhat similar to that which the menial servants received at the hands of their masters. But one notorious practice prevalent in those days was traffic in slaves, particularly by the Portuguese and the Mags of Arracan.[180] Calcutta was a slave market in the eighteenth century.

In 1789, the Government of Lord Cornwallis issued a proclamation forbidding the collection of adults and children for export as slaves to different parts of India or outside, a practice which 'many natives and some Europeans' followed.[181] Various efforts were made to stop the growing traffic in slaves. In 1832, the purchase and sale of slaves 'brought from one district to another was made a penal offence'. By Act V of 1843 legal recognition of slaves was prohibited, and by the Indian Penal Code of 1860 keeping of or trafficking in slaves was made a criminal offence.[182]

The Government of the first Lord Hardinge took steps to stop the atrocious and cruel practice of human sacrifices (under the name of *meriah*) practiced by the Khonds of Orissa on the wrong belief that the fertility of the soul would be increased thereby. But it took some years more to remove it completely through the energetic efforts of Campbell and some other officers who were specially appointed for this purpose between 1847-1854.

The abolition of the cruel and atrocious practice of human sacrifices prevalent among the Khonds in Orissa and certain parts of the Madras Presidency was one of the humane acts of the Company's Government in India. The Hob'ble Mr. Russell was the first to draw the attention of the Madras Government to the subject of the Khonds in his first report of August 1836, and he submitted another Report about it to the Madras Government on 11 May 1837. Russell recommended cautious steps. Adopting his views, the Government, while admitting that 'the evil was a crying one, could not but feel persuaded that the remedy must necessarily be of slow operation, and that the extinction of the practice must be gradual and voluntary'.[183] From then on, some enthusiastic officers of the Bengal and Madras Governments and also of the Calcutta Government tried their best, through conciliatory measures in most cases, to put a stop to the horrible practice. Most of them submitted reports to the Government based on their personal enqueries at places where the practice was rampant. On 12 November 1837, Arbuthnot, the Acting Collector of Vizagapatam, wrote to the Government suggesting that the *zamindars* should be urged to use their influence within their own territories to prevent it', that its suppression 'must be a work of difficulty and of time', and that the persons who perpetrated it should be 'brought within the influence of civilization'. Some other officers engaged in this task were Mr. Banerman, Magistrate of Ganjam, Mr. Inglis, Joint-Magistrate of Ganjam, Captains Miller and Campbell, and Lieutenant Hill of the Survey Department. On 3 May 1841, the Secretary of the Company's Government thus addressed the Chief Secretary to the Government of Fort St. George: 'The Governor-General-in-Council entirely participates in the strong anxiety evinced by Lord Elphinstone (Governor of Madras) and the Government of Fort St. George, to put an end to the savage practice of human sacrifice unfortunately so prevalent among the wild tribes of Ganjam and the neighbouring districts of Orissa and Berar, and believes with His Lordship that the best hope of success is in cautious and gradual measures, by which, without any direct attack upon national customs or religious prejudices, the natural march of civilization may be securely facilitated.[184] To carry out the instructions of the Government regarding the Khonds, Lieutenant McPherson was appointed an Assistant to the Commissioner's or Governor's Agent in Ganjam.

In Orissa also some energetic officers of the Bengal Government dealt with this matter with great earnestness from 1837. They were Ricketts, the Commissioner of Cuttack, Mills, the Superintendent of the Tributary Mahals, Cuttack and immediate successor to Ricketts, and Lieutenant Hicks, the Assistant Superintendent of the Tributary Mahals, Cuttack. The abominable practice was ultimately abolished by the Government of the first Lord Hardinge.

REFERENCES

1. *Calcutta Review,* 1851.
2. *Ibid.*, p. 240.
3. Frazer, *Literary History of India,* p. 390.
4. *Calcutta Review,* 1851, p. 242.
5. *Calcutta Review,* 1851, pp. 242 and 245.
6. *Ibid*.

7. S.C. Sarkar, *Some Aspects of the Earliest Social History of India,* pp. 82-83.
8. *Ibid.*, pp. 186-97. For early texts on the subject of *sati, see* H.H. Wilson's *Essays and Lectures Chiefly on the Religion of the Hindus,* 1881, Vol. II, p. 270 ff., and Max Muller's *Selected Essays on Language, Mythology and Religion,* 1881, Vol. 1, p. 32.
9. *Ibid.*, pp. 291-93.
10. Foster, *Early Travels in India,* pp. 14, 17 & 22.
11. V.A. Smith, *Akbar, the Great Moghul,* p. 382.
12. Foster, op. cit., p. 119.
13. *Ibid.*, p. 219.
14. *Voyage to East India* (1665, reprint ed.,), pp., 302-307. The Rev. Edward Terry was in his youth a Chaplain to Sir Thomas Roe; he lived with his master during his embassy for two years and wrote his account soon after his return. The first edition of his account, entitled. *A Voyage to East India,* did not appear before 1965.
15. Francois Bernier, *Travels in the Moghul Empire,* ed. Archibald Constable, pp. 306-15.
16. This is a correct appreciation of the policy of the Muslim state in India, for Muslim scriptures and law require all Muslims to see that no widow remains unmarried; but since the Muslim state in India had a large majority of Hindu subjects, this scriptural injunction could be conformed to only indirectly in the manner described above. This point of view was clearly different from that of the British administration when it sought to reform Hindu Society.
17. *Travels in India,* ed. V. Ball (1887), Chapter IX.
18. (a) *'Sati was* about to burn herself in the burning fire, when she heard a voice form heaven.' Bharatacandra's *Granthavali* (Basumati ed.), p. 65.
19. Bolts, *Considerations on Indian Affairs,* p. 7.

20. *Sketches of Hindoos,* Vol. II, pp. 17-18.
21. Stavorinus, *Voyage to the East India,* Vol. I, pp. 448-49.
22. Op. cit., Vol. II, pp. 15-16. See also Bolts, op. cit., p. 7.
23. *Reflections on the Government of Indostan,* pp. 110-11.
24. Op. cit., Vol. II, p. 448.
25. *Ibid.*
26. Craufurd, op. cit., Vol. II, p. 19; Beveridge, *Comprehensive History of India,* Vol. II. pp. 185-86.
27. *Memories of Central India,* Vol. I, pp. 190-91. Malcolm went to the spot with Baramul Dada, who had been with Ahalya Bai at the time when her daughter burned herself. In the *Asiatic Annual Register,* 1800, we get an eye witness account of a *sati* case; Poona 24 July, 1786.
28. Malcolm, op. cit., Vol. I, pp. 90-91.
29. *Ibid.*
30. Smith, *Oxford History of India,* p. 665.
31. Tod, *Annals and Antiquities of Rajasthan,* ed. by William Crooke, Vol. II, pp. 737-39.
32. Kaye, *Administration of the East India Company,* p. 128.
33. Malcolm, op. cit., Vol. I, p. 191.
34. *Account of the District of Shahabad in 1812-13* by Francis Hamilton Buchanan (published by the B. and O. Research Society in 1934), pp. 212-13. He saw such *stupas* in the Patna District also.
35. This village stands upon the Dasan (Dasarna) river, which rises in Bhopal State and falls into Betwa after a course of about 220 miles.
36. It was probably a lotus and not a rose, as the latter is not used in Hindu symbolism.
37. Maj. Gen. Sir W.H. Sleeman, *Rambles and Recollections of an Indian Official,* Vol. I, pp. 132-133. Drawings of such *sati*

pillars are given in *F.A.S.B.*, Vol. XLVI, Part I; Cunningham's *Archaeological Reports,* Vol. III, p. 10, Vol. VII, p. 137., Vol. X, p. 175.

38. *Some Records of Crime.* Vol. I. p. 209.
39. *Cambridge History of India,* Vol. VI, p. 132.
40. *Ibid.*, Vol. II, p. 452.
41. *Ibid.*, Vol. VI, p. 132.
42. *Ibid.*
43. *Ibid;* Forbes, *Oriental Memoirs,* Vol. I, p. 57 & Vol. II. p. 26.
44. *Cambridge History of India,* Vol. VI, p. 133. Sivanath Sastri, *History of the Brahmo Samaj,* Vol. I, p. 48.
45. *Ibid.*
46. *Travels in India,* pp. 426-68; Walker, *Life of Carey,* pp. 245-46; *Cambridge History of India,* Vol. VI, p. 134.
47. *Ibid.*
48. *Ibid.*
49. *Ibid.*, p. 135.
50. *Ibid;* B.N. Banerjee, *Sambad Patre Sekaler Katha,* part I, p. 145.
51. Kaye, *History of India under the East India Company,* p. 123.
52. *Ibid.*
53. *Lord Minto in India,* p. 96.
54. L.S.S.O. Malley, *History of Bengal, Bihar and Orissa under British Rule,* p. 341.
55. Robinson, *Daughters of India,* Appendix S.
56. *Cambridge History of India,* Vol. VI, p. 135; Sivanath Sastri, op. cit., Vol. I, p. 48.
57. Quoted from *Parliamentary Papers 1821,* Vol. XVIII, 29-30 in *Cambridge History of India,* Vol. VI, p. 136.

58. *Ibid.*, p. 137.
59. Copy preserved in the Magistrate and Collector's record room, Balasore.
60. *See* Appendix L, and B.N. Banerjee, *Sambad Patre Sekaler Katha,* Part I, p. 146.
61. *English Works of Raja Rammohan Roy,* ed. J.C. Ghose, Introduction p. vii.
62. 'It is true that this insane practice is much more in vogue on the banks of the Gangas than anywhere else. In the southern parts of the Peninsula of India suttees are seldom seen. I am convinced that in the Madras Presidency which numbers at least thirty millions of inhabitants, not thirty widows allow themselves to be thus burnt during a year.' Abbe J.A. Dubois, *Hindu Manners, Customs and Ceremonies,* p. 361, footnote. We have already noted that in the Maratha country widow burning was often sought to be prevented, whereas in Rajputana it flourished. It would seem that in mainly Hindu and secure parts of India the practice did not flourish to the extent that it did in those parts of the country which were either fully subject to alien rule or exposed to continuous attacks (like the Gangetic plains or Rajputana).
63. B.N. Banerjee, op. cit., Part I, p. 145.
64. *See* Appendix L.
65. *Cambridge History of India,* Vol. VI, p. 138.
66. *Shahabad Report,* p. 213 (B. and O. Research Society Publication). It should be noted that the custom of the wife burying herself in the grave of her husband was prevalent among some castes. Abbe Dubois, op. cit., pp. 364-65.
67. Martin, *Eastern India,* Vol. 2, p. 130.
68. *Ibid.*, p. 475.
69. *Ibid.*, Vol. III, p. 166.
70. *Ibid.*, p. 556.
71. *Bengal: Past and Present,* Jubilee Number, 1957, pp. 108-109.

72. *Calcutta Review,* February 1868.
73. *Ibid.*
74. B.N. Banerjee, op. cit., Part I, p. 145.
75. *Cambridge History of India,* Vol. VI, p. 137.
76. B.N. Banerjee, op. cit., Part I, p. 146.
77. *Cambridge History of India,* Vol. VI, p. 137.
78. Sleeman, *Rambles and Recollections, etc.,* Vol. I, pp. 29-30.
79. *Cambridge History of India,* Vol. VI, p. 139.
80. *Ibid.*
81. *Ibid.,* p. 139.
82. *Ibid.,* p. 139.
83. *Ibid.*
84. *Calcutta Review,* 1868.
85. Sophia Dobson Collect, *Life and Letters of Raja Rammohan Roy,* Dilip Kumar Biswas and Prabhat Chander Ganguli (eds.), 3rd, ed., p. 194.
86. *Ibid.*
87. *Bengal: Past and Present,* October-December 1933.
88. *Cambridge History of India,* Vol. VI, p. 139.
89. *Ibid.*
90. Collect, op. cit., p. 199.
91. *Ibid.*
92. *Quoted in Collect, op. cit., p. 253;* Auber, *Rise and Progress of the British Power in India,* Vol. II, p. 610; Boulger, *Lord William Bentinck,* pp. 84-85. *Calcutta Review,* February 1868;
93. Collet, op. cit., p. 199.
94. *Ibid.,* p. 252.
95. *Ibid.*
96. J.C. Marshman, *History of India,* Part II, p. 397.

97. Collect, op. cit., p. 252.
98. Letter to Court, 25 July 1827, quoted in Auber, op. cit., Vol. II, p. 611.
99. Preserved in the Orissa Commissioner's Office.
100. *Rambles and Recollections of an Indian Official,* Vol. I, p. 23.
101. Boulger, op. cit., p. 85.
102. Sivanath Sastri, *History of the Brahmo Samaj,* Vol. I, p. 4.
103. R.C. Dutt, *Literature of Bengal,* (1895) p. 148.
104. Sivanath Sastri, *History of the Brahmo Samaj,* Vol. I, p. 47; Collect, op. cit., p. 48.
105. *Ibid.*, p. 47.
106. *Ibid.*, p. 48.
107. *Ibid.*, p. 49. Two such cases have been recorded in the *Asiastic Journal,* March 1818.
108. *The English Works of Raja Rammohan Roy,* ed. Ghose, Vol. 2, pp. 123-28.
109. *Ibid.*, pp. 139-80.
110. For discussion about this date *see Rammohan Roy Centenary* Volume. (1933), Part II, p. 47.
111. *The English Work of Rammohan Roy,* Vol. II, p. 200.
112. Collect, op. cit., p. 198.
113. *Ibid.*, p. 199.
114. For details about the orthodox and the reform parties *see* Sivanath Sastri's *Ramtanu Lahiri O Tatkalin Bangasamaj,* Chapter V.
115. *Literature of Bengal.*, p. 143.
116. Kaye, *Life of Metcalfe,* Vol. II, pp., 172-73.
117. Boulger, *Lord William Bentinck,* p. 87; Collet, op. cit., p. 254.
118. *Ibid.*
119. *Ibid.*

120. *Cambridge History of India,* Vol. VI, p. 141.
121. Quoted in *Ibid.*
122. B.N. Banerjee, *Sambad Patre Shekaler Katha,* Part I, pp. 147-49.
123. *Ibid*; Colleut, op. cit., 3rd, ed., p. 256 (1962).
124. Lord William Bentinck's Minute of 8 November 1829.
125. Collet, op. cit., p. 257.
126. Lord William Bentinck's Minute of 8 November 1829.
127. *Ibid.*
128. *Cambridge History of India,* Vol. VI, p. 142.
129. Judicial Despatch from Bengal, 4 December, 1829, laid before Parliament on 4 June, 1830, Quoted in Auber, op. cit., Vol. II, p. 611.
130. Collet op. cit., p. 260 is of the opinion that 'the researches and the agitation carried on 'by Raja Rammohan Roy made it possible to include those expression in the preamble of the Regulation.
131. *Cambridge History of India.* Vol. VI, p. 142.
132. Papers laid before the Select Committee in 1832 on the affairs of the East India Company, p. 331.
133. *History of India,* Part II, p. 339.
134. Quoted from *Sambad Kaumudi* in B.N. Banerjee, op. cit., Part II, pp. 391-92. The *Sambad Kaumudi* expressed gratification at this.
135. For Short Accounts of Some Prominent Bengalis of this Period *see* Sivanath Sastri's *Ramtanu Lahiri O Tatkalin Bangasamaj.*
136. Collet, op. cit., p. 267, B.N. Banerjee, op. cit., Part I, pp. 147-48.
137. *Ibid.*
138. *Ibid.*
139. *Cambridge History of India,* Vol. VI, p. 142.

140. Sivnath Sastri, *History of the Brahmo Samaj,* Vol. I, p. 54; Collet, op. cit., p. 262.

141. Collect, op. cit., p. 263; Sivanath Sastri, *History of the Brahmo Samaj,* Vol. I, p. 54; B.N. Banerjee, op. cit., Part I, p. 153.

142. *Ibid.*

143. *Ibid.*

144. *Ibid.*

145. Sivanath Sastri, *History of the Brahmo Samaj,* Vol. I, p. 55.

146. B.N. Banerjee, op. cit., Part I, p. 154.

147. Collet, op. cit., p. 264.

148. *Ibid.*, p. 265.

149. B.N. Banerjee, op. cit., Part 1, p. 148.

150. For a list of the subscribers *see* B.N. Banerjee, op. cit., Vol. I, pp. 150-52. For the organisation of the Dharmasabha, *see Ibid.*, pp. 154-56; Sivanath Sastri, *Ramtanu Lahiri O Tatkalin Bangasamaj,* pp. 109-10; Sivanath Sastri, *History of the Brahmo Samaj,* Vol. I, pp. 42-44, & *The Indian Spectator.*

151. *The English Works, etc.*, Vol. II, pp. 181-92.

152. *The English Works,* Vol. II, pp. 333-34.

153. *Ibid.*, Vol. I, p. 320; *Asiatic Journal,* May 1831, pp. 20-21.

154. *Rammohan Centenary Booklet* (1933), p. 62.

155. B.N. Banerjee, op. cit., Part II, pp. 347-48.

156. Chailley, *Administrative Problems of British India,* p. 145; Marshman, *History of India,* Part II, p. 651.

157. Robinson, *Daughters of India,* p. 113; *Calcutta Review,* No. II: Lepel Griffin, *Ranjit Singh,* pp. 66-67.

158. *Ibid.*

159. I.R. Ouseley to S.R. Tickell, 31 August 1839; I.R. Ouseley to H.T. Prinsep, Secretary to the Government of India, 28 August 1839, (preserved in the record room of the

Commissioner of Chota Nagpur, and now in the Bihar State Archives, Patna) *see* Appendix 3.

160. *Ibid.*

161. *Bengal: Past and Present,* April-June 1932, p. 133.

162. Quoted in John Malcolm Ludlow's *British India: Its Races and Its History,* Vol. II, p. 136 from *Widow Burning* by H.J. Bushy, p. 21.

163. *The Bengal Spectator,* 10 October 1843, p. 294.

164. John Malcolm Ludlow, op. cit., Vol. II, p. 149.

165. *Ibid.*

166. Secretary to the Government of India to E.H. Townsend, Acting Secretary to the Government of Bombay, Political Department, 30 November 1835, No. II, *see Appendix 6.*

167. L.R. Reid, Acting Chief Secretary to the Government of Bombay to the Secretary with the Right Honourable the Governor-General of India, Simha, Bombay Castle, 4 October 1839. *See* Appendix 7.

168. John Malcolm Ludlow, op. cit., Vol. II, p. 149.

169. *Ibid.*

170. William Lee-Warner, *The Life of the Marquis of Dalhousie,* Vol. II, p. 211.

171. *Ibid.*

172. Tod, *Annals and Antiquities of Rajasthan,* Vol. II, pp. 653-54.

173. *J.R.A.S.,* Vol. XVI, pp. 201-15. (Compare his views of 1819 A.D.)

174. *Ibid.*, Vol. XVII, pp. 209-20.

175. L.S.S.O. Malley, *History of Bengal, Bihar and Orissa,* p. 346; E.J. Thompson, *Suttee,* Chapter IX.

176. *India in 1930-31,* p. 543.

177. *Cambridge History of India,* Vol. VI, p. 131.

178. *Calcutta Review,* 1844.

179. S.R. Mitra, *Types of Early Bengali Prose.*
180. K.K. Datta, *Bengal Subah,* Vol. I, pp. 498-99.
181. Ross, *Cornwallis Correspondence,* Vol. I, p. 547; *Cambridge History of India,* Vol. VI, p. 128.
182. *Cambridge History of India,* Vol. VI, p. 129.
183. *Calcutta Review* July-December 1846, p. 52.
184. *Ibid.*, pp. 78-79.

12. *British Paramountcy and Indian Renaissance*

Among the factors contributing to Renaissance an important place must be given to the growing knowledge of the glory and greatness of the ancient Hindus. When the Indians first began to learn English, little was known of their ancient history, and even the comprehensive and standard history of India like that written by James Mill about that time unhesitatingly expressed the view that the Hindus had ever been in the same abject condition in which the Englishmen found them in the eighteenth century.[1] The very poor knowledge that the Indians themselves possessed about their own past history is shown by the history of the Hindu kings written by Mrityunjay Vidyalankar, a Pandit of the Fort William College in Calcutta. In the year 1808.[2] The works of early oriental scholars like Sir William Jones, Prinsep, Bohtlingk and other Europeans had not yet reached or impressed the general public. But the regular archaeological explorations and excavations, commencing in A.D. 1861 under the personal supervision of Alexander Cunningham, and the writings of Max Müller, Wilson, Fergusson, Rajendra Lal Mitra and others in a more popular form, brought home to the educated Indians a very vivid picture of the past glory and greatness of ancient India which placed her on the same pedestal with Greece and Rome. This inspired the Hindus with a sense of their rich heritage from the past and the leading part they once played as a great nation in the history of the world. It necessarily generated in their minds a spirit of self-confidence and held out before them a bright vision of their future destiny. The views promulgated by

European scholars that the forefathers of the Hindus belonged to the same group of mankind from which were derived all the nations of Europe famous in ancient and modern times; that the Vedas, the sacred literature of the Hindus, were the oldest literary works in the world; that the Upanishads contained the most profound philosophical speculations that human mind has ever conceived; [3] That Emperor Asoka united the whole of India and Afghanistan under one rule, as testified to by his own records engraved on stone more than two thousand years ago; and that, thanks mainly to his efforts, Buddhism, originating in India, played a great role in civilizing a large portion of the population of the world, so much so, that even today one-fifth of the human race still profess that faith;—all these could not fail to stir deeply the hearts of the Hindus with the result that were imbued with a spirit of nationalism and ardent patriotism. The revelation of India's past was one of the strongest foundations on which Indian nationalism was built, and gave it that stamp of Hindu character which made its influence felt in many ways at different stages of political evolution in India.

Another factor that must have stimulated the growth of nationalism in India was the strong current of nationalist ideas which passed over the whole of Europe and South America during the nineteenth century. The momentous revolutions in U.S.A. and France during the last quarter of the eighteenth century. which the English-educated Indians read in their books, roused their patriotic feelings. But they were far more deeply stirred the national revolts happening in their own times, reports of which were regularly received in India. It was a happy confidence that the period during which the English education spread in India also witnessed that phase in the history of Europe and America of which the most distinctive feature was the development of the idea of nationality. About a dozen national States sprang into existence between 1822 and 1830, mostly out of the Turkish, Spanish and Portuguese empires. All these as well as the ideas and events culminating in the struggles for freedom in different regions of Europe in 1830 and 1848, and the stories of heroic resistance and untold sufferings associated with them, made a profound impression upon the

English-educated Indians. In particular, the liberation from foreign yoke of Greece and Italy, two ancient centres of culture like India, and the fight for freedom by the Irish, subject to servitude under a common master, deeply stirred the emotion of the Indians, and evoked feelings of nationalism of the same type. The visit of Indians to Europe in increasing numbers contributed to the same end by making them familiar with the nationalist movements and the working of the free political institutions of Europe.

The introduction of printing press was another important factor. The growth of vernacular literature and the important role it played in the political education of the people has been mentioned in Chapter V. The printing press made the books accessible to a large number of people and stimulated their interest. The printing press also facilitated the growth of periodical literature which was a powerful factor in the development of nationalistic ideas.[4] The opening up of communication between distant parts of India by the introduction of railways, post and telegraph also helped the cause of Indian nationalism by developing the sense of unity among the diverse peoples of the great subcontinent.

Apart from these important factors, the spirit of nationalism was intensified by the growing volume of discontent and disaffection against the British rule due to a variety of causes mentioned above.[4a] The grinding poverty of the people, punctuated by periodical famines was naturally ascribed to the British policy of destroying Indian trade, industry and manufacture by unfair means dictated by the interest of their own country.[5] The galling distinctions between Indians and Europeans in the eye of the law, and the united opposition offered by the latter to the so-called "Black Acts" which sought to remove them, were bitterly resented by the Indian intelligentsia, and they were further estranged by the failure of the Government to concede even the most moderate demands for administrative reforms. The terrible tales of oppression by the indigo-planters, the haughty attitude of the English officials, the arrogant conduct of Englishmen towards Indians, not unoften resulting in brutal assaults and rupture of spleens of the latter, and the acquittal or very nominal punishment of the criminals with white skin by British Judges, produced an intense anti-British feeling among all classes of people which fed the current of national feeling among Indians.[6]

There were many other contributory causes. Among these may be mentioned the effect of the outbreak of 1857-58. There is no doubt that the social and political relations between the Indians and the British, bad as they were before, grew much worse owing to that event,[7] and thus it indirectly helped the growth of national feeling. But it is a moot point to decide how far the mutiny or revolt of 1857-58 directly stimulated the growth of such a feeling. For the nationalistic feeling first appeared among the intellectuals who were, generally speaking, indifferent and even unsympathetic, if not positively hostile, to the movement, and were not therefore likely to be affected by it.[8]

It is in Bengal, which was least affected by the incidents of 1857-58, that we find the distinct growth of a truly nationalist movement during the sixties, *i.e.* almost immediately after the suppression of the outbreak of 1857-58. It was not directed towards the advancement of political status or the achievement of administrative reforms, but it had a higher aim, namely, the regeneration of Indians on the basis of a true conception of nationality.

One of the important factors in the development of nationalism in Bengal was the new movement in Brāhma Samāj, initiated by Keshab Chandra Sen, which carried one step further the ideal of freedom not only in respect of religious ideas—which was already developed by the older section—but also in social ideas and personal conduct. B. C. Pal, who was intimately connected with this movement, thus refers to it:

"The Brahmo Samaj, under Keshub Chunder Sen, had proclaimed a new gospel of personal freedom and social equality, which reacted very powerfully upon this infant national consciousness and the new political life and aspirations of young

Bengal. Keshub's controversies with the Christian missionaries were widely read and greatly enjoyed not only by his own followers and co-religionists but by the entire body of our English-educated countrymen. In his victories over the Christian missionaries in these controversies, Keshub's countrymen, even outside his church and community, felt a genuine pride, which powerfully fed their national conceit. Keshub's English visit and the way he was lionized by the British public and the British press also reacted very powerfully upon the mind of his people in India. The old paralyzing sense of superiority of their new political masters over them was visibly replaced by a new self-confidence in our educated countrymen in consequence of Keshub's successful missionary propaganda in England."[9]

The all-India tour of Keshab also fostered the ideas of national unity by bringing together on a common platform diverse peoples of India in different regions. He was the first great all-India figure symbolizing the unity of Indian culture. This was proved beyond doubt by the high regard in which he was held all over India—a fact strikingly demonstrated after his death. Sir Henry Cotton justly remarks: "The death of Keshub Chunder in January, 1884, was one of the earliest occasions for the manifestation of truly national sentiment in the country. The residents of all parts of India, irrespective of castes and creed, united with one voice in the expression of sorrow at his loss and pride in him as member of one common nation".[9a]

But great as were the services of Keshab Chandra. His contribution to the growth of nationalism was both limited and indirect. In the first place his appeal was "exclusively to the religious and moral sensibilities of the rising generations",[10] and he deliberately eschewed politics. "If anything, Keshab's politics accepted the British subjection of Indian as due to the intervention of God's special providence for the salvation of India", and he openly proclaimed "loyalty to the British Government" as an article of the creed of his church.[10a] Secondly, he derived his inspiration soley from the West, and his leanings towards Christianity were such that not only Christian missionaries hoped, but the Indians also feared, that he would erelong embrace Christianity. Whatever we might think of this popular impression, there is no doubt that Keshab's theology was "built partly upon the Intuitionalist school of European philosophy and partly upon Carlyle's *Hero Worship* and *Emerson's Representative Men.*[11] For these reasons as well as the new doctrinal developments and other personal affairs, Keshab and his church steadily lost popular sympathies. "In fact, Keshub Chunder had almost as many detractors among young Bengal of his as he had admirers."[12]

At this crisis of our national life, "when Keshub and his progressive Brahmos developed unmistakable tendencies towards the modern European or Christian ethics and rationalism,"[12a] the tide was turned by Rajnarain Bose,[13] himself a product of the Western education. He boldly proclaimed "the superiority of Hindu religion and culture over European and Christian theology and civilization."[14] The Hindus, said he had forgotten their past to such an extent that they had no recollection of the fact that rational thinking and ideas of social and personal freedom were not wanting in the history of their own culture. Rajnarain Bose boldly asserted that "not only have we the most perfect system of theism or monotheism in our ancient theology and religion, but Hinduism presented also a much higher social idealism, all its outer distinctions of caste notwithstanding, than has as yet been reached by Christendom".[15] How far his views were historically correct, we need not discuss in the present context. It will suffice to state that these ideas were catching and his clarion call rallied round his banner a large number of Hindus who accepted his views with enthusiasm, and probably without argument or discussion. Rajnarain held before them a complete ideal of nationalism to be realised in every department of life. He gave a concrete picture of his ideas in a prospectus which he issued in 1866 with a view to the establishment of a "Society for the Promotion of National Feeling among the Educated Natives of Bengal".

The following extracts from this prospectus sufficiently illustrate his ideas, though the whole document deserves a careful study.[16]

"Now that European ideas have penetrated Bengal, the Bengalee mind has been moved from the sleep of ages. A restless fermentation is going on in Bengalee Society. A desire for change and progress is everywhere visible. People discontented with old customs and institutions are panting for reform. Already a band of young men have expressed a desire to sever themselves at once from Hindu Society and to renounce even the Hindu name. It is to be feared that the tide of revolution may sweep away whatever good we have inherited from our ancestors. To prevent this catastrophe and to give a national shape to reforms, it is proposed that a Society be established by the influential members of native society for the promotion of national feeling among the educated natives of Bengal. Without due cultivation of national feeling no nation can be eventually great. This is a fact testified to by all history.

"The Nationality Promotion Society shall first of all use their best endeavours to revive the national gymnastics exercises...The Nationality Promotion Society shall establish a Model School for instruction in Hindu Music...the Nationality Promotion Society shall also establish a school of Hindu Medicine, where Hindu Materia Medica and practice of physic will be taught freed from the error and absurdities that disfigure them...The teacher of the proposed Hindu School of Medicine should be one who is acquainted with both English and Hindu Medical Sciences.

"The Nationality Promotion Society will publish in Bengalee the results of the researches of the Sanskrit scholars of Europe in the department of Indian Antiquities, giving special prominence to their description of prosperity and glory of Ancient India, physical, intellectual, moral, social, political, literary and scientific....

"The Nationality Promotion Society shall afford every encouragement in their power to the cultivation of Sanskrit. It shall patronize the publication of important Sanskrit works, cooperating with the Asiatic Society of Bengal in this respect, and shall offer pecuniary reward or panegyrical addresses to the best Sanskrit scholars of Bengal.

"The Nationality Promotion Society shall make it binding upon its members to ground the knowledge of their sons in their mother-tongue before giving them an English education. Education both in Bengalee and English, if carried on simultaneously, does great injury to the Bengalee education of a student, as he pays greater attention to the English than to the Bengalee language...

"The Nationality Promotion Society shall try its best to prevent daily increasing corruption of the colloquial of the educated natives who mix, in common conversation, English words with Bengalee in the most ridiculous manner imaginable...

"The Nationality Promotion Society shall endeavour to prevail upon their countrymen to hold in the Bengalee language the proceedings of such societies as do not require the co-operation of Englishmen, and are exclusively composed of Bengalees, or have not as their object the improvement of youth in English speaking or writing...

"The Nationality Promotion Society shall publish tracts in Bengalee containing proofs of the existence of liberal and enlightened customs in Ancient India, such as female education personal liberty of females, marriage by election of the bride, marriage at adult age, widow-marriage, inter-marriage, and voyage to distant countries. It will try to introduce such foreign customs into educated society as have a tendency to infuse national feeling into the minds of its members such as that of holding festivities in honour of men of genius as is done amongst European nations... The Nationality Promotion Society shall, in a few words, try, firstly to prevent the introduction of evil foreign customs into educated native community; secondly, to introduce such foreign customs as have a tendency to infuse national feeling into the minds of its members; thirdly, to give, if possible, to foreign customs already introduced a national shape; fourthly, to aid social reformation by citing old precedents in its favour; and fifthly, to prevent the abolition of such old customs of the country as are beneficial in their nature.

"The Nationality Promotion Society will not overlook even such trifling points as the regulation of etiquette, with a view to give a national shape to the same. It would be impossible to abolish all foreign modes of etiquette that have crept into educated native society, such as the hearty handshake, but the members of the Nationality Promotion Society shall give the preference to our national *numuskar* and *pranam* on all occasions on which it is practicable to do so....

"It would be the duty of the Nationality Promotion Society to reprobate the practice of frequenting European hotels so common among our educated countrymen. This practice shows a greedy hankering after European food, and demeans us in the eyes of foreigners. It must appear ridiculous in the eyes of all Europeans except hotel-keepers."

The ideas preached by Rajnarain Bose in this remarkable document were enthusiastically taken up by a young man named Naba Gopal Mitra, editor of the *National Paper* founded by Devendranath Tagore in 1865. He started an institution known as "Hindu Melā" to promote the national feelings, sense of patriotism, and a spirit of self-help among the Hindus. It was an annual public gathering on the last day of the Bengali year. The special features of the annual gathering were patriotic songs, poems and lectures, a detailed review of the political, social, economic, and religious condition of India, an exhibition of indigenous arts and crafts, and performance of different forms of physical exercises and feats of physical strength. It had an all-India outlook and specimens of arts and crafts were collected from Banners, Kashmir, Jaipur, Lakhnau, and Patna. Rewards were also offered for good books written in Bengali and Sanskrit, which were calculated to promote the welfare of the country. Thus intellectual development through fine arts and literature, and economic progress by means of industrial development formed the main planks of the Hindu Melā.

The Hindu Melā met altogether fourteen times from 1867 to 1880. Its importance gradually declined owing to the establishment of other associations more directly connected with the political and national movement in Bengal. But it is impossible to overestimate the importance of its contribution to the growth of national feeling in Bengal. The patriotic songs and poems, sung and recited in this Melā, including one or two by Rabindranath, then a boy of 18, are still regarded as treasures of Bengali literature.

An association, called the 'National Society', was founded after the fourth session of the Melā. Its avowed object was the promotion of unity and national feeling among the Hindus. The National Society arranged a monthly discourse. In one of these monthly meetings, presided over by Devendranath Tagore, Rajnarain Bose delivered an address on the "Superiority of Hinduism" embodying his main views as mentioned above...It evoked a keen controversy, and meetings were held not only by Christians but also by advanced Brāhmas to his views. As the Melā was confined to the Hindus, objection was taken to the use of the word 'National'. Against this, the *National Paper,* the organ of the Melā, observed as follows:

"We do not understand why our correspondent takes exception to the Hindus who certainly form a nation by themselves, and as such a society established by them can very properly be called a National Society."

This was not an isolated expression of views, casually formed, but rested on a deep-seated conviction which, at first confined to a small section, was gradually imbibed, consciously or unconsciously, by a large majority of educated people.

Naba Gopal elaborated his view of Hindu nationalism through his writings. This has been summed up as follows: "Naba Gopal holds that the chief criterion of nationalism is unity. This unity according to him, is brought about, sustained and promoted in different peoples by different means and on different principles. The principle which promoted nationalism amongst the Greeks was love of country, amongst the Jews the Mosaic Law, amongst the Romans the love of liberty and renown, and amongst the English the love of liberty. He maintains that the basis of national unity in

India has been the Hindu religion. 'Hindu nationality is not confined to Bengal. It embraces all of Hindu name and Hindu faith throughout the length and breadth of Hindustan; neither geographical position, nor the language is counted a disability. The Hindus are destined to be a religious nation".[17]

But, side by side with the idea of Hindu nationalism, there was a broader outlook which sought to embrace the whole of India in one nationality. Indeed, this was a dominant and characteristic feature of nationalism in Bengal even at the very beginning, and was never lost sight of throughout the chequered course of its evolution. The school represented by Naba Gopal Mitra was at first insignificant, but gradually gained strength for reasons discussed later.

The contribution of the Brāhma Samāj to the development of nationalism, after Keshab Chandra Sen, cannot be regarded as very significant. Nevertheless, the founders of the third Samāj, notably Shiva Nath Sastri and Ananda Mohan Bose, in their personal capacities did much to further its cause. Reference will be made to A. M. Bose in connection with the growth of political organization discussed in the next chapter. B. C. Pal, an eminent political leader of Bengal at a later date, has preserved an interesting reminiscence of his close personal contact with Shiva Nath Sastri and the influence exercised upon him by the latter. Shiva Nath held that "freedom is one and indivisible", "political emancipation is impossible without social emancipation and personal purity". In all this he agreed with the current Brāhmaism. But he proceeded further and maintained that the realization of a man's spiritual destiny or his salvation was equally impossible unless the ideas of equality, liberty, and fraternity were fully organized in his personal life, his social relations, and in the constitution of his national State. To realize this completer ideal of freedom, a Society was organized by Shivanath in 1876. Its members were to take a pledge which was embodied in a formal document. The first article pledged the members to put up a strenuous fight against image-worship and castedomination. The next article started with the declaration that "self-government is the only form of political government ordained by God." Logically interpreted, it meant that the British Government had no moral title to the allegiance of the people. But it was not a practical declaration of revolt, for the removal of social and religious evils be the condition precedent to the reconstitution of the national State upon a truly democratic basis. Till then they should obey the laws of the present Government, but would not "take service under this Government." The next article discussed ways and means for advancing the country to the goal of self-government. This comprised education, including that of women and the masses, introduction of widow-remarriage, abolition of purdah, and other social reforms. Lastly, emphasis was laid on the development of physique and ability to defend the country. The signatories therefore pledged themselves to learn how to ride and shoot, and preach the duties of acquiring these military trainings and aptitudes to their fellow-countrymen.[18]

In spite of the fact that the actual achievement of this Society was very little or nothing, its idealism commands our attention. While the Brāhma Samāj confined its activities to the religious and ethical life to the exclusion of political life, and political leaders ignored or belittled the ethical and social aspects, Shiva Nath combined all of them in his ideal of complete freedom. To him belongs the credit of viewing religion as a formative force in worldly life in all its aspects, and also of bringing to our new patriotism and politics the inspiration of a lofty ethical ideal. Probably such an ideal was never preached again till we come to the days of Swāmi Vivekānanda and Mahātmā Gandhi.

Reference may be made to an innovation of Shiva Nath Sastri which signifies the change of spirit introduced by him. In the liturgy of Keshab Chandra Sen there was a prayer for universal humanity. Shiva Nath, as a minister of Sādhāran Brāhma Samāj replaced it by a special prayer, offered every week, for the uplift and emancipation of his own country and his people.[19]

The other religious movements also directly or indirectly helped the growth of nationalism. The Ārya Samāj founded by Dayananda gave a great impetus to nationalism in the Punjab. It imbued the people with a spirit of self-confidence. B. C. Pal, who witnessed the early stages of its development, has described it as follows:

"The fact of the matter is that the new generation of Hindus in the Punjab felt a keen humiliation in their inability to meet the attacks of Moslem and Christian propagandists, who condemned their religion as idolatry and polytheism. In the message of Pandit Dayananda they discovered, first a powerful defensive weapon by which they could repudiate the claims to superiority of Christianity and Islam over their national religion. Dayananda. In the second place, did not only find a weapon of defence to the Punjab Hindu in his *Satyārtha-Prakāśa,* he made a violent attack on Christian and Moslem propaganda showing up the unreason of both these alien systems and exposing what he believed to be their moral lapses also. All this helped to feed the pride of the race of the Punjabee Hindu, who had previously found himself in a completely helpless position under the attacks of Christian and Moslem propaganda."[20]

As noted above, the Ārya Samāj was a militant sect from the very beginning. Its "chef inspiration came from its intense patriotism. This patriotism has always carried with it a spirit of intolerance of, if not virulent antagonism to, other religious systems, particularly the Moslem. Its attitude towards Christianity is not less hostile, though certainly not so open as it is towards Islam".[21] Ere long it developed an anti-foreign sentiment which was particularly strong among the younger section. "The young Arya Samajists openly declared that they were waiting for the day when they would settle their account both with Moslems and the Britishers."[22]

But the Ārya Samāj had also a positive approach to nationalism. "Political independence was one of the first objectives of Dayānanda. Indeed, he was the first man to use the term Swarāj. He was the first to insist on people using only swadeshi things manufactured in India and to discard foreign things. He was the first to recognize Hindi as the national language of India".[23] Whatever one might think of these claims put forward by the biographer of Dayananda,[24] there is no doubt that the Ārya Samāj aimed at the creation of an Indian nation by establishing a common religion and culture all over India. For this it adopted *Suddhi* or reconversion into Hinduism of all those who had once renounced it, either willingly or under duress.

Similarly, a great impetus was given to nationalism by the Theosophical Society as well as by the great spiritual leader Ramakṛishṇa Paramahaṁsa and his disciple Svāmī Vivekananda, to which reference will be made later.

Though the spirit of nationalism was first evolved in Bengal it soon spread to other parts of India, but the positive evidence afforded by contemporary records is not as adequate or as easily available as in Bengal. In Bombay the writings and activities of Vishnu Krishna Chiplunkar, who died in 1882, Mahadev Govind Ranade, Gopal Ganesh Agarkar and Bal Gangadhar Tilak, as well as the ideas preached by Gopal Hari Desmukh and Bhaskar Pandurang Tarkhadkar, to whom reference has been made in the Preceding chapter,[25] definitely indicate the growth of a strong national feeling. This is only what could be normally expected. For the People of Maharashtra occupied a high and honourable position in Indian polities even within living memory. Less than a century ago they had made a bold bid for political supremacy such as the British then enjoyed in India, and the last descendant of the Peshwas, though in exile, continued as a living symbol of their political glory and greatness till 1853.

For similar reasons the Muslims were also inspired by a national feeling from the very beginning of the British rule. But it was dominated by class consciousness at the very outset, as it was based solely on the memory of their political greatness and historical traditions, and not broadbased on those ideas of patriotism and nationalist feeling which the Hindus of Bengal imbibed through Western education. The nationalism of Maharashtra was saved from this narrowness by the influence of Western ideas, and was gradually merged into the widely developing Indian nationalism. As this nationalism was a product of English education, and the Muslims as a class lagged far behind the Hindus in taking advantage of it, there was a marked divergence in the growth of nationalism among the Hindus and Muslims. The Wahabi movement in the first half of the nineteenth century was a genuine national movement, but it was exclusively Muslim in character. On account of this Muslim exclusiveness and the greater influence of English education and Western ideas upon the Hindus, the Western type of nationalism, which was a characteristic feature of the political growth in India during the latter half of the nineteenth century, gradually partook more and more of a Hindu character. This process was hastened by the fact, mentioned above, that the past glory and greatness of the Hindus came to form the solid basis of this nationalism. This was quite natural, for in every country the memory of past greatness binds the people together into a national unity. But in India this historic consciousness operated upon the two major elements of the population, the Hindus and the Muslims, in diametrically opposite ways. Every historical incident in the past which reflected glory upon the one was a humiliating memory to the other. The triumphs of Mohammed ibn Qāsim, Sultan Mahmūd of Ghaznī, and Mohammed Ghūrī which swelled the pride of the Muslims as a great conquering nation of the world, only evoked painful memories of national degradation and humiliation in the minds of the Hindus.

A very striking illustration of what has been stated above is afforded by the development of nationalism in Bombay. Here, too, as in Bengal, it was the English education that fostered the spirit of nationality as the people imbibed, along with western culture, the love of freedom, the spirit of patriotism, the idea of self-government, the higher duty of self-sacrifice for the preservation of national honour and national liberty, and similar ideas which permeated Western literature, but were comparatively strangers to our own. Bal Gangadhar Tilak, the great nationalist leader of Bombay, gave expression to these ideas through his paper, the *Kesarī*. As far back as 1885 he wrote:

"We are, at present, gradually being inspired by the spirit of patriotism. The birth of patriotism among us is due to English rule and English education. English education has imparted to us knowledge of ancient and modern history; it has enabled us to know what were the fruits of patriotism among the ancient Greeks and Romans. We have also learned from their histories how, when they lost their patriotism, they were subjected to foreign domination and became ignorant and superstitious. English rule has made us realise the necessity of cultivating patriotism in our national concerns....The spirit of patriotism has not as yet permeated all classes. It is only those who have come under the influence of English education and begun to realise the defects of British administration that have been inspired by that spirit. Patriotism is not our national quality: it is the product of the influences to which we have been subjected after the introduction of British rule".

Tilak made it the great object of his life to diffuse the spirit of patriotism and nationalism among the masses. Two expedients adopted by him for this purpose were the inauguration of Shivāji festival and the transformation of the traditional worship of Ganapati into an altogether new form. Thus he requisitioned to the national service two of the great forces which are calculated to deeply stir the national mind, namely, religion and history. But both the institutions produced diametrically opposite effects upon the Hindus and Muslims. The images of Hindu gods have always excited the Muslims with iconoclastic fury, and their traditional role in Indian history has been to break them to pieces rather than make them serve any national purpose. Even though bereft of any power to do any mischief, their religion forbade them to derive any good out of it. As Shivāji had founded the Maharashtra kingdom in the teeth of opposition from the most powerful Muslim Emperor in India, a festival in his honour was well calculated to inspire the masses in Maharashtra. But Shivāji and the Maratha power founded by him were rightly regarded by the Muslims as the main causes of the decline and downfall of the greatest Muslim Empire in India, and their national vanity was sure to be wounded by doing any honour to the great Maratha leader. As a matter of fact, though

Tilak did yeoman's service to the cause of Indian nationalism. He was never forgiven by the Muslims for instituting the Shivāji festival. In Bengal also the new spirit of nationalism was gradually assuming a Hindu character. This first came into prominence in connection with the Hindu Melā whose founder definitely asserted that the Hindus formed a nation by themselves. This view, of course, did not go unchallenged, as the criticism of the use of the title 'national' by Hindu Melā, noted above,[26] clearly demonstrates. But the further progress of nationalism in Bengal leaves no doubt that it did not, or rather could not, shed its Hindu character, as a genuine pride in the old history and culture of the Hindus formed its very basis.

This is quite clear from the Bengali literature which made the greatest contribution to the development of national and patriotic feeling during the last quarter of the nineteenth century. The name of Bankim Chandra Chatterji stands foremost in this connection. His famous novel *Ānandamath* contains the hymn *Bande Mātaram* which had been the national anthem of India up to 1947. During the long and arduous struggle for freedom from 1905 to 1947 *Bande Mātaram* was the rallying cry of the patriotic sons of India, and thousands of them succumbed to the *lāthi* blow of the British police or mounted the scaffold with *Bande Mātaram* on their lips. The main theme of the novel inspired the Bengali youths to supreme self-sacrifice during the hectic days of the Swadeshi movement. The central plot moves round a band of *sannyāsins,* called *santānas* or children, who left their hearth and home and dedicated their lives to the cause of their motherland. They worshipped their motherland as the Goddess Kālī;—they knew no other deity save the land of their birth, and no other religion except the service of their motherland. That is why they called themselves *santānas* or children (of the mother). In their temple they placed three images of the Goddess Kālī representing the motherland,—Mother that was, great and glorious in her majestic grandeur; Mother that is, wretched and groveling in the dust; and the Mother that will be, in her pristine glory. No other Bengali book—or, for the matter of that, no book written in any language—so profoundly moved the Bengali youths save perhaps Sarat Chandra's Pather Dābi, written half a century later. The later novel was an emotional protest against the British rule, as the earlier one was, at least ostensibly, against the Muslim rule. This aspect of the *Ānandamath* and the imagery of Goddess Kālī leave no doubt That Bankim Chandra's nationalism was Hindu rather than Indian. This is made crystal clear from his other writings which contain passionate outbursts against the subjugation on India by the Muslims. From that day set the sun of our glory—that is the refrain of his essays and novels which not unoften contain adverse, and sometimes even irreverent, remarks against the Muslims. The plots of some of his novels are based on historical fights between Hindus and Muslims, such as Bakhtyar Khaljī invasion of Bengal, Aurangzeb's fight with the Rajputs, etc., and his readers were never left in doubt as to where his sympathies lay. The following confession of the great Bengali leader, B. C. Pal, echoes the sentiment of every young Hindu reader of Bankim's novels:

"*Durgesh-nandini* quickened my earliest patriotic sentiments. Our sympathies were all entirely with Birendra Singha, and the court-scene where the Moslem invader was stabbed through his heart by Vimala (widow of Birendra Singha) made a profound impression upon my youthful imagination."[27]

Bengali lyric poems of the period gave a clarion call to patriotism. Rangalal's famous Ode to Liberty is a notable instance. Its opening line, which has been in the mouth of every Bengali ever since, may be translated as follows: "Breathes there the man who would like to live, though shorn of liberty?" And this was put in the mouth of a Rajput fighting for his country against the Muslims. Nabin Chandra Sen, another famous poet of Bengal, wrote a long poem on the occasion of the visit of the Prince of Wales (future Edward VII) to India. He mades Mother India recount in stirring verses to her guest her lost glory of the past, and the heroic achievements of the Marathas, Sikhs, and her other children; but no mention is made of the Muslims. But the broad

Western type of nationalism which embraced India as a whole, irrespective of creeds and communities, was also faithfully reflected in Bengali literature. The greatest name in the field is that of Hem Chandra Banerji whose national lyrics, now become almost classic, drew a lurid picture of the Indians as contrasted with the Chinese and even the "uncivilized Japanese", who were free nations while India was asleep. The burthem of his poems was a passionate appeal to India to awake and arise. His brilliant satires on the Anglo-Indian agitation against the Ilbert Bill and the presentation of the ladies of his family to the Prince of Wales by a Bengali gentleman of Calcutta were really strong appeals to the national sentiments and feeling of self-respect of the Indians.

B. C. Pal describes as follows Hem Chandra's influence upon him:-

"Hem Chandra, however, was our special favourite. The intense patriotic passion that breathed through his poems captured our youthful minds in a way which no other Bengalee poems had done. The new generation of English-educated Bengalees had already commenced to advance themselves to positions of trust and responsibility in the new Administration. In the learned professions of law and medicine, also, they were gradually asserting themselves as against the British members. A new spirit of independence and self-assertion was increasingly manifesting itself in the conduct and conversations of the English-educated Bengalee. All these had already commenced to provoke a racial conflict in the country. Hemchandra was, in a special sense, the poet of this new conflict and of the new racial self-respect and sensitive patriotism, born of it."[28]

The new-born patriotism and national sentiments found expression in, and were deeply stimulated by, a number of beautiful national songs which have survived to the present day. The Bengali dramas and the public stage also played a great part in fostering the national sentiments. There were social dramas written with the deliberate object of drawing pointed attention to the many social evils which were eating into vitals of the nation, for in those days "a new passion for freedom,—personal, social, and political—h d possessed the Bengali mind."[29] But they were also dramas with a distinctly national appeal. Reference may be made to the *Bhārata-mātā* (Mother India) which proclaimed the gospel of the religion of motherland. The following specimen of songs in this drama illustrates the anguish of a patriot's heart which it was the deliberate design of the author to evoke:

> "O India, gloomy is thy face,
> Beautiful that was as the moon;
> Tears flow from thine eyes
> throughout the day and night.''[30]

Some of the worst evils of the British rule which deeply stirred the feelings of the people formed the theme of dramas. The best illustration is the *Nīla-darpana* by Dina Bandhu Mitra which depicted the terrible oppression of the indigo-planters.[31] B. C. Pal writes in his autobiography:

> "When it was put upon the board of the new Bengalee theatres, the audience got wild with passion against the White Planters; and sometimes they so far forgot themselves that they threw their shoes at the poor actor on the stage."[32]

In general, the Bengali dramas, unable, on account of press laws, to portray directly sentiments and actions against the British, took resort to a subterfuge. They either portrayed heroic historical fights by the Rajputs against the Muslims who invaded or conquered their motherland, or invented purely imaginary pictures of struggle against foreign rulers or conquerors. The scenes and speeches and actions were devised in such a manner that no spectator was under any illusion as to the real objective.

The glaring evils of the British rule were overtly or covertly emphasised in poems, dramas, novels, and songs. Reference may be made to one particular national song which was an "open condemnation of foreign economic exploitation. The burthen of it was that India was becoming poorer and poorer every day owing to the loss of her national freedom." It was taken from a novel by

Manmohan Bose, *Baṅgādhipa-parājaya,* depicting the conquest of Bengal by a foreign people who came from a high island on the sea called Tuṅgadvīpa. "The weaver and the blacksmith are crying day and night. They cannot find their food by plying their trade. Even threads and needles come from distant shores. Even match-sticks are not produced in the country. Whether in dressing themselves or producing their domestic utensils or even in lighting their oil-lamps,—in nothing are the people independent of their foreign masters......Swarms of locusts from Tuṅgadvīpa coming to these shores have eaten up all its solid grains leaving only the chaff for the starving children of the soil."[33]

Among the important factors that contributed to the development of patriotic and national feelings must be reckoned the activities of some great personalities. The chief among these, during the period under review, was undoubtedly Surendra Nath Banerji.

Dismissed from Indian Civil Service for what is now generally regarded as a very minor offence of technical character, Surendra Nath had proceeded to England to appeal to the higher authorities. He failed in his mission, but during his stay in England he had made a special study of the history of the national movements in Europe and realized the important role played by young men in these movements. In particular the "Young Italy" movement by Mazzine made a deep impression upon him. Surendra Nath joined the Calcutta students' Association founded by Ananda Mohan Basu, and soon became the life and soul of it. B. C. Pal, himself a student in those days, has recorded his impression as follows. "Surendra Nath's eloquence and burning patriotism lent to it a new strength and inspiration. Surendra Nath's first appearance on the platform of the Students' Association at once established his claims to the leadership of a new youth movement."[34]

The subject of Surendra Nath's first lecture was the rise of the Sikh power in the Punjab. This and several other eloquent lectures that followed made Surendra Nath the leader of a new political movement, which practically supplanted the new religious movement of Keshab Chandra Sen which had hitherto caught the imagination of Young Bengal. The spirit of freedom which had been dominating the educated intelligentsia of Bengal was largely diverted from religion and social spheres and "Surendra Nath found a new and larger scope for its fulfilment in the political propaganda which he initiated.[35] It was nothing short of a silent but powerful revolution in the intellectual atmosphere in Bengal which gave a great stimulus to the newly awakened sense of national and patriotic fervour.

At this distance of time, with the situation so profoundly changed, it is difficult to assay properly the value of the inspiring addresses of Surendra Nath For what really matters is not so much the logic of arguments, or the accuracy of facts in the light of what we know today, but the effect it produced on the impressionable minds of the young men who listened to them, and the activities which they stirred up. Fortunately, there is a first-hand record of these impressions by one who was a student in those days but later became a distinguished nationalist leader, *viz.* Bipin Chandra Pal. The following is an extract from his autobiography.

"The materials for his lecture on the 'Rise of the Sikh Power' were, no doubt, drawn from English sources, particularly from Malcolm's History of the Sikhs. But the Sikh movement was Practically unknown to us. Our school text-books on Indian History did, no doubt, notice the story of the Sikhs in connection with Ranjit Singh. But these references had no inspiration for us. Surendra Nath for the first time presented the Sikh movement as really a movement of freedom, first, against the current ceremonialism and Brahminical domination of the Hindu community; second, against the oppression of the Moguls, who tried to crush a movement of religious and spiritual freedom by the organised brute force of an alien Government; and lastly, against British aggression. British historians of the Sikhs had glossed over the wonderful military skill and velour of the Sikh army, describing signal defeats of the British as draws, and what were really draws as defeats of the Sikhs. Surendra Nath in his address on the 'Rise of the British Power in the Punjab' exposed the unreliable character of British historians and painted in burning words the justice of the Sikh cause, the deathless devotion of the Sikh people to their *Khalsa* or Commonwealth, and the signal defeats which they inflicted on the British at Chilianwala and Gujarat. Our school histories never confessed frankly these defeats. This revelation of the history of the Sikhs made a very powerful appeal to our infant patriotism and lent new strength and even bitterness to the anti-British feeling that had already commenced to possess our youthful minds. I was not present at this first lecture of Surendra Nath's, but those who were, carried with them from this meeting a new patriotic fervour. A friend characterised this lecture of Surendra Nath's as creating, by deafening rounds of applause that followed in quick succession his rapidly flowing periods, almost a literal storm about College Square. Surendra Nath's position as the most powerful orator of his generation was at once established by this performance."[36]

"But the greatest and the most inspiring message of Surendra Nath's early propaganda was delivered through his lectures on Joseph Mazzini and the Young Italy movement organised by him. Mazzini's life and particularly his extremely sensitive patriotism which so worked upon his youthful imagination that even as a school boy he refused to join in any form of gaiety of his family and his community, in the face of the bondage in which his country lay under Austrian domination, drew out all the latent passion for national freedom in us. The tyrannies of the Austrian army of occupation in Italy, who showed scant regard for the ordinary rights and liberties of the Italian people and treated even the Italian intellectuals of the middle class as members of an inferior race, indeed literally as helots and slaves, made a profound impression upon our sensitive minds. Neither the person nor the property of the Italian in the neighbourhood of the Austrian military camps, nor even the honour of their women, were safe from the wanton insults and outrages of Austrian officers and soldiers. We saw or imagined a great similitude between the position of the Italians under Austrian domination and our own position under British rule. In the outlying districts in cases between Europeans and Indians the latter could hope to receive practically no justice. The differential treatment accorded to Indians and Europeans even when they happened to be members of the same Covenanted Civil Service rankled in our heart. The plight of the indentured labourers in the tea gardens of Assam had already commenced to be agitated in our vernacular press. The *Amrita Bazar Patrika* was circulating broadcast tales of magisterial high-handedness all over the province. All these things working upon our youthful imagination created a profound sympathy in us with the struggle for national freedom in Italy led by Mazzini, when the story was presented to us by Surendra Nath."[37]

Another effect of Surendra Nath's lecture on *Mazzini*, although little noticed at the time, and less known in later days, was big with future consequences. The familiarity of young Bengalis with the Young Italy movement led to the growth of secret political societies, Here also let Bipin Chandra Pal speak of his own youthful days:

"We commenced to read the writings of *Mazzini* and the history of the Young Italy movement. Here we saw also the earlier organisations for Italian freedom, particularly those of the Carbonari, with which *Mazzini* had himself been associated at the beginning of his patriotic career. The Carbonari were secret societies. They hoped to win their national freedom by covering the whole country with a network of secret revolutionary organisations, whose idea was to free their fatherland from the Austrian yoke by striking at the Austrian rulers. Secret assassinations were the main objective of these Carbonari organisations....But though without any real revolutionary motive or any plan of secret assassinations as the way to national emancipation, the new inspiration imparted to young Bengal by Surendra Nath's presentation of the life of *Mazzini* and the Italian freedom movement led many of us to form secret organisations. Calcutta student community was at that time almost honeycombed with these organisations. Secrecy has a strange fascination for youthful minds. And this was the real psychology of our *penchant* for these secret societies. Surendra Nath was himself, I think, the President of quite a number of these secret societies.....Surendra Nath's connection with quite a number of the new secret societies among the youthful intellectuals of Calcutta proved the unique confidence which he enjoyed of his young followers. Though without any serious plan or policy of political action aiming at the liberation of their people from the British yoke, these societies were, however, not lacking in seriousness. Their patriotism was serious, and how seriously they took it was seen in the vows and rituals of many of these societies. I knew of one such society, though I was not myself a member of it, whose initiatory rites were almost Masonic in some aspects. Every member of this society had to sign the pledge of membership with his own blood drawn at the point of a sword from his breast."[38]

These societies did not achieve any practical result by way of organising revolution or political assassinations. But they left a rich legacy in this respect to the next generation.

Surendra Nath's nationality was of the Western type and it was predominantly political and free from any Hindu bias. In a speech he delivered in 1878 he urged the young men of India to dedicate their lives to the good of their country and laid special emphasis on the unity among different creeds. Here are a few passages:

"Young men, your country expects great things from you. Now I ask, how many of you are prepared, when you have finished your studies at the College, to devote your lives, to consecrate your energies to the good of your country? (Cries of "all," "all")....There comes a time in the history of a nation's progress, when every man may verily be said to have a mission of his own to accomplish. Such a time has now arrived for India. The fiat has gone forth. The celestial mandate has been issued that every Indian must now do this duty, or stand condemned before God and man. There was such a time of stirring activity in the glorious annals of England when....(refers to Hampden, Algernon Sidney, and the Seven Bishops).....

"It is not indeed necessary for us to have recourse to violence in order to obtain the redress of our grievances. Constitutional agitation will secure for us those rights and privileges which in less favoured countries are obtained by sterner means. But peaceful as are the means to be enforced, there is a stern duty to be performed by every Indian. And he who fails in that duty is a traitor before God and man.....

"Three hundred years ago, in the Punjab, the immortal founder of Sikhism, the meek, the gentle, the blessed Nanak preached the great doctrine of Indian unity and endeavoured to knit together Hindus and Musulmans under the banner of a common faith. That attempt was eminently successful. Nanak became the spiritual founder of the Sikh Empire. He preached the great doctrine of peace and good will between Hindus and Musulmans. And standing in the presence of his great example we too must preach the great doctrine of peace and good will between Hindus and Musulmans, Christians and Parsees, aye between all sections of the great Indian Community.

......"In the name then of a common country, let us all, Hindus, Musulmans, Christians, Parsees, members of the great Indian Community, throw the pall of oblivion over the jealousies and dissensions of bygone times and, embracing one another in fraternal love and affection, live and work for the benefit of a beloved fatherland".[39]

The eloquence of Surendra Nath and the voice of many other leaders put this broad view of nationalism in the forefront of the young Indians, and it exercised great influence upon the political evolution of India.

The great leaders of Bengal had hitherto laid stress on social, religions, and personal freedom. The emphasis of Surendra Nath's appeal was far more on political freedom. This constitutes his principal contribution to the regeneration of Bengal. He brought a new message and inspiration of political freedom and carried young Bengal with him. Bipin Chandra Pal, himself a Brāhma, admits that "Surendra Nath's political propaganda gathered a much larger following than that of the religious and social revolt of Keshub Chandra Sen and the Brahmo Samaj."[40]

Surendra Nath was not insensible to social reform, but he was against violent changes. "We must", he said, "so far as practicable, take the community with us, by a process of steady and gradual up lift, so that there may be no sudden disturbance or dislocation, the new being adapted to the old and the old assimilated to the new. That has been the normal path of progress in Hindu society through the long centuries."[40a]

Another great personality who advanced the cause of nationalism in India broadbased on the unity of all communities was Mahadev Govind Ranade (1842-1901). He held the office of a Subordinate Judge under the Government of Bombay and could not there fore take any active part in politics. But he devoted himself to the social and economic uplift of the country. In respect of social reform, as noted above,[41] he steered a middle course between the overzealous enthusiasts who would rather secede from the Hindu society than tolerate its evils, and the orthodox who would oppose any reform. Ranade made a deep study of the economic problems of India and advocated a vigorous policy of industrial and commercial development. In 1890 he inaugurated the Industrial Association of Western India. His life and activities were not so spectacular as those of Surendra Nath Banerji, but like the latter he greatly advanced the cause of nationalism in Bombay and inspired and initiated men like Gokhale to the service of the motherland.

Indian nationalism proved to be a dynamic force and gathered momentum as years rolled on. In general it may be said that the further development of nationalism was mainly due to the rapid expansion of those very influences which gave birth to it. Among these specific mention may be made of the English education and the consequent impact of Western culture, religious and social reforms, vernacular literature, press and periodical literature, and political associations and organisations, which have been dealt with separately in different chapters. The phenomenal development of the Bengali literature and its reaction on the development of nationalism has been sketched above. In the same way the rapid expansion of English education through the Universities established in 1857 served as a potent instrument for developing nationalist ideas on a very much wider scale than before. Bankim Chandra Chatterji, one of the earliest products of the Calcutta University, made a philosophical study of nationalism as an abstract idea. In his view nationalism consists of two essential elements: first, the identification of individual interest with that of a particular community, so that every individual regards the welfare of the community as his primary duty. The second is a grim determination on the part of the individual to promote the interest of his own community even when it clashes with that of another and can be safeguarded only by doing harm to other nations. Such a spirit might be good or bad, but historical examples show that only the nations inspired by it achieve greatness. The unification of Italy and Germany was pointed by Bankim Chandra as the result of such a spirit of nationalism, and nobody can possibly fail to understand that in all this abstract discussion his main objective was to draw the public attention to the case of India. This is rendered crystal clear when Bankim Chandra adds, that neither of the two elements of nationalism mentioned by him was ever present in India. This he seeks to prove by reference to the events of Indian history, and concludes that the ideas of independence and nationalism are new to India and have been taught to the Indians by the English Tilak's searching analysis of the profound effect of English education on the growth of patriotism and nationalism, even so late as the eighties of the nineteenth century, has been quoted above. The great poet Rabindra Nath has described, in his inimitable way, the inspiration he received from the English literature in his younger days, *i.e.* in the seventies and eighties. Indeed any one who studies the Indian books and periodicals of the period cannot fail to be struck with the powerful force exerted upon Indian minds by the passionate outbursts for the ideals of human liberty and violent denunciations of despotism in all shapes and forms by poets like Wordsworth and Shelley, and in general by the writings, speeches, and activities of celebrated English men. A vernacular paper in Bengal felt almost a religious reverence for the Englishmen. "It is their Wilberforces, Hampdens, Mills, Brights, Metcalfes, Macaulays, and hundreds of other great men, whose liberal principles have captivated us, and we have regarded them as the very model of morality, and hold them in veneration."

The last three decades of the nineteenth century also saw a remarkable growth of Indian-owned newspapers—daily and weekly, and both in English and vernacular—whose role in developing nationalism was very great indeed, and detailed reference to it has been made in Chatper VI. Growth of political associations, described in Chapter XII, and the development of nationalism acted and reached upon each other. It is the growing sense of nationalism which led to the development of powerful political organizations, and these, in their turn, further stimulated the Indian nationalism and made it a political force which even the mighty British Government had soon to reckon with.

In addition to these powerful forces which worked from within these were others supplied by current evens in the history of the world. The defeat of Italy in Abyssinian War, the rise of Japan as a great power, and the defeat it inflicted upon a mightly European power like Russia, had a great repercussion upon Indians. All these shattered the myth of European invincibility in war against non-Europeans and infused in the heart of the Indians hope and faith in their own power. The early discomfitures of the British in the Boer War were hailed with delight in India, though the Boers were no friends of India, and probably hated the Indians even more than the British. Here, again, a minor power successfully defying the authority of Britain, served as an object-lesson to the Indians that they could also rely on their own strength. The Irish struggle for independence against the British also served as a great inspiration to the Indians.

While nationalism in India was making rapid strides, it received a great momentum from two special circumstances during the closing decade of the nineteenth century. The first was the degraded status and the miserable lot of the Indians who migrated to the British Colonies in South Africa, Australia and elsewhere, and were subjected to great hardships and disabilities by the Colonial Governments, to which a detailed reference will be made in Chapter XVII. Every Indian felt with bitter and poignant sorrow that such humiliating treatment of the Indians was possible only because they were a subject people and not an independent nation. This idea quickened the consciousness of the Indians to the great value of nationalism and independence.

The second circumstance, of far greater importance, was the meteor-like rise of Swāmi Vivekananda as a great Messiah, Reference has been made above[42] to his religious career, but he shone no less brilliantly as a great nation-builder. It is not possible here to describe in detail the manifold ways in which he contributed to the development of Indian nationalism, and only a brief outline must suffice. As mentioned above, he championed the cause of Hinduism in the great Parliament of Religions, held at Chicago in U.S.A. in 1893 in connection with the celebration of the 400th anniversary of the discovery of America by Columbus. There, in the presence of the representatives of all the religions from almost all the countries in the world, the young monk from India expoudned the principles of Vedānta and the greatness of Hinduism with such persuasive eloquence that from the very first he captivated the hearts of the vast audience. It would be hardly an exaggeration to say that it was Swāmī Vivekananda who made a place for Hinduism in the cultural map of the modern world. The civilized nations of the West had hitherto looked down upon Hinduism as a bundle of superstitions, evil institutions, and immoral customs, unworthy of serious consideration in the progressive world of today. Now, for the first time, they not only greeted, with hearty approval, the lofty principles of Hinduism as expounded by Vivekananda, but accorded a very high place to it in the culture and civilization of the world. The repercussion of this on the vast

Hindu community can be easily imagined. The Hindu intelligentsia were always very sensitive to the criticism of the Westerners, particularly the Christian missionaries, regarding the many evils and shortcomings of the Hindu society and religion, as with their rational outlook they could not but admit the force of much of this criticism. They had always to be on the defensive and their attitude was mostly apologetic, whenever there was a comparative estimate of the values of the Hindu and Western culture. They had almost taken for granted the inferiority of their culture *vis a vis* that of the West, which was so confidently asserted by the Western scholars. Now, all on a sudden, the taste was turned, and the representatives of the West joined in a chorus of applause at the hidden virtues of Hinduism which were hitherto unsuspected either by friends or foes. It not only restored the self-confidence of the Hindus in their own culture and civilisation, but quickened their sense of national pride and patriotism. This was evident from the sentiment echoed and re-echoed in the numerous public addresses which were presented to Swāmī Vivekananda on his home-coming by the Hindus all over India, almost literally from Cape Comorin to the Himālayas. It was a great contribution to the growing Hindu nationalism.

On his return to India, Swāmī Vivekananda made it a mission of his life to preach the spiritual basis of Hindu civilization. He pointed out in his writings and speeches that the spirituality of India was neither less valuable, nor less important for the welfare of humanity, than the much vaunted material greatness of the West which has dazzled our eyes. He was never tired of asking the Indians to turn their eyes, dazed by the splendour of the West, to their own ideals and institutions. By careful comparison between the real values of the Hindu ideas and institutions and those of the West, he maintained the superiority of the former and asked his countrymen never to exchange gold for tinsels. Referring to the conflict between Westernized India and the true India of the old, he said: "On one side, New India is saying: 'If we only adopt Westerrn ideas. Western language, Western food. Western dress and Western manners, we shall be as strong and powerful as the

Western nations'. On the other, Old India is saying 'Fools! By imitation, other's ideas never become one's own—nothing, unless earned, is your own. Does the ass in the lion's skin become the lion?'

"On one side, New India is saying: 'What the Western nations do are surely good, otherwise how did they become so great?' On the other side, Old India is saying: 'The flash of lightning is intensely bright, but only for a moment; look out, boys, it is dazzling your eyes. Beware!"

But Vivekanand was not prejudiced against the West, nor insensible to the great value of her achievements. He frankly admitted that Indian culture was neither spotless nor perfect,—it had to learn many things from the West, but without sacrificing its true character.

Swāmī Vivekananda combined in himself the role of a great saint and fervid nationalism. He placed Indian nationalism on the high pedestal of past glory, but it embraced the teeming millions of India, both high and low, rich and poor. He devoted his life to the awakening of national consciousness and many of his eloquent appeals would stir the national sentiments of India even today to their very depths. Here is one specimen:

"India!...Wouldst thou attain, by means of thy disgraceful cowardice, that freedom deserved only by the brave and the heroic? O India! forget not that the ideal of thy womanhood is Sītā, Sāvitrī, Damayantī; forget not that the God thou worshippest is the great ascetic of ascetics, the all-renouncing Śaṅkara, the Lord of Umā; forget not that thy marriage, thy wealth, thy life are not for sense-pleasure, are not for thy individual personal happiness; forget not that thou art born as a sacrifice to the Mother's alter; forget not that thy social order is but the reflex of the Infinite Universal Motherhood; forget not that the lower classes, the ignorant, the poor, the illiterate, the cobbler, the sweeper are thy flesh and blood, thy brothers. Thou brave one, be bold, take courage, be proud that thou art an Indian and proudly proclaim, 'I am an Indian, every Indian is my brother.' Say, 'The ignorant Indian, the poor and destitute Indian, the Brahman Indian, the Pariah Indian, is my brother.' Thou, too, clad with but a rag round thy loins proudly proclaim at the top of thy voice. 'The Indian is my brother, the Indian is my life, India's gods and goddesses are my God. India's society is the cradle of my infancy, the pleasure-garden of my youth, the sacred heaven, the Vārāṇasī of my old age.' Say, brother, "The soil of India is my highest heaven, the good of India is my good.' And repeat and pray day and night, `O Thou Lord of Gaurī, O Thou Mother of the Universe, vouchasafe manliness unto me. O Thou Mother of Strength, take away my weakness, take away my unmanliness, and—*Make me a Man*."[43]

Though an ascetic, Vivekananda was a patriot of patriots. The thought of restoring the pristine glory of India by resuscitating among her people the spiritual vitality which was dormant, but not dead, was always the uppermost thought in his mind. His great disciplc, Sister Niveditā (an Irish lady named Margaret Noble). Who was his constant companion, has remarked: "Throughout those years, in which I saw him almost daily, the thought of India was to him like the air he breathed". A saint and an ascetic have always exercised a profound influence upon Indian minds. No wonder, therefore, that the prophecy of Vivekananda that India, with all her shortcomings, and in spite of the present dismal outlook, shall rise to the statue of a great nation in the modern world, went home and quickened the national impulses of the people of India. There seems to be a great deal of truth in the following tribute paid to him by a recent historian of India's struggle for *Swaraj:*

"Swāmī Vivekananda might well be called the father of modern Indian Nationalism: he largely created it and also embodied in his own life its highest and noblest elements."[44]

An important contribution to the growth of Indian nationalism, was also made by the Theosophical Society, to which reference has been made above.[45] Its effect on Indian mind is thus described by B.C. Pal:

"This Society told our people that instead of having any reason to be ashamed of their past or of the legacies left to them by it, they have every reason to feel justly proud of it all, because their ancient seers and saints had been the spokesmen of the highest truths and their old books, so woefully misunderstood today, had been the repositories of the highest human illumination and wisdom. Our people had hitherto felt perpetually humiliated at the sense of their degradation. This new message, coming from the representatives of the most advanced peoples of the modern world, the inheritors of the most advanced culture and civilisation the world has as yet known, at once raised us in our own estimation and created a self-confidence in us that commenced to find easy expression in a new propaganda which, instead of apologising for our current and mediaeval ideas and institutions and seeking to reform and reconstruct these after modern European ideals, boldly stood up in defence of them."[46] Elsewhere Pal says: "But the greatest contribution of Theosophy to the development of our national consciousness was in its new and strange gospel of Ancient Indian Wisdom and in its announcement of a great world purpose and world mission which India yet had for the races of the modern world."[47]

The most talented representative of the Society in India was Mrs. Annie Besant. Apart from revealing the past glory and greatness of the Hindus, she offered justification even for the many customs and institutions, which were generally tolerated by the educated Hindus though regarded by them as evil or superstitious and openly condemned as such. The justification of these customs and institutions by new interpretation of their significance and *raison d'être* from the pen of a talented European lady, noted for profound learning and wisdom, naturally flatered the wounded vanity of the Hindus, the pride in their national glory being further enhanced by her dictum, repeatedly asserted, that the Hindu culture was essentially superior to the European.

It has been pointed out above that the newly born Indian nationalism was gradually assuming a decidedly Hindu character. This received further stimulus from the activities of Vivekananda and the teachings of the Theosophical Society. The latter, in particular, gave it a tinge of orthodoxy which was disapproved by Vivekananda himself. Referring to the Theosophical Society he said, "foolish depreciation is surely vicious, but fulsome praise is equally loathsome."[47a] It was also disliked by a section of the nationalists. Nevertheless, towards the close of the nineteenth century, one could clearly distinguish a spirit of revivalism, *i.e.* an attempt to reconstruct the Hindu society on the model of the old.[48] This, as noted above, was strongly opposed by Mahadev Govind Ranade.[40]

But whatever one may think of this drawback, there is no doubt that patriotism was lifted to a high spiritual level by Swāmī Vivekananda. Although he was mainly a religious devotee, and a *sannyāsin* who had renounced the world, his speeches, writings and activities had a direct bearing on the devotion to motherland. He emphasized the greatness of the spiritual idea enunciated in the Vedānta, and the important role it was destined to play in elevating the whole mankind. But, he said, this great mission of India would remain unfulfilled so long as India continued in her present state of slavery and abject poverty. The political and material greatness of India was, therefore, indissolubly bound up with the spiritual regeneration of India and mankind. Vivekananda restarted the old ideas of Vedānta in a new form. The fundamental concept of Vedānta was the essential unity of God and man and the realization of this truth by man by removing his illusion or ignorance. In the past, such realization was sought through metaphysical abstractions and renunciation of social and civil life. It is against this prevailing view that Vivekananda raised his voice of protest. Realization of God is to be achieved, said he, not by retirement into hills and forests and negation of worldly life, but by the spiritualization of the normal contents and actualities of life. He put it in a more concrete form by laying emphasis on the fact that one should not run away from the world in order to seek God, but try to recognize Him in his fellow-beings, who were the images of God Himself, as taught by the Vedānta. The true worship of God was the service of the people whom we have hitherto neglected or trodden under food. He therefore asked every Indian to realize God in the nation and to dedicate himself to its service, in a spirit of religious reverence and without any pride or fear, irrespective of all earthly consequences. He gave a living tough to the idea by using the world *Daridra-Nārāyana* i.e. the God symbolised by the poor and the humble. This great *sannyās'n,* who had left his hearth and home at the call of his spiritual *guru,* Śrī Rāmakrishna, and delved deeply into spiritual mysticism, was never tired of preaching that 'what India needs today is not so much religion or philosophy, of which she was enough, but food for her hungry millions, social justice for the low classes, strength and energy for her emasculated people, and a sense of pride and prestige as a great nation of the world.'

Vivekananda put Indian nationalism firmly on the five bed-rocks, viz, yearning for political independence, pride in the past glory and greatness of India, unity of Indians on the conception of brotherhood, awakening of the masses, and development of physical strength and vigour. To a group of young men who met him, seeking his guidance and blessing, he said: "Man-making is my mission of life. You try to translate this mission of mine into action and reality. Read Bankim Chandra and emulate his *deśabhakti* (patriotism) and *sanatānadharma* (activities of the band of patriots depicted in the *Ānandamatha*). Your duty should be service to motherland. India should be freed politically first." "For the next fifty years", he said elsewhere, "this alone shall be our key-note—this, our great Mother India. Let all other vain Gods disappear for that time from our mdins".[49a]

Again and again Vivekananda asserted that weakness, real or fancied, has been the bane of Indian national life in the past. "What I want", said he, "is muscles of iron and nerves of steel, inside which dwells a mind of the same material as that of which the thunderbolt is made." Again, "First of all, our young men must be strong. Religion will come afterwards. Be strong, my young friends; that is my advice to you. You will be nearer to Heaven through football than through the study of the *Gitā.*" But he held out the Kṛishṇa of the *Bhagavad-Gītā* as our national ideal of dynamic energy based on true religion.

The uplift of the masses seems to have been the key-note of his programme of national regeneration. "The only hope of India," he said, "is from the masses. The upper classes are physically and morally dead."

Again, he said, "Keep the motto before you—'Elevation of the masses'. . . Work among those young men who can devote heart and soul to this one duty—the duty of raising the masses of India." Vivekananda put it in the forefront of his social programme. "Our modern reformers", said he, "are very busy about widow remarriage. Of course, I am a sympathiser of every reform, but the fate of a nation does not depend upon the number of husbands their widows get, but upon the condition of the masses."

Vivekananda made a trumpet call to all Indians to shed fear of all kinds and stand forth as men by imbibing *śakti* (energy and strength), and reminded them that they were the particles of the Divine, according to the eternal truth preached by the Vedānta.

As for himself, he was even prepared to forego his own salvation for the sake of the masses. "Who cares for your *Bhakti* and *Mukti?"*, he once exclaimed, "I will go into a thousand hells cheerfully, if I can rouse my countrymen, immersed in *Tamas,* to stand on their own feet. "What I now want", he wrote in a letter in 1895, "is a band of fiery missionaries," and he gave a practical shape to the idea a few years later. In the Rules which he had himself drawn up for the Belur Math, the centre of his organization, the last one runs as follows: "The root of all misery in India is the wide gulf between the lower and upper classes. Unless this difference is made up, there is no hope of any well-being for the people. Therefore we must send preachers to all places to give the masses education and religious teaching." In pursuance of this he engaged the monks recruited mostly from the educated middle class for social service under an allied, but distinct, organisation known as the Rāmakrishna Mission, whose activities extend throughout India. The precepts and example of this great *sannyāsin* galvanied the current of national life, infused new hopes and inspirations, and placed the service to the motherland on a religious level. His voice had a special appeal to the Indians as they are always attracted by a saintly life, more particularly as his teachings, inspired by Śri Rāmakṛishṇa, were highly honoured even in Europe and America.

Swāmī Vivekananda thus gave a spiritual basis to Indian nationalism. The lessons of Vedānta and the *Bhagavad-Gitā* permeated the lives and activities of many a nationalist, and, as will be seen later, many a martyr, inspired by his teachings, endured extreme sufferings and sacrifices with a cheerful heart, fearlessly embraced death, and calmly bore the inhuman tortures, worse than death, which were sometimes inflicted upon them.

Not only religion and philosophy but also history was enlisted in the cause of nationalism. As Bengal had no knowledge in those days of her own great heroes, the lives of Rājput, Marāṭhā and Sikh heroes took their place. The patriotism of Rāṇā Pratāp and the heroic deeds of Shivāji were household words in Bengal. It would be difficult to find in any literature such stirring poems as Rabindranath wrote on Shivāji and the Sikh leaders Bāndā and Guru Govinda.

The ground was thus prepared in Bengal for the emergence of a mighty wave of nationalism which soon revolutionised the political movement in India. But it was in Maharashtra where the new spirit of nationalism first manifested itself in a practical form. This is best illustrated by the career of Wasudeo Balwant Phadke sketched above.[60]

Wasudeo Balwant Phadke set the example of militant nationalism which took deep root in the soils of Maharashtra and Bengal a quarter of a century later, as will be described in another chapter. His activities, however, had no immediate effect on the progress of nationalism as an ideal and motive force in political and social life, such as has been described above.

A review of the progress of nationalism in India was made by Gopal-krishna Gokhale in 1905, in the following passage: "The growth, during the last fifty years, of a feeling of common nationality, based upon common tradition, common disabilities and common hopes and aspirations, has been most striking. The fact that we are Indians first, and Hindoos, Mahomedans, Parsees, or Christians afterwards, is being realised in a steadily increasing measure, and the idea of a united and renovated India, marching onwards to a place among the nations of the world worthy of her great past, is no longer a mere idle dream of a few imaginative minds, but is the definitely accepted creed of those who form the brain of the community—the educated classes of the country."[51]

The most significant trait of the new nationalism was an intense love of the motherland, based on a conception of its past glory and future greatness. But it was often distinguished from patriotism of the Western type by being elevated to a religious level. This was clearly preached by Bankim Chandra in his famous novel *Ānandamaṭh,* to which reference has been made above. His has depicted therein the lives of a band of patriots who had left their hearth and home, wives and children, and dedicated their lives to the service of their motherland, conceived as the goddess Kālī the source of all power and energy. The only form of worship acceptable to her was the selfless service to the motherland. They revered no other deity, and no other form of worship was known to them.[62] Thus Bankim Chandra converted patriotism into religion and religion into patriotism.

Gokhale tried to give a practical shape to this high ideal by founding the 'Servants of India Society' in 1905. While inaugurating it, he described the progress of nationalism in the extract quoted above, and then observed: "The results achieved so far are undoubtedly most gratifying, but they only mean that the jungle has been cleared, and the foundations laid. The great work of rearing the superstructure has yet to be taken in hand...One essential condition of success is that a sufficient number of our countrymen must now come forward to devote themselves to the cause in the spirit in which religious work in undertaken. Public life must be spiritualised. Love of country must so fill the heart that all else shall appear as of little moment by its side. A fervent patriotism which rejoices at every opportunity of sacrifice for the motherland, a dauntless heart which refuses to be turned back from its object by difficulty or danger, a deep faith in the purpose of Providence that nothing can shake,—equipped with these, the worker must start on his mission and reverently seek the joy which comes of spending oneself in the service of one's country."

The object of the 'Servants of India Society' was to train such men—men who would be "prepared to devote their lives to the cause of the country in a religious spirit", and, "as national missionaries," promote "by all constitutional means the national interests of the Indian people." Every member of the Society had to take seven vows at the time of admission. The first four of these are: (1) That the country will always be the first in his thoughts and he will give to her service the best that is in him. (2) That in serving the country he will seek no personal advantage for himself. (3) That he will regard all Indians as brothers, and will work for the advancement of all, without distinction of caste or creed. (4) That he will be content with such provision for himself and his family, if he has any, as the Society may be able to make. He will devote no part of his energies to earning money for himself.

—*R.C. Majumdar*

REFERENCES

1. See p. 338.
2. *Bengal Past and Present,* LXVII (1948), pp. 40-5.
3. "If I were asked under what sky the human mind has most fully developed some of its choicest gifts, has most deeply pondered on the greatest problems of life, and has found solutions of some of them which well deserve this attention even of those who have studied Plato and Kant—I should point to India, And if I were to ask myself from what literature we, here in Europe, we who have been nurtured almost exclusively on the thoughts of Greeks and Romans, and of one Semitic race, the Jewish, may draw that corrective which is most wanted in order to make our inner life more

perfect, more comprehensive, more universal, in fact more truly human, a life, not for this life only, but a transfigured and eternal life—again I should point to India." F. Max Müller, *What Can India Teach Us?* 2nd Edn. Oxford, 1892, p. 6.

4. Cf. Ch. VL
4a. Cf. Ch. XL and Vol. IX, Chs, XIII, XXIX.
5. Cf. Vol. IX, pp. 412 ff.
6. Ch. IX and the Chs. mentioned in f.n., 4a.
7. See pp. 349-51.
8. Vol. IX, Ch. XX; Griffiths, p. 259.
9. B.C. Pal-I, I. 229.
9a. Cotton-II, 222.
10. B.C. Pal-I, I. 233.
10a. *Ibid*, I. 315; II. XV.
11. *Ibid*, I. 237.
12. *Ibid*, 234.
12a. *Ibid*, 259-60.
13. This is the popular form of the name of Rāj-nārāyan Basu mentioned on p. 176.
14. *Ibid*, 260.
15. *Ibid*, 261-2.
16. The text of the Document is reproduced in the *Modern Review,* June, 1944, pp, 444 ff.
17. B. Majumdar, 293-4.
18. B.C. Pal-I, I, 310-14.
19. B.C. Pal-II, 66.
20. B.C. Pal-I, II, 70-1.
21. *Ibid*, 84.
22. *Ibid*, 85.

23. H.B. Sarda—*Dayananda,* p. cxxii.
24. It may be noted that Keshab Chandra Sen and Bhudev Mukherji recommended Hindi as national language, and several others recommended *swadeshi,* before Dayānanda.
25. See pp. 456 ff.
26. See pp. 472-3.
27. B.C. Pal-I, I. 227.
28. *Ibid*, 228.
29. *Ibid*, 252.
30. *Ibid*, 256.
31. Cf. Vol. IX, pp. 917, 922, 933.
32. B.C. Pal-I, I, 253.
33. *Ibid*, 256. I have substituted 'Tuṅgadvīpa', the original word, for 'a distant island' in Pal's transition.
34. *Ibid*, 233.
35. *Ibid*, 237-8.
36. *Ibid*. 242-3.
37. *Ibid*, 245-6.
38. *Ibid*, 246-48.
39. Speeches and Writings, 227-31.
40. B.C. Pal-I, I. 235.

40a. *A Nation in Making,* pp. 397-8.

41. See p. 256.
42. See pp. 123-31.
43. For the extracts quoted from the writings and speeches of Vivekananda, and others of similar import. cf. *Complete Works of Vivekananda,* IV (7th Ed.) pp. 477-80; Bhupendranath Datta, *Swami Vivekanands,* pp. 314-42, 371-99; Eknath Ranade, *Swami Vivekananda's Rousing Call to Nation* (a compilation of select passages).

44. Pradhan, 60.
45. See pp. 131-4.
46. B.C. Pal-I, I. 425.
47. *Ibid*, II LV.
47a. *Complete Works of Vivekananda,* Vol. IV (7th Ed.). p. 318.
48. See pp. 115-6.
49. See pp. 257-8.
49a. Complete Works, III (8th Ed.), 300-01.
50. Cf. Vol. IX, pp. 908-14.
51. *Speeches of Gokhale*, Appendix, pp. 182-4.
52. See pp. 257-8.

13. *Renaissance of Tamil Culture*

The term Renaissance is applied in a narrower sense to the revival of classical art, learning, and literature and in its wider sense, to the resurgence of the secular, individualistic and spirit of classical antiguity, involving the social, political and religious systems and institutions. In India, generally speaking, the systematization of intellectual and religious tradition which was spawned by such men as Ram Mohan Roy, Dayananda Saraswathi, Vivekananda, Tilak, B.C. Pal and Mahatma Gandhi can be termed as 'renaissance' because it involved a recrudescence of interest in Hinduism and in its importance both for individuals and for India as a nation.[1] These founders of Indian Renaissance were initially stimulated by the western educational systems, though in varying degrees.

In Tamil Nadu, the impact of the Indian renaissance was no doubt felt, but that was not all. The concept and ideology covered a wider field of action with a larger time span. Two parallel levels were in operation in Tamil Nadu, one the national and the other regional. On the political side the national level asserted itself over the regional level during the early faces, though the regional level succeeded at a later stage[2]. The former tried for the establishment of an Indian national identity, by pointing to certain commonly acclaimed religious texts of India's golden past as providing the sacred legitimization to this new understanding of India as a spiritual nation[3]. The greatest exponent of this phenomena was, of course, Gandhi. The nineteenth century through the introduction of western education had prepared the ground for him that he could channel and model it into an ideology for both social reform and political revolution. Gandhi made these symbols (of identity and unity) politically potent on a scale not imagined before 1919.

The situation in Tamil Nadu was slightly different. The political phase identified itself with what was covering the whole nation. But on the cultural front, the Tamils felt a little different from the rest of the country, since they appear as a distinct cultural stratum around 3000 B.C. even before the pre-Vedic Aryans entered the country[4]. They had trade connection with Sumeria and China and were sending ivory and muslin to the Pharaobs of Egypt, about the time of Moses[5] Later when the Aryans had not yet penetrated the South, the Tamils were exporting pearls, precious stones and peacocks to the Court of Solomon.[6]

Even when the Aryanisation process of the South commenced, the Tamil society seems to have had a highly sophisticated culture[7]. The Sangam literature (first three centuries of the Christian era) reflect the culture of the Tamils. Apart from the political and social contents, the Sangam classics reverberate the cultural trends of the Tamils. The Tamil bards with an evangelical style of writing idylls called Aarrupadai, which consisted essentially announcing the good things one has received to those who were in search for them pointed out to them the way. This became in fact the motto of Tamil culture. "Yam perra inbam peruga iv vaiyagam" (May the wide world share the happiness that has been granted to us!)[8]. Sharing with others anything of truth, goodness, beauty or happiness which are found by one, was a cultural and religious urge of the Tamils[9].

The typical Tamil society was essentially aristocratic. Desire of fame and fears of shame were the distinguishing marks of the Sangam literature. Like Pugaze (glory), vamai (truth) and nermai (honesty) were generally valued. Determination, bravery, liberality, munificence and mercy were also highly valued. The position of women was higher than what it became latter. The Tamil language itself stood not merely as the vehicle of communication of ideas but as the whole asthetic achievement of the people. Hospitality was so highly valued. The Sangam classics also furnish information about assemblies, debate (pattimanrams), pastimes, sports and festivals.[10] Evidences of institutionalised irrigation and public works through the ages are also recently discovered.[11] On top of it, all tolerance formed the basis of Tamil culture.

Culture depicted in Silapathikaram and Manimekalai is different from that of the Sangam works. Urban life with the pomp and grandeur of the fine arts, state functions like Indira Vila, centralised administration with councils to assist like Enperayam (high power council of eight), Iymperngulu (committee of five) are the few of the additions.[12]

During the Pallava period, which was the era of Rock cut temples and temple art, the literature underwent a change. The secular tolerant literature was replaced by religious intolerant literature.[13]

Then dawned the second empire of the Pandyas and the reign of Imperial Cholas. This was the age of conquests and consolidation, overseas expansion of political authority and cultural trends.[14] This was the saga of big temples and fine arts, decentralised administration—King, provincial governors, district chiefs (Kottams), local units (wariyams) etc.[15] It is during this period a sort of electoral system (kodavolai system) was followed for selecting members of the village councils.[16] During this period epics like Kamba Ramayanam, Puranams like Thiruvilayadal Puranam etc., dominated the scene.

After the fall of the Cholas and the pandyas, the Muslims, the Nayaks, and the Marathas ruled Tamil Nadu, while the Europeans were already making their appearance on the coastal areas. The Telugu Nayaks and Tanjore Marathas definitely contributed to Tamil culture, but the exclusiveness of the Tamils was best.[17] Literature which has been the mainstay of Tamil culture was at its lowest ebb.

With the advent of the Europeans drastic changes in the cultural trend were witnessed. During the Portuguese period, changes in agriculture, trade and industry were effectively made—changes were that deep that even food habits and dress patterns were changed.[18] Thanks to the Christian missionaries, education was imparted to the down-trodden, which gradually changed the cultural stratum of the masses. When the country came under the British rule, western educational systems were followed all over. Institutional changes in the administrative set up resulted in adaptation of western methods and ways of life. As Telugu, Persian and English became the officials language, (in the order mentioned), Tamil was somnolent. So also Tamil culture. The alien domination was at its peak.

However, a fillip was given to the Tamil language by the European scholars from the 17th century. The Europeans played an important role in the history of Tamil literature generally in Tamil prose and particularly in the methods of studies and writings of Tamil literature.[19] Tamil prose which remained in a secondary position, to poetry was made popular by he European scholars. As for the Tamil language is concerned, the Renaissance was born with the advent of the European scholars Rev. Fr. Robert De Nobili (1605-1656), Rev. Fr. Constantine Joseph Beschi (1680-1747) are the pioneers among the European Tamil Scholars. The latter was known as Virama Munivar. Following them, protestant missionaries Zieganbalg, Schwartz, Bishop Caldwell and G.U. Pope did yeoman services to tamil language.

From the foregoing account it is evident that the Tamil language has registered a steady growth from the 17th century onwards. It must be remembered that the Tamil country from the period referred above was under alien rule. While the language was growing, becoming more scientific than it was, the Tamil culture was undergoing a change. The Portuguese colonial rule has changed the charter of the occupational pattern in Tamil Nadu.[20] Education was no more the monopoly of a specified few. In the schools run by the missionaries the Brahmin and the untouchable were fellow students.[21] Western education was on the ascendency and lucrative jobs in the Government were given to people educated in the western system.

Although, education was available to everybody, the Brahmins because of the tradition and the lower castes because of the missionaries were the first to occupy such positions. Generally the social status of the educated man in public was quite enviable to others, who belonged to the upper classes but not employed in the Government. At the national level those who were enjoying such status wanted more jobs and participation in the Government and the Indian National Congress was grounded in 1885.[22] The first meeting of the Congress was held in Bombay and 72 men attended, half of them from Bombay; over 20 from Madras; 3 from Bengal, Orissa and Bihar; 3 from the Punjab and 7 from U.P.; the London Times reported, "For the first time since the world began, India as a national met together."[23] And Congress never lost the consciousness that it was India as a nation meeting together. As it was an elite organisation, the Congress in Madras was dominated by the Brahmins.

Just at this Juncture, the non-Brahmin elite, mostly caste Hindus, started feeling the dominance of the Brahmins in all walks of life. After the fall of G. Subramania Iyer from leadership in 1908, Mrs. Besant was looked upon as the alternative to lead the Madras Congress and she accepted it.

In 1915, Mrs. Besant embarked on a campaign pressing for political reform through her two Madras based news papers—New India and Commonwealth. Following Tilak's 'Indian Home-Rule League', Mrs. Besant in September 1916, inaugurated Home-Rule League in Madras.

In Madras, the Home-Rule League was dominated by Brahmins. The Brahmins who had been in subordinate positions, seized the opportunity to provide leadership.[24] The Home-Rulers began to circulate pamphlets in Tamil and Telugu with a view to enlist the support of the masses. This was something different from the usual approach of the Brahmins. The non-Brahmin elite which was already agitating in their minds to arrest the domination of the Brahmins in educational, administrative and occupational channels of mobility provided by the British rule, now became alarmed at the emergence of the Brahmins as political leaders through Home-Rule League. Therefore, the non-Brahmins decided to counteract.

It was composite Madras then, and non-Brahmin leader drawn from Tamil Nadu, Kerala and Andhra decided to start a political association to "advance, safeguard and protect the interests of the non-Brahmin community".[25] (20th November 1916). *The Justice,* in English; *The Dravidian* (in Tamil and the *Andhraprakasika* in Telugu[26] were started to propagate the creed of the party. The non-Brahmin's association started a political party—South Indian Liberal Federation,[27] which came out with a manifesto attacking the traditional position of the Brahmins in South Indian society. The manifesto went to exhort the non-Brahmins to organize and mend their own house before throwing in with the Brahmin nationalists.[28] This attitude continued during the national movement also. Starting with the twenties when under the leadership of Gandhi the Congress Party started agitating for freedom from the British, the South Indian Liberal Federation, later on the Justice Party and the Dravida Kalagam, started agitating against the Brahmins. This ended up in a conflict, between nationalism and regionalism in the political front and that reflected in the cultural front too.

The non-Brahmins adopted the theories and ideologies of the Tamil Renaissance to support their attack on the Brahmins' domination in Madras. Thiagaraya Chetty, one of the leaders of the non-brahmin movement, used to elaborate the earlier theories of P. Sundaram Pillai to condemn the local Brahmins as "the local representative of the Aryans".[29] When the South Indian Liberal Federation became the Justice party, they worked in cohesion with the British, as opposed to the Congress. Under the Government of India Act of 1919, elections took place in 1920 and the Justice Party was called upon to form the Government. With the limited powers they succeeded in enacting the Hindu Religious Endowment Act (to curb the exclusive rights of the brahimins in the temples) and the Madras University Act of 1924.[30] The Annamalai University came into being (1929) to serve the non-brahmin interest. On top of it all the communal G.O. to regulate government service in favour of the non-brahmins was issued. The Tamil language however, did not attract much attention from this group, because the leaders were more anglicised. Their support to the British Raj is a phenomenon which cannot have any rationale. On the contrary the Congress party in Tamil Nadu through Bharathiar, Namakkal Ramlingam Pillai, V.O. Chidambaram, Jeeva, Rajaji, Dr. Varadarajalu, Kothamangalam Sabbu, Raya Chockalingam, Kalyana Sundaranar and a host of others did yeomen service to Tamil language, both Prose and Poetry.[31]

When the Justice Party was routed in the 1937 elections, it realised that fighting against the congress was futile and it twisted its stand from the political to social. Yet regionalism was vehemently observed. E.V. Ramasamy Naicker, popularly known as 'Thanthai Periyar' had left the congress and became the leader of the Justice Party (1940). Even before this he was associating himself with the Justicits from 1937 onwards, and under his leadership 'Hindi' was opposed. C.N. Annadural became the chief aide of Periyar. The ferver for Social Reforms and regionalism ended up in changing the name of the Party as "Dravida Kazhagam" (1944).

The nomenclature "Dravida Kazhagam" indicates, that it was an association of Tamils, Malayalis, Andras and the Karnatakas, and its chief motto was to achieve a separate 'Dravida Nadu. But in practice it was popular in Tamil Nadu alone.[32] They preached that through religion the Brahmins have enslaved the Tamils and the religious rituals were nothing but the manipulation of the brahmins to exploit the Tamils economically. They recalled the glory of the Tamils of the past in support of their claims. Adulation of the past naturally attracted the masses. The Sangam classics were recited to prove the bravery, heroism, hospitality and humanism of the Tamils. The histories of Emayavaramban, Ariya Padaikadantha Nedunchelian etc. were recited to make the Tamils feel that the north was subjucated by the Smouth in those days and because of the Brahmins the South has lost its glory and is being subjucated by the North Rama was depicted as Aryan hence Brahmin and Ravana was glorified as a Dravida. Idol worship was condemned as the creation of the brahmins. The purity of Tamil blood was often reminded of. The followers of Periyar, led by Annadurai could use their pen vehimently against social injustice and irrational behaviour of a section of the people. The platform Tamil was improved greatly and the pure Tamil movement was on.[33] The untouchables were sought to be treated as equals. In this respect the congress party did not lag behind. When Annadurai and his followers left the Dravida Kazhagam on differences with Periyar and founded the D.M.K. (1954), they continued their services through newspapers, Novels, Dramas and regular platform speeches. The demand for a separate Dravida country and the anti-Hindi posture sounded in all their endeavours.

In the late 50s their labours started yielding results. Youths were drawn in large numbers towards their social ideology. Marriages were performed without priests. Widow remarriage was advocated. Poet Bhrarati Dhasan's[34] service through his writings in this connection was remarkable.

The oft repeated citing of the past glory kindled the ego of the Tamils. Many people changed their religious, sanskritized names into that of pure Tamil Name.[35] Vedachala Swami, a renamed Tamil Scholar changed his name as Marai Malai Adigai. He also started a pure Tamil movement.[36] Name of Sangam Kings were adopted very commonly. Pure Tamil names have become the order of the day.

The D.M.K. rejuvenated Tamil Culture Its leaders and followers wore Dhoti and Towel, which is typical Tamil dress. In public life the justice gentlement with a Western suit, was replaced by a respectable politician gentleman in dhodhi, shirt and towel. It must be remembered that the Congress party also adopted non-brahminism and local culture from the thirtees of this century.[37] because of the thrust by the non-Brahmin groups. Tamil festivals like the Tamil New Year's Day, Pongal Day, Mattuppongal etc. are celebrated with greater importance these days. Pattimanrams as in the Sangam Age[38] are revived.

From 1967 to 1976 the D.M.K. was in power, and from 1977 the A.I.A.D.M.K. an offshoot of D.M.K. is in power. Even before they came to power they have given up the demand for a separate state. Anti Hindi is still there and both give vent to their feelings periodically. While in power the D.M.K. changed the name of Madras State into 'Tamil Nadu' State. The Foreshore Estate, a Government Quarters is called 'Pattinapakkam'—a typical Tamil name of the past. Revenue division are called Kottams Corporate bodies are called Wariyams, reminding us of the Imperial Cholas. Road and Streets are replaced with local men's names. Tamil is made official language for State purposes. State festivals at places like Kaviripoompattinam are conducted to remind the glory of the past; traditional games of the Tamils such as Jallykattu, Wrestling etc; the Republic day, the Tamil festival Pongal, is also celebrated by the Government. Monuments are erected in honour of Great Tamil saints, the 'Valluvar Kottam' is a fitting example. 'Poompuhar', constructed by the Government is yet another example. The A.I.A.D.M.K. Government does not lag behind. They continue the services started by the D.M.K. Party Politics could not make them deviate[29] because the common man is aware of himself.

Over enthusiasm leads to linguistic chauvinism. This should be curtailed. To look back it is interesting and encouraging, but we have many more miles to go.

—Dr. S. Kadhirvel

REFERENCES

1. Nichoals B. Dirks. 'The Hindu Renaissance'. Unpublished Paper.
2. I am not going into the discussion of the merits and demerits of this case.

3. Dalton, D. "Gandhi and Roy: The interaction of Ideologies in India" in Sibnarayun. *Gandhi India and the World*, Philadelphia, Temple University Press, 1970, p. 156.

4. Ignatius Hindayam Christianity and Tamil Culture. University of Madras, Madras 1977 p. 2.

5. *Ibid*.

6.. *Ibid*.

7. Sangam classics, Passim.

8. Akin to the slogan 'Share the poverty'.

9. Ignatius Hirudayam, Op. cit., p. 4.

10. K.K. Pillay, *Social History of the Tamils,* University of Madras, 1975, Passim.

11. S. Kadhirvel, 'Sources for the History of Tamil Nadu' in South Asian Village Studies, Vol. V, Tokyo, 1980, p. 73.

12. K.A.N. Sastri, *The Cholas,* Univesity of Madras.

13. This period witnessed religious persecution in Tamil Nadu (Saivism vs Jainism.)

14. R.C. Mazumdar: Indian Culture in "South East Asia".

15. K.A.N. Sastri, op. cit. Chapter on Administration.

It is pointed out by some scholars like Burton Stein, that Proof. Sastri's assertion of central, provincial and district administration has to be reviewed since the link between them has not been explained so far.

16. Uthiramerur Inscription.

17. Those who subscribe to the alien origin of the Pallavas may say that Pallava art is not exclusively indigenous. For that matter, impact of alien elements in any culture is unavoidable.

18. Fr. D.'Souza S.J., 'Agriculture in Goa during the Portuguese times', Paper presented at the Annual conference of the Institute of Historical Studies, Calcutta held in Panjim, Goa, November, 1975.

19. K. Meenakshisundaram, *The Contribution of European Scholars to Tamil.*, p. 5.
20. Supra, 18.
21. Social status of the traditional type was maintained even in the beginning of the 20th Century.
22. Detailed discussion of the National Congress will be redundant for this paper.
23. Cited in Eleanor Zellior "Regional Aspects of the Nationalist Movement", University of Minnesota, 1968.
24. Eugene F. Irshick, *Politics and Social Conflict in South India. The non-Brahmin Movement and Tamil Separatism, 1916-1929,* Berkeley, 1969, p. 30.
25. Justice Party Golden Jubilee Souvenir, 1968, Madras, p. 12.
26. *Ibid.*
27. The Hindu, 18 November 1916.
28. The Hindu, 20 December 1916.
29. S. Kadhirvel; "The South Indian Liberal Federation" paper presented at the 16th annual conference of the Institute of Historical Studies, Calcutta, 1978.
30. No Brahmin Vice-Chancellor was elected until the Act was modified in 1966.
31. K. Dhiraviyam: *Thesiyam Valartha Tamil,* Madras, 1974 Passim. Besides, Starting with O.V. Swaminatha Iyer, many scholars like R.P. Sethu Pillai, T.K. Chidambaranatha Mudaliar, A.C. Chettiar, T.P.M. Ka. Su. Pillai; have done remarkable service to Tamil. The Annamalai University deserve special mention.
32. The Justice party had links all over South India.
33. Back numbers of Party organisations.
34. Names of deceased persons alone are mentioned.
35. Out of love for Tamil, Suryanarayana Sastri, a Brahmin changed his name as Parithima Kalaigner. It is an exceptional case.

36. K. Siva Thambi, *Thami Tamizh Eyakka Arasial Pinnani* Madras. 1979. p. 39.

37. Supra. 28.

38. T.P. Meenakshi Sundaram, Op. cit. p. 41.

39. The First World Tamil Conference at Madurai (1980) by the AIADMK Govt. was conducted on a competitive basis with more pump and Vanity than that of the Second World Conference held at Madras (D.M.K. Govt.) 1968.

14. Premchand: And Indian Resurgence

I

Premchand (1880-1936) left behind an enormous corpus at the end of a literary career that spanned over three decades, which witnessed the resurgence of the national struggle against alien rule. He wrote about three hundred short stories, nearly a score of novels, a number of biographies and plays, besides a large body of journalistic pieces on different issues of both national and international importance. If we go through this corpus we get valuable insights into the vicissitudes through which the country passed during this phase; insights that are remarkable because they show us, as perhaps only realistic literature can show, the dialectical relationship between the individual and the objective reality.

While seeking inner tranquility.[1] Premchand was not at peace with himself, primarily because he was not at peace with his times. He was experiencing and responding to diametrical pulls. Contradictory, and perhaps discrete elements, consequently, got lodged in his mind. The pattern and implications of such contradictions suggest interesting historiographic possibilities. This paper seeks to indicate those possibilities by tracing the evolution of a paradox in Premchand's writings. The paradox relates to the question of peasantry under the zamindars.

Writing for Premchand was a mission. He looked upon himself as an idealistic realist, describing his brand of realism as *adar shonmukhi yatharthavad.*[2] It was the duty of the writer, he maintained, to feel for 'the oppressed, the persecuted, and the deprived'.[3] For long, the reins of society had been in the hands of religious leaders, and the politicians were begging to take over the leadership; neither of them, however, could be trusted. As such it was for the writers to constitute the 'advance guard' of politics and work for a humane restructuring of society. It was they who would have to endeavour to make the world a better place for people to live and die in; a world that anchored neither slavery nor poverty; and promised freedom and happiness to all its inhabitants.

Premchand defined these aims in 1936, the year of his death, in the course of his presidential address delivered at the first convention of the Progressive Writers' Association. Obviously, he had stopped dreaming. And he knew this.[5] But this was a dream that required a great effort of will in order to salvage some hope in the midst of a situation where optimism seemed to be a function of self-delusion.[6] In fact, even on the eve of exhorting his fellow *litterateurs* to follow this lofty ideal, he had been plagued with the fear that his address might turn out to be too pessimistic.[7] Premchand's was the dream of a man who had seen the pervasive ugliness of reality; but had not yet lost faith in the liberating effect of hope. Rooted in the reality—the seamy reality—around him, he kept struggling to find ways of changing it. In sum, however, he provided escapist millenarian solutions, although at times, he made determined efforts at stark confrontations, but seldom did he offer a way out from this dilemma.

Premchand was committed to the underdog. Again and again, he turned to the wretched of his society be they women, workers or peasants. It was, however, the peasants who attracted him irresistibly. He viewed himself as the chronicler of peasant society.[8] Himself a villager, he thought he owed a debt to his village brethren. Most of his literary effort was directed toward the discharge of this debt.[9]

Personal compulsions apart, Premchand felt that the peasants needed special attention because they were the most neglected and the worst exploited segment of Indian society. Workers had their organization. Government employees had formed their associations. So had the zamindars and the money-lenders. But the peasants were without an organization of their own. Their power lay scattered. If at all any attempt was made to organize them, the scare of Bolshevism was raised and everyone got nettled, be it the government, its officials, zamindars; or money-lenders.[10] Even the nationalist movement under the Congress, Premchand felt, was dominated by leaders who, as zamindars and capitalists, found their own interests in conflict with the interests of kisans.[11]

Implicit in this understanding of the wretched lot of the kisans was a comprehension of the quality of nation and class[12] Here was a network of exploitation in which were woven, relationships of dependence and collaboration between the imperial masters and the native exploiters. Premchand saw this clearly, and realized that cessation of British connection would not *ipso facto* mean liquidation of exploitation. As early as February 1919, he had felt obliged by the selfishness of the 'leaders of the *Swaraj* movement' to warn them: 'There is no reason for the public to prefer your governance to the governance of foreign rulers.'[13] In *Karmabhumi* (1932) he declared that transference of power from one group to another did not, by itself, constitute liberation;[14] a theme that can be discerned even in *Godan* (1936), a novel not directly concerned with the problem of *Swaraj*.

As a nationalist, Premchand was thus conscious of the two levels at which the fight for liberation had to be waged. Judging by his writings, fictional as well as journalistic, it is clear that he saw no reason to postpone this fight at one level until it had been won at the other. Even as a nationalist, his sympathies were with those who were being denied the fruits of their labour. Yet, though Premchand was familiar with socialism and tended to be progressively drawn toward the Soviet experiment,[15] he remained a nationalist with broad Gandhian sympathies. Herein lay the crux of a dilemma that obtruded upon him with increasing inconvenience and pressed for a resolution.

To follow the unfolding of this dilemma in Premchand's writings is to understand him at two planes; as a creative writer with an abiding concern for the deprived of his society; and as an intellectual with certain class affiliations and a mental orientation, who was perhaps unconsciously constrained by his locus in the society, which he was trying to view from the viewpoint of the wretched. By watching him at these two planes, it may be possible to gain some understanding of the interplay of the ideal and the material interests, during an important phase of the Indian national movement.

II

It was in *Premashram* that Premchand had his first close look at the rural society. Written between May 1918 and February 1920, it was published in 1921. Gandhi had by then emerged on the Indian political scene, though the non-cooperation movement had not yet been launched during the period when *Premashram* was written. In addition to Gandhian influence,[16] Premchand seems to have been inspired by Tolstoy also. Read along with 'Purana Zamana: Naya Zamana', and article Premchand wrote during this period, *Premashram* suggests the working of a mind that was angered by the ugliness of the reality, but seemed lost when confronted with the need for a solution.

The picture that emerges from *Premashram* is one of merciless exploitation of kisans who were denied even a subsistence level of existence. What is the cause of their misery? In answering this question, Premchand absolves the kisans of all responsibility. Through Premshankar, who is frequently used as a proxy for the authorial voice, Premchand says:

> The responsibility for their poverty rests not with them but with the conditions under which their life is spent. And what are these conditions? Mutual discord, selfishness, and an institution which has fettered them. But if you consider the matter a little more carefully, all the three branches would seem to have sprung from a single stem; and that stem is this institution which depends for its very existence on the blood of peasants.[17]

Obviously the only solution was the abolition of this institution. Particularly so when it had a no justification for its existence. Premshankar, a benign visionary who has come back from the United States with aspirations of reconstructing his society, asks the younger brother, Gyanshankar, who is an unscrupulous villain and an avaricious zamindar: 'What justice is this that while someone toils and someone else protects him, it is we who collect the money?'[18] Premchand maintained that the land belonged to the tiller and the ruler could claim a share in return for ensuring peace and order in the country. No third group could have a place in society.[19]

Premchand knew that this formulation would raise the bogey of revolution.[20] But he could think of no alternative. It is possible that in arguing for abolition of *zamindari* he was influenced by the U.P. Kisan Sabha which, having been founded towards the end of 1917, had asked the Indian National Congress in 1919 to plead for the bestowal of proprietary rights on the actual cultivators of land. This supposition is strengthened by the manner in which the Kisan Sabha is mentioned by a tahsildar in *Prem ashram.*[21] It would seem from this reference that the Kisan Sabha activities had begun to bother the administration; certainly its petty officials. Premchand might have felt further emboldened by the example of the Russian Revolution to put forward the ultimate solution of zamindari abolition. This would be suggested by 'Purana Zamana: Naya Zamana' and by the fact that Balraj, the angry young villager in *Premashram,* did feel inspired by the example of Russia where 'cultivators are the rulers'.[22]

Yet, in one sense, *Premashram* is without a solution. Premashankar certainly knew the source of the kisans' misery, but he also knew that it was 'beyond human power' to eliminate this source.[23] Moreover, after entering the Legislative Council as the leader of an influential group within it, Premshankar could think of nothing more drastic than a resolution intended to deprive the Zamindars of the right to evict their tenants. Even this he could not move for fear of antagonizing his kith and kin.[24]

But the idealist in Premchand would not let him leave the story on a note of despire, which is what a solution that was 'beyond human power' would have meant. So he brought about a series of conversions of heart which could entitle Premshankar to say that he had found every bad person essentially good.[25] To this Premchand added his own direct bit by philosophizing that human character was neither altogether black nor altogether white.[26] To emphasis that this was no empty hope, he provided a millenarian finals to *Premashram.* This was done by making Mayashankar, the idealistically inclined son of villainous Gyanshankar, renounce the vast estates to the direct administration of which he had become entitled on attaining majority. 'Land', says the young self-abnegating zamindar, 'belongs either to God or to the kisan who makes use of it as a result of divine will'. In accordance with this faith, Mayashankar frees the kisans of the bondage imposed upon them by his rights as a zamindar, and makes them proprietors of the land cultivated by each one of them.[27]

Though it described the wretched lot of the rural poor, *Premashram* failed to highlight the grim tragedy to which they had been condemned by the institutionalisation of exploitation. Faithful in its portrayal of actual details of rural life, it nevertheless misrepresented the existential reality by taking away the inescapability and unmitigability of exploitation under the system. Flights of idealism apart, it would seem that Premchand genuinely believed at this time that the mediation of benevolent zamindars would mitigate the miseries of kisans in spite of the essentially exploitative nature of the system.[28] That would explain why, after threatening a radical reconstruction of society, his 'Purana Zamana: Naya Zamana' ended with a whimper; appealing to the good sense and enlightened self-interest of the zamindar in order to ensure a better deal for the *kisans.*

In *Rangbhumi* (1922-24), Premchand managed to curb his idealism. Unlike *Sevasadan* (1917-18) and *Premashram, Rangbhumi* did not report to the *ashram* and change of heart techniques. In fact, most of its formidable 'villains' remain unrepentant till the end; though some of them tried to serve their own purposes by pretending to have undergone a change of heart. But the *Rangbhumi* did not take up the problem of *kisans*.

Premchand came back to the kisans in *Karmabhumi* (1931-32). Apart from the civil disobedience movement, a major development that provided the backdrop for this novel was the slump in the prices of agricultural products. Even before this slump, as Premchand tells us in *Karmabhumi, kisans* had barely managed to get one meal a day. But with the slump the value of their produce feel short of their investments and the rent they had to pay.[29] In some cases, the value of the produce was not even equal to the rent the cultivator was obliged to pay.[30] Still, 'cursing their fate, remaining naked and starved, and dying like dogs, people continued to till the fields. What else could they do? Many had migrated to the cities and taken up employment there. Many others had taken to wage labour. But there still was no dearth of tenants. In a predominantly agricultural country farming is not merely a means of earning livelihood; it is also a status symbol'.[31]

Going deeper than the extraordinary situation created by the price fall, Premchand brought out in *Karmabhumi* the basic irreconcilability of interests between the zamindars and *kisans*. He was beginning to see the futility of reliance on the goodwill of zamindars. He showed this with his penchant for the kind of simple but telling, metaphors that the villagers used and understood so well. Atmanand, a militant leader who moved away from the city to settle in a village, asks his audience: "If the *roti* in your plate asks you not to eat it, would you oblige'? There are cries of 'no' from all around. Atmanand thereupon clinches the argument. 'How can then those oblige you for whom you are the *rotis* in their plates.'?[32]

But if, in *Karmabhumi*, Premchand was beginning to see the ineffectuality of individuals in the face of a grinding system of which they were but instruments. He was also wary of trusting the educated non-*kisan* leaders of *kisans*. He recognized the idealism of these young men and women; but the realist in him was quick to see the less noble dimension of their motivation. He felt concerned for *kisans* when he saw the idealism of these leaders play a second fiddle to their vanity, love for power, and mutual jealousies. That Premchand's fictional transcreation corresponds, in this respect, to the objective reality would be borne out by the testimony of Sampurnanand who had himself taken part in the kind of activities described in *Karmabhumi.*[33]

Given this new reluctance to rely on the benevolence of zamindars and his weariness against trusting the leaders of *kisan satyagraha,* Premchand was in a quandary about the means of securing relief to *kisans.* He offered a virtual spate of change of heart in *Karmabhumi* and made the *satyagraha* in the city a success. But he could not bring himself to offer such easy relief to the agitating *kisans.* In fact, through none other than Amarkant, the main leader of the *kisans,* Premchand expressed doubts about the very prudence of having launched *satyagraha* for providing relief to the suffering *kisans.* These doubts, it may be noted, did not stem from a feeling that the possibilities of negotiations with the zamindars had not been exhausted; they arose from a realization that the government had not been given sufficient time to look into the grievances of the *kisans.* Even when the *satyagraha* was withdrawn, the withdrawal was made possible by the willingness of the government to reach a peaceful settlement.[34]

Premchand's non-fictional writings of this period would confirm that he was veering toward the belief that the government alone could provide whatever relief was possible under the circumstances.[35] This belief rested on his assessment of the pragmatism of the government. In a picturesquely written article that could compare with the best in his fiction, Premchand likened the zamindars to a mistress whose youth was on the wane. They had been supported whole-heartedly by the government so long as it believed that they were the natural leaders of the society. But now that it had realized that instead of being a source of strength they had become and obstacle in its way, its interest had waned. Though, as a matter of policy, it could not afford to set them aside, the government could also not ignore the growing discontent of the peasantry.[36]

Karmabhumi offers clearer glimpses of the sombre tragedy that had got diffused in the millenarian escapism of *Premashram.* It is, however, not without a glimmer of hope. But even as he was writing *Karmabhumi,* Premchand was finding it difficult to retain this glimmer. The tone of his journalistic writings during this period—as also their content—would suggest that he was hoping against hope.

Increasingly, Premchand was awakening to the realization that, bolstered as it was by the government, the institution of *zamindari* had become dysfunctional and counter-productive. His *'Poos ki Raat'* (1930) constitutes a definite movement towards this realization. Halku is a typical farmer: poor and heavily indebted. Every night he goes out, along with his dog, to keen a vigil over his standing crops. Unable to bear the cold and wind of the winter night, ill-clad Halku manages to get together a fire for himself and his dog. Son a heard of animals enters his fields and the dog begins to bark furiously, but Halku refuses to move. He would rather have the crops destroyed than leave the transient warmth he had so painstakingly managed. But that is not the climax of the story. Morning comes. Munni, Halku's wife, is disconsolate. But Halku is now permanently happy. He will no more be required to brave the cold of night.[37]

Premchand unfolded the tragic drama of peasant life in *Godan* (1932-36) with an austere ruthlessness that could brook no sentimentalism. He was still worried by problems of idealism but he could not bear to soil the truth of his story with a hope that did not exist. He had, at long last, realized the ideal of an artist that he had set before himself way back in 1906. The ideal was to inspire the reader without seeming to do that.[38] 'The description of an incident', he had then written, 'is so often a conclusion in itself'.[39] In *Godan,* Premchand succeeded in describing the utter starkness of the variegated wretchedness of the rural poor.

The tragedy of Hori, the Protagonist of *Godan,* is not an individual tragedy. He is the tragic lot of his class, transcending the two villages within the confines of which tragedy is enacted. Here is Premchand's portrayal of the village;[40]

There was not a man whose face was untouched by sorrow, as if grief, not life, was manipulating them like they were so many puppets. They would walk, work, suffer, and be crushed because suffering and oppression was their destiny. Life held out to them no hope, nor excitement; the very springs of their life had run dry....

Premchand could now see with a clarity that had earlier eluded him that no amount of goodwill on the part of individual zamindars could help the *kisans*. The zamindar of Semari and Belari, the two Godan villages, is a good-hearted person who had resigned from the Legislative Council in order to take part in the Gandhian movement. He is convinced that nothing could be a achieved for the *kisans* by depending on the goodness of zamindars. For as he puts it succinctly: 'I cannot set aside my self-interest. I want that my class should be obliged to renounce its selfishness through the instrumentality of the administration and ethics.'[41]

Premchand had ruled out, in *Karmabhumi* the effectiveness of the instrumentality of ethics.[42] The message is writ large in *Godan* itself. As for the administration. It would move only under pressure. Revealing powers of discernment which hinted at radical potentialities, Premchand showed in *Godan* the futility of expecting that such a pressure would come from a nationalist movement dominated by the moneyed classes.[43]

Could such pressure come from the very people who were groaning under this iniquitous system? Premchand was pessimistic. He had shown the fate of discontent produced by the sheer weight of injustice and exploitation. In *Premashram,* Manohar, Qadir and Sukkhu had laboured under such discontent. In *Godan,* Dhaniya had acted similarly; even Hori, the very picture of docile resignation, recalled having stood up to injustice in his youth. This kind of orthogenetic discontent neither derived from, nor resulted in, the questioning of the system as such.

There was another kind of discontent that questioned the very foundations of the existing system. Balraj, in *Premashram,* felt this type of discontent as a result of the little knowledge he had obtained of happenings in the outside world, especially Russia. Gobar felt this in *Godan,* but only after he had run away from his village and acquired in the city some understanding of the nationalist movement. Judging what Balraj and Gobar were able to achieve, Premchand seems to have entertained no hopes of the *kisans* themselves exerting pressure on the administration. He found the peasants in general a passive lot whom only terrible blow could make active.[44]

What could have been more terribal than the tale told in *Godan?* If, however, something had remained unsaid in *Godan,* it was said by Premchand in *Kafan* (1936). He had now laid bare the dysfunctionality of the system. The exploited components of the system were now beginning to ask why, at all, they should retain their links with it as active participants if their lot was going to remain the same, irrespective of whether they worked or idled away.[45]

III

From the innocuous romanticism of *Premashram,* Premchand had gradually moved in his literary universe towards a logic that was explosive in its implications. *Swaraj* could not mean the replacement of external by internal oppressors. Logically, it would entail the liquidation of both. In terms of the internal oppression involving the *kisans,* the only solution was the abolition of the *zamindari* system. Premchand had himself suggested this in *Premashram,* as also in 'Purana Zamana: Naya Zamana'. This he had done in spite of his faith in the possibility of relief to the *kisans* through the benevolence of individual zamindars.

After *Premashram,* Premchand could see with growing clarity the dysfunctional character of the institution of *zamindari.* There was, therefore, greater reason for him to press for its abolition. But ironically, neither in his fiction nor in his journalistic writings did he broach the subject again. Like Gandhi, he would now talk of liquidating the oppression, so far as internal oppression was concerned, without liquidating the oppressors. He would see, and show, in his fictional world the futility of reliance on the zamindars. But in his journalistic pieces he would make desperate appeals to their good sense and enlightened self-interest, hoping to lure them to behave with assurances that their rights would continue 'for ages' even after independence;[46]

> If the *zamindars* would not stain themselves so much with their injustices that their existence is disgusting in the eyes of others, they would for ages remain the chiefs, the leaders and the protectors of the *kisan*. After independence, of course, land rents will be somewhat reduced—the *kisans* will not accept less than 50 per cent, and among with that the zamindar's wealth will be reduced, but will self-rule be so empty of justice and righteousness that it will snatch away the proper rights of any group? This is not possible.
>
> The zamindars will remain, their honour and respect will remain. Of course free labour will not remain, free gifts will not remain, secret looting will not remain, but they will still be the kings of their homes. Those greetings flatteries, bowings, payments of cash, which in the past they have had to give to their rulers, will all vanish. To be sure, wealth will be somewhat less, but in exchange for this their honour will increase and they will become true leaders of society.

Gandhi's attitude can be understood more easily. As one called upon to fight the colonial regime in a plural society riven by a wide variety of divisions, he was obliged to contain internal fissility. But judging from his letters and writings, he was not altogether unaware of who he might be compelled to fight once the colonial exploiters were gone. As early as 1928, he had written to Nehru who was getting impatient with the inequalities and injustices obtaining within Indian society: 'I am quite of your opinion that some day we shall have to start an intensive movement without the rich people and without the vocal educated class. But that time is not yet.'[47]

Premchand was not constrained as Gandhi was. It is possible. Moreover, that he could see more clearly and closely than Gandhi the counterproductive nature of the system. Besides, judging from his fiction, he was also moving away from Gandhi's idea of trusteeship as far as the problem of kisan-zamindar relations was concerned. *Premashram* may be seen as having elements of trusteeship. But in *Karmabhumi,* as we have seen, whatever hope is entertained rests on the pragmatism of the government. In *Godan,* family, the message is one of almost unrelieved despair; a message confirmed beyond doubt in *Kafan.*

How then could—or why did—Premchand short-circuit the logic of his fiction? On the answer to this question may hinge much of our appraisal of the dynamics of Indian society in Premchand's time; an answer that may even have more than merely historical significance.

It seems that scholars have come tantalizingly close to this paradox of the inversion of relationship between the clarity of Premchand's perception of the plight of *kisans* and the radicalism of his prescription; but without having really faced it. Their questions have primarily been addressed to Premchand's massive fiction. Their answers, consequently, stop at the speculation that only if he had lived long enough to complete his last novel, *Mangalsutra*—of which he could write only four chapters—Premchand probably would have offered an explicit enunciation of the implicit revolutionism of his later writings.[48]

Mangalsutra does betray a kind of frenzied lucidity that can be discerned in *Kafan.* Yet, any speculation based on what message it might have provided constitutes only a futile and needless exercise. It is futile because it is in the nature of what might have been, to which there can possibly be no meaningful answer. It is needless because it consigns to the realm of what might have been a discussion that can satisfactorily be conducted within the framework of what actually was.

Between *Sevasadan* and *Premashram* on the one hand and *Godan* and *Kafan* on the other, Premchand showed marked development as a creative writer. There is a progressive diminution—though not as a rule—of idealism as an extraliterary factor. The story often gives the impression of having an autonomous movement of its own without having been extraneously twisted by the writer's idealism.[49] Hence the contrast between the vague millenarianism of *Premashram* and the sombre austerity of *Godan*. In terms of prescription, Premchand took the most radical position when his fictional world least demanded it. Quietly, but stubbornly, he turned his back on it when his transcreation of reality demanded it the most.

What held Premchand back even when he could see the reality in its utter nakedness? In the absence of direct evidence—Premchand never discussed this problem—one can only speculate. The most important clue for such a speculation is provided by chronology. Premchand suggested the abolition of *zamindari* at a time when the non-cooperation movement had not been launched. Though he never joined the Congress as an active worker, his sympathies always remained with it. He was not oblivious to the sordidness within the nationalist movement: he could even criticize Gandhi.[50] He saw the constraints within which the Congress operated because of the class interest of its leadership. Still he not only supported the Congress but also—even while criticizing it—so trimmed his writings as to keep them in consonance with the programme of the Congress.

This may be illustrated by comparing Premchand's journalistic writings with the programmatic policy pronouncements of the Congress. Having defined *swaraj* as complete independence and having decided to embark on a movement intended to enlist the common people, the Congress was obliged to make declarations that were likely to have a popular appeal. It declared, in 1929, that in order to remove 'poverty and misery and to ameliorate the condition of the Indian masses, it is essential to make revolutionary changes in the present economic and social structure of society and to remove gross inequalities'.[51] In 1931, the Congress thought in necessary 'to enable the masses to appreciate what swaraj', as conceived by it, would mean to them, and declared: 'In order to end the exploitation of the masses, political freedom must include economic freedom of the starving millions.'[52] But when the zamindars and capitalist demurred at these radical pronouncements, the Congress hastened to lay their misgivings at rest. It disavowed any intention to countenance either a class war or confiscation of private property, because both were contrary to its creed of non-violence.[53]

Premchand's journalistic writings of this period show that his observations on problems of land and labour bore a marked resemblance to the socio-economic programme outlined by the Congress.[54] He often seemed to echo, in their Hindi translation, the very words of the Congress statements. For example, in the very year that the Congress had felt obliged to eschew class war, Premchand wrote: 'We do not want a war between classes'.[55]

It would thus appear that once, Premchand decided to follow Gandhi, during the non-cooperation movement, his writings began to be constrained by the tactical demands of the national movement. To this extent, his inability to follow the logic of his fiction was rooted in the colonial situation. In terms of its logical implications, this kind of a rooting implied the acceptance by Premchand of the dominance of certain vested interests within the nationalist movement. How could he accept this dominance in spite of having seen through the selfishness of these interest and in spite of his commitment to 'the oppressed, the persecuted, and the deprived'?

Premchand must have been conscious of the subordination, in his post 1919 non-fictional writings, of the logic of his fiction to the logic of the national movement. But at the conscious level, this was subordination to the dominant ideology of the national movement—as represented by the Congress under Gandhi's leadership—and not to the narrow material interest that he knew were camouflaged behind the national movement. Because he continued, even in his non-fictional pronouncements, to expose the selfishness of the entrenched nationalist leadership, Premchand could justifiably believe that in supporting the national movement he was promoting the cause of the poor and the exploited in his society. He could not have realized the logical implications of the conscious lessening of the thrust of his fiction. It is only in retrospect that these implications acquire clarity. In fact, the very lessening of the thrust seems, in retrospect, to have been sharper than could ever have been realized by Premchand.

But implicit in the acceptance of the dominant nationalist ideology were some assumptions regarding the nature of a national consensus for carrying on the struggle for freedom. These assumptions produced a consensus that was built around vaguely radical promises for the masses and concrete concessions for the classes. Nehru was able to see this when he complained in 1928: 'Whenever vital questions affecting the masses have arisen, they have been postponed till Swaraj has been attained'.[56] But the pattern of consensus remained unaffected by such stray insights. Nehru himself did precious little to change it.[57]

If, in spite of his understanding of the cheerless lot of the poor and the selfish character of the nationalist leadership, Premchand could accept the national consensus sought by the Congress, his locus in society was not without its contribution in making this acceptance possible. It seems improbable that there was no connection between his own material situation and his acceptance of the programmatic constraints of the Congress. Ideally Premchand would like to ensure a better deal for the poor, but there were limits beyond which he would not go. These limits were defined though not always consciously, by his perception of what was possible without eroding peace and order in society. As he moved from his earlier concern to both portary and prescribe towards the realization that to portray was to prescribe, he could work on his fiction with increasing freedom from considerations of what was possible. Having, as a creative writer, portrayed what *was,* as a nationalist political commentator he had to be concerned with the possible and the pragmatic. It was at this level that he could vaguely sense that acceptance of the logic of his fiction would entail the kind of upheaval he was unprepared to risk.

A letter written by Premchand less than two years before his death would lend credence to this speculation. He wrote: 'I believe in social evolution our object being to educate public opinion. Revolution is the failure of saner methods....It is the peoples' character that is the deciding factor. No social system can flourish unless we are individually uplifted. What fate a revolution may lead us to is doubtful. It may lead us to worse forms of dictatorship denying all personal liberty. It do want to overhaul, but not destroy.[58]

Premchand wrote this letter when he had been more than two years at work on *Godan.* And nothing could have refuted this exposition more convincingly than the underlying thrust of this novel.

Not obtrusively but through his preferences for certain alternatives as against other—including the ones suggested by his own creative universe—was Premchand held back by the mediation of material interests and processes of socialization. Apart from influence the choice of alternatives, this mediation also produced a kind of intellectual fuzziness which tended to strengthen the retrogressive hold of Premchand's preferences.

As an example may be cited Premchand's response to the decision of the Congress to adopt complete independence as its goal. In a letter written at this time he hailed the momentous Lahore resolution; but in the same breath expressed his inability to appreciate the boycott of councils.[59] That he should have missed the connection between the two decisions is in itself astonishing. But still more astonishing is the fact that he should have failed to appreciate the boycott six years after he had himself provided, in *Rangbhumi,* a most devastating *expose* of the councils.[60]

So effective was this retrogressive hold—and so sharp, for that reason, the gap between his fiction and non-fiction that even while following the policies and programmes of the Congress, Premchand was cautious enough not to follow its most radical elements. It is noteworthy that after 1919 he refrained from explicitly advocating the abolition of *zamindari* in spite of the fact that Nehru was, between 1928 and 1936, unsparing in his criticism of the U.P. zamindars and categorical in his demand for their elimination as proprietors of land.[61] Interestingly enough, Premchand supported Nehru's economic programme in general, but avoided any reference to the proposed abolition of *zamindari.*[62] His radicalism was apparently subject to hidden reins.

—*Sudhir Chandra*

REFERENCES

1. Premchand to Banarasi Das Chaturvedi, 1 Dec. 1935, in Premchand, *Chitthi Patri,* (Allahabad, 1978), Vol. II, p. 93.
2. See Premchand's presidential address at the first convention of the Progressive Writers' Association, Apr. 1936, in Premchand, *Kuchh Vichar* (Allahabad, 1973), pp. 5-25.
3. *Ibid.,* p. 10.
4. *Ibid.,* pp. 5-25, 79-84.
5. I have not stopped dreaming', he wrote to Chaturvedi in the letter cited above.
6. In the last chapter of *Rangbhumi,* Premchand makes Dr. Ganguli say that 'In the present situation optimism is little more than more self-delusion'. (This and the other translations form Hindi, except the one indicated in note 46, are by the author.) Between 1924, when *Rangbhumi* was published, and 1936 Premchand seems to have moved towards greater pessimism.
7. Premchand wrote this to Sajjad Zaheer, one of the chief organizers of the convention. See Amrit Rai, *Kalam ka Sipahi,* (Allahabad, 1976), p. 582.

8. Premchand to Banarasi Das Chaturvedi, 3 Jun. 1932, n. 1. p. 76.
9. Premchand to Sri Ram Sharma, 9 Feb 1931, *ibid.*, p. 211.
10. Premchand, *Vividh Prasang,* (Allahabad, 1978), vol. II, pp. 42, 507.
11. This is recurring theme in Premchand's novels. See, for example, *Premashram,* (Allahabad, 1979), pp. 265-66; *Godan,* (Allahabad, 1975), pp. 91-2, 137, 155, 266. See also *Vividh Prasang,* Vol. II, pp. 331-32, 496.
12. There is an interesting passage in *Godan* in which Premchand shows Gobar, a young villager who has migrated to Lucknow, to be aware of the distinctions of class and nation, p. 191.
13. *Vividh Prasang,* Vol. I, p. 267.
14. *Karmabhumi,* Allahabad, 1978, p. 312. see also *Chitthi Patri,* Vol. I, p. 93; 'Ahuti' in Premchand *Kafan,* (Allahabad, 1973), pp. 104-05. This may be compared what what Jawharlal Nehru said in 1928: 'Our educated classes have so far taken the lead in the fight for Swaraj, but in doing so they have seldom paid heed to the needs of the masses.... But what shall it profit the masses of India—the peasantry, the landless labourers, the artisans—if everyone of the offices held by Englishmen in India today is held by an Indian?' S. Gopal, ed. *Selected Works of Jawaharlal Nehru,* (New Delhi, 1942), Vol. III, p. 371.
15. *Premashram,* pp. 51-2, 400; *Vividh Prasang,* Vol. I, pp. 258-69; Vol. II, p. 217; *Chitthi Patri,* Vol. I, p. 93. For Premchand's most spirited defence of the Soviet experiment see 'Mahajani Sabhyata', an article published a month after his death and written a few months earlier; in *Mangalsutra va Anya Rachanayan,* (Allahabad, n.d.), pp. 365-68. But a reading of Premchand would make it difficult to believe that he was more than a progressive liberal. See also Robert O. Swan, *Munshi Premchand of Lahmi Village,* (Durham, 1996), pp. 109 ff.
16. See Shivrani Devi Premchand, *Premchand: Ghar Mein,* (Delhi, 1956), pp. 47 ff.
17. *Premashram,* p. 199.

18. *Ibid.*, p. 141.
19. *Ibid.*, p. 150.
20. *Ibid.*, p. 150, 403.
21. *Ibid.*, p. 182.
22. *Ibid.*, p. 51.
23. *Ibid.*, p. 200.
24. *Ibid.*, p. 398.
25. *Ibid.*, p. 295.
26. *Ibid.*, p. 386.
27. *Ibid.*, pp. 403-4.
28. Premchand, 'Upadesh' (1917), *Mansarovar,* (Allahabad, 1980), Vol. VIII, 276 ff.
29. *Karmabhumi,* p. 301.
30. *Ibid.*, p. 241.
31. *Ibid.*
32. *Ibid.*, p. 243.
33. Sampurnanand, *Memories and Reflections,* (Bombay, 1962), pp. 66-70, Cf *mabhumi,* p. 32.
34. *Karmabhumi,* pp. 334-39.
35. *Vividh Prasand,* Vol. II, pp. 489-92.
36. *Ibid.*, pp. 500-3.
37. *Mansarovar,* (Allahabad, 1971), Vol. I, pp. 157-63.
38. *Vividh Prasang,* Vol. I, pp. 64-7.
39. *Ibid.*, p. 64.
40. *Godan,* p. 336.
41. *Ibid.*, p. 153.
42. *Karmabhumi,* p. 27.
43. *Godan,* pp. 91-2, 137, 155, 226.
44. *Ibid.*, p. 294.

45. *Kafan*, pp. 5-14.

46. *Vividh Prasang*, Vol. II, pp. 42-3. The English translation of these passages has been taken from Swan, n. 15; p. 111.

47. Gandhi to Nehru, 1 Apr. 1928, in *The Collected Works of Mahatma Gandhi*, Vol. 36, (Delhi, 1970), p. 174. For a discussion that Gandhi could see this; see N.K. Bose, *My Days with Gandhi*, (Calcutta, 1953).

48. Amrit Rai, n. 7; Also Shachi Rani Gurtu, ed. *Premchand aur Gorki*, (Bombay, 1955).

49. Premchand's work is to uneven to permit any generalization in this respect. Even his masterpiece, *Godan*, suffers from uneveness of quality.

50. *Vividh Prasand*, Vol. II, pp. 233, 257.

51. Zaidi, A.M., and S.G., (eds.) *The Foundations of Indian Economic Planning*, (New Delhi, 1979,) p. 59. Writing in 1928, Jawaharlal Nehru emphasized the need for enlisting the masses: 'Even from a narrow point of view it is now recognized that no effective pressure can be brought to bear on the British Government without mass support but there is fear of the masses and little is done. Mass support cannot come from vague ideals of Swaraj. It is essential that we must clearly lay down an economic programme for the masses with socialism as its ideal' S. Gopal (ed.), n. 14, p. 371.

52. Zaidi, n. 51, pp. 59-60.

53. *Ibid.*, p. 65.

54. *Ibid.*, pp. 61-1 for the Congress programme; and *Vividh Prasang*, Vol. II, pp. 479-512 for Premchand's advocacy of the cause of labour and kisan; also pp. 216-217, 263-64, 270-83.

55. *Vividh Prasang*, Vol. II, p. 487.

56. S. Gopal, (ed.) n. 14, p. 371.

57. This is a serious problem that has hampered the emergence of a radical perspective for the study of modern Indian history. I have dealt with this aspect of modern Indian historiography

with reference to the late nineteenth century in 'The Secular Potential of Early Indian Nationalism', *Economic and Political Weekly,* Vol. xv, No. 17, Apr. 26, 1980, pp. 773-75. What I have written about the late 19th century holds true of the later period also. Even a perceptive scholar like N.K. Bose who had seen through the *status quoist* implications of the ideology of Indian nationalism, failed to apply this insight to the study of Gandhi. He accepted the assumption that within the constraints of the colonial presence, Gandhi had no option but to defer the working out of his more radical ideas of social reconstruction until *Swaraj* had been achieved. He, too, avoided the question: Why was this particular approach to a national consensus adopted? If the assumptions underlying the dominant nationalist ideology continued to be taken for granted even after 1947, it is not surprising that Premchand could not rise above them in spite of the radical thrust of his fiction. See N.K. Bose, *Problems of Indian Nationalism,* (Calcutta, 1969), and also *My Days with Gandhi.*

58. Premchand to Indranath Madan, 26 Dec. 1934, *Chitthi Patri,* Vol. II, Appendix, p. 2. This latter is in English.
59. Premchand to Keshoram Saberwal, n.d., *ibid.,* p. 208. The letter appears to have been written in January 1930.
60. Explaining the failure of Prabhu Sevak, to realize in practice his theoretical commitment to the welfare of the common man, Premchand writes in *Rangbhumi;* 'He was wanting in the circumstances in which he had been brought up, and the values on which had rested his mental and spiritual development'. (p. 404) Could it be that Premchand himself lacked the moral courage and audacity to face the logic of his fiction? And that, in spite of the suffering he had seen and recorded, he could not transcend the socialization that had shaped his values and assumptions?
61. Nehru said: 'We in this province have to face especially the zamindari and *kisan* problem. To our misfortune we have zamindars everywhere and they have prevented all healthy

growth.... It is a feudal relic of the past utterly out of keeping with modern conditions'. He had no hesitation in recommending the only solution possible under the circumstances: 'The abolition of landlordism must, therefore, occupy a prominent place in our programme and instead of that we should have small holdings ordinarily enough for a family to cultivate'. S. Gopal, (ed.), *op. cit.*, pp. 258-59.

62. *Vividh Prasang,* Vol. II, pp. 220-21.

Appendix I

Excerpts form Mrs Annie Besant's Presidential Address at the Calcutta Session of the Indian National Congress in 1971

Fellow-Deligates and Friends

Everyone who has preceded me in this chair has rendered his thanks in fitting terms for the gift which is truly said to be the highest that India has it in her power to bestow. It is the sign of her fullest love, trust, and approval, and the one whom she seats in that chair is, for his year of service, her chosen leader. But if my predecessors found fitting words for their gratitude, in what words can I voice mine, whose debt to you is so overwhelmingly greater than theirs? For the first time in Congress history, you have chosen as your President one who, when your choice was made, was under the heavy ban of Government displeasure, and who lay interned as a person dangerous to public safety. While I was humiliated, you crowned me with honour; while I was slandered, you believed in my integrity and good faith; while I was crushed under the heel of bureaucratic power you acclaimed me as your leader; while I was silenced and unable to defend myself you defended me, and won for me release. I was proud to serve in lowliest fashion, but you lifted me up and placed me before the world as your chosen representative. I have no words with which to thank you, no eloquence with which to repay my debt. My deeds must speak for me, for words are too poor. I turn your gift into service to the Motherland; I consecrate my life anew to her in worship by action. All that I have and am, I lay on the Altar of the Mother, and together we shall cry, more by service than by words VANDE MATARAM!

There is, perhaps, one value in your election of me in this crisis of India's destiny, seeing that I have not the privilege to be Indian-born, but come from that little island in the northern seas which has been, in the West, the builder-up of free institutions. The Aryan emigrants, who spread over the lands of Europe, carried with them the seeds of liberty sown in their blood in their Asian cradleland. Western histrorians trace the self-rule of the Saxon villages to their earlier prototypes in the East, and see the growth of English liberty as up springing from the Aryan root of the free and self-contained village communities.

Its growth was crippled by Norman feudalism there, as its millennia-nourished security here was smothered by the East India Company. But in England it burst its shackles and nurtured a liberty-living people, and a free Commons' House. Here, it similarly burgeoned out into the Congress activities, and more recently into those of the Muslim League, now together blossoming into Home Rule for India. The England of Milton, Cromwell, Sydney, Burke, Paine, Shelley, Wilberforce, Gladstone; the England that sheltered Mazzini, Kossuth, Kropotkin, Stepniak, and that welcomed Garibaldi; the England that is the enemy of tyranny, the foe of autocracy, the lover of freedom, that is the England I would fain here represent to you today. Today, when India stands erect, no suppliant people, but a Nation, self-conscious, self-respecting, determined to be free; when she stretches out her hand to Britain and offers friendship, not subservience; co-operation, not obedience; today let me, Western born but in spirit Eastern, cradled in England but Indian by choice and adoption, let me stand as the symbol of union between Great Britain and India, a union of hearts and free choice, not of compulsion, and, therefore, of a tie which cannot be broken, a tie of love and of mutual helpfulness, beneficial to both Nations and blessed by God.

India's great leader, Dadbhai Naoroji, has left his mortal body and is now one of the company of the Immortals, who watch over and aid India's progress. He is with W.C. Bannerjee, and Ranade, and A.O. Hume, and Henry Cotton, and Pherozeshah Mehta, and

Gopala Krishna Gokhale—the great men who, in Swinburne's noble verse, are the stars which lead us to Liberty's alter:

> These, O men, shall ye honour,
> Liberty only and these.
> For thy sake and for all men's and mine,
> Brother, the crowns of them shine,
> Lighting the way to her shrine,
> That our eyes may be fastened upon her,
> That our hands may encompass her knees.

Not for me to praise him in feeble words of reverence and of homage. His deeds praise him, and his service to his country is his abiding glory. Our gratitude will be best paid by following in his footsteps, alike in his splendid courage and his unfaltering devotion, so that we may win the Home Rule which he longed to see while with us, and shall see, ere long, from the other world of Life in which he dwells today.

INDIA AND THE WAR

The Great War, into the whirlpool of which Nation after Nation has been drawn, has entered on its fourth year. The rigid censorship which has been established makes it impossible for any outside the circle of Governments to forecast its duration, but to me, speaking for a moment not as a politician but as a student of spiritual laws, to me its end is sure. For the true object of this War is to prove the evil of, and to destroy, autocracy and the enslavement of one Nation by another, and to place on sure foundations the God-given right to Self-rule and Self Development of every Nations, and the similar right of the Individual, of the smaller Self, so far as is consistent with the welfare of the larger Self of the Nation. The forces which make for the prolongation of autocracy—the rule of one—and the even deadlier bureaucracy—the rule of a close body welded into an iron system—these have been gathered together in the Central Powers of Europe—as of old in Ravana—in order that they may be destroyed; for the New Age cannot be opened until the Old passes away. The new civilization of Righteousness and Justice, and therefore of Brotherhood, of ordered Liberty, of Peace, of Happiness, cannot be built up until the elements are removed which have brought the old civilization crashing about our ears. Therefore it is necessary that the War shall be fought out to its appointed end, and that no premature peace shall leave its subject unattained. Autocracy and bureaucracy must perish utterly in East and West, and, in order that their germs may not resprout in the future, they must be discredited in the minds of men. They must be proved to be less efficient than the Governments of Free People, even in their favourite game of war, and their iron machinery—which at first brings outer prosperity and success—must be shown to be less lasting and effective than the living and flexible organizations of democratic Peoples. They must be proved failures before the world so that the glamour of superficial successes may be destroyed for ever. They have had their day and their place in evolution, and have done their educative work. Now they are out-of-date, unfit for survival, and must vanish away.

When Great Britain sprang to arms, it was in defence of the freedom of a small Nation, guaranteed by treaties, and the great principles she proclaimed electrified India and the Dominions. They all sprang to her side without question, without delay; they heard the voice of old England, the soldier of Liberty, and it thrilled their hearts. All were unprepared, save the small territorial army of Great Britain, due to the genius and foresight of Lord Haldane, and the readily mobilized army of India, hurled into the fray by the swift decision of Lord Hardinge. The little army of Britain fought for time, fought to stop the road to Paris, the heart of France, fought, falling back step by step, and gained the time it fought for, till India's sons stood on the soil of France, were flung to the front, rushed past the exhausted regiments who cheered them with failing breath, charged the advancing hosts, stopped the retreat, and joined the British army in forming that unbreakable line which wrestled to the death through two fearful winters—often, these soldiers of the tropics, waist-deep in freezing mud—and knew no surrender.

India, with her clear vision, saw in Great Britain the champion of Freedom, in Germany the champion of despotism. And she saw rightly. Rightly she stood by Great Britain, despite her own lack of freedom and the coercive legislation which outrivalled German despotism, knowing these to be temporary, because un-English, and therefore doomed to destruction; she spurned the lure of German gold and rejected German appeals to revolt. She offered men and money; her educated classes, her Vakils, offered themselves as volunteers, pleaded to be accepted. Then the never-sleeping distrust of Anglo-Indian rejected the offer pressed for money, rejected men, And, slowly, educated India sank back, depressed and disheartened, and a splendid opportunity for knitting together the two Nations was lost.

Early in the War, I ventured to say that the War could not end until England recognized that autocracy and bureaucracy must perish in India as well as in Europe. The good Bishop of Calcutta, with a courage worthy of his free race, lately declared that it would be hypocritical to pray for victory over autocracy in Europe and to maintain it in India. Now, it has been clearly and definitely declared that Self-Government is to be the objective of Great Britain in India, and that a substantial measure of it is to be given at once; when this promise is made good by the granting of the Reforms outlined last year in Lucknow, then the end of the War will be in slight. For the War cannot end till the death-knell of autocracy is sounded.

Causes with which I will deal presently, and for which India was not responsible, have somewhat obscured the first eager expressions of India's sympathy, and have forced here thoughts largely towards her own position in the Empire. But that does not detract from the immense aid she has given, and is still giving. It must not be forgotten that long before the present War, she had submitted—at first, while she had no power of remonstrance, and later, after 1885, despite the constant protest of Congress—to an ever-rising military expenditure, due partly to the amalgamation scheme of 1859, and partly to the cost of various wars beyond her frontiers, and to continually recurring frontier and trans-frontier expeditions, in which she had no real interest. They were sent out for supposed Imperial advantages, not for her own.

The financial burden incurred in consequence of the above conflicts, and of other causes, now to be mentioned, would not have been so much resented, if it had been imposed by India on herself, and if her own sons had profited by her being used as a training ground for the Empire. But in this case, as in so many others, she has shared Imperial burdens, while not sharing Imperial freedom and power. Apart from this, the changes which made the Army so ruinous a burden on the resources of the country were the system of "British reliefs", the using of India as a training ground for British regiments, and the transfer of the men thus trained, to be replaced by new ones under the short service system, the cost of the frequent transfers and their connected expenses being charged on the Indian revenues, while the whole advantage was reaped by Great Britain. On the short service system the Simla Army Commission declared: "The short service system recently introduced into the British army has increased the cost and has materially reduced the efficiency of the British troops in India. We cannot resist the feeling that, in the introduction of this system, the interest of the Indian taxpayer was entirely left out of consideration."

The remark was certainly justified, for the short service system gave India only five years of the recruits she paid heavily for and trained, all the rest of the benefit going to England. The latter was enabled, as the years went on, to enormously increase her Reserves, so that she has had 4,00,000 men trained in, and at the cost of, India.

In 1863 the Indian army consisted of 1,40,000 men, with 65,000 white officers. Great changes were made in 1885-1905, including the reorganistion under Lord Kitchener, who became Commander-in-Chief at the end of 1902. Even in this hasty review, I must not omit reference to the fact that Army Stores were drawn from Britain at enormous cost, while they should have been chiefly manufactured here, so that India might have profited by the expenditure. Lately, under the necessities of War, factories have been turned to the production of munitions; but this should have been done long ago, so that India might have been enriched instead of exploited. The War has forced an investigation into her mineral resources, that might have been made for her own sake, but Germany was allowed to monopolies the supply of minerals that India could have produced and worked up, and would have produced and worked up had she enjoyed Home Rule. India would have been richer, and the Empire safer, had she been a partner instead of a possession.

Since 1885, the Congress has constantly protested against the ever-increasing military expenditure, but the voice of the Congress was supposed to be the voice of sedition and of class ambition, instead of being, as it was, the voice of educated Indians, the most truly patriotic and loyal class of the population. In 1885, in the First Congress, Mr. P. Rangiah Naidu pointed out that military expenditure had been £ 11,463,000 in 1857 and had risen of £ 16,975,750 in 1884. Mr. D.E. Wacha ascribed the growth of the amalgamation scheme of 1859, and remarked that the Company in 1856 had an army of 2,54,000 men at a cost of £ 11½ millions, while in 1884 the Crown had an army of only 1,81,000 men at a cost of £ 17 millions. The rise was largely due to the increased cost of the European regiments, overland transport service, stores, pensions, furlough allowances, and the like, most of them imposed against the resistance of the Government of India, which complained that the changes were "made entirely, it may be said, from Imperial considerations, in which Indian interests have not been consulted or advanced".

Year after year the Congress continued to remonstrate against the cost of the army, until in 1902 after all the futile protests of the intervening years, it condemned an increase of pay to British soldiers in India, which placed an additional burden on the Indian revenues of £ 7,86,000 a year, and pointed out that the British garrison was unnecessarily numerous, as was shown by the withdrawal of large bodies of British soldiers for service in South Africa and China. The very next year Congress protested that the increasing military expenditure was not to secure India against internal disorder or external attack, but in order to carry out an Imperial policy; the Colonies contributed little or nothing to the Imperial military expenditure, while India bore the cost of about one-third of the whole British Army in addition to her own Indian troops. Surely these facts should be remembered when India's military services to the Empire are now being weighed.

In 1904 and 1905, the Congress declared that the then military expenditure was beyond India's power to bear, and in the latter year prayed that the additional ten millions sterling, sanctioned for Lord Kitchener's reorganization scheme, might be devoted to education and the reduction of the burden on the raiyats. In 1908, the burdens imposed by the British War Office since 1859 were condemned, and in the next year it was pointed out that the military expenditure was nearly a third of the whole Indian revenue, and was starving Education and Sanitation.

Lord Kitchener's reorganization scheme kept the Indian Army on a war footing, ready for immediate mobilization; and on January 1, 1915, the regular army consisted of 2,47,000 men, of whom 75,000 were English; it was the money spent by India in maintaining this army for years in readiness for war which made it possible for her to go to the help of Great Britain at the critical period to which I alluded. She spent over £ 20 millions on the military services in 1914-15. In 1915-16 she spent £ 21.8 millions. In 1916-17 her military budget had risen to £ 22 millions; and it will be largely exceeded.

With such a record of deeds as the one I have boldly sketched, it is not necessary to say much in words as to India's support of Great Britain and her Allies. She has proved up to the hilt her desire to remain within the Empire, to maintain her tie with Great Britain. But if Great Britain is to call successfully on her manpower, as Lord Chelmsford suggests in his Manpower Board, then must the man who fights or labours have a man's rights in his own land. The lesson which springs out of this War is that it is absolutely necessary for the future safety of the Empire that India shall have Home Rule. Had her Manpower been utilized earlier there would have been no War, for none would have dared to provoke Great Britain and India to a contest. But her Man-power cannot be utilized while she is a subject Nation. She cannot afford to maintain a large army, if she is to support an English garrison, to pay for their goings and comings, to buy stores in England at exorbitant prices and send them back again when England needs them. She cannot afford to train men for England, and only have their services for five years. She cannot afford to keep huge God Reserves in England, and be straitened for cash, while she lends to England out of her Reserves, taken from her over-taxation, £ 27,000,000 for War expenses, and this, be it remembered, before the great War Loan. I once said in England: "The condition of India's loyalty is India's freedom." I may now add: "The condition of India's usefulness to the Empire is India's freedom." She will tax herself willingly when her taxes remain in the country and fertilise it, when they educate her people and thus increase their productive power, when they foster her trade and create for her new industries.

Great Britain needs India as much as India needs England, for prosperity in Peace as well as for safety in War. Mr Montagu has wisely said that "for equipment in War a Nation needs freedom in Peace". Therefore I say that, for both countries alike, the lesson of the War is Home Rule for India.

Let me close this part of my subject by laying at the feet of His Imperial Majesty the loving homage of the thousands her assembled, with the hope and belief that, are long, we shall lay there the willing and grateful homage of a free Nation.

THE NEW SPIRIT IN INDIA

Apart from the natural exchange of thought between East and West, the influence of English education, literature and ideals, the effect of travel in Europe, Japan and the United States of America, and other recognized causes for the changed outlook in India, there have been special forces at work during the last few years to arouse a New Spirit in India, and to alter her attitude of mind., These may be summed up as: (a) The Awakening of Asia; (b) Discussions abroad on Alien Rule and Imperial Reconstruction; (c) Loss of Belief in the Superiority of the White Races; (d) The Awakening of the Merchants; (e) The Awakening of the Women to claim her Ancient Position; (f) The Awakening of the Masses.

Each of these causes has had its share in the splendid change of attitude in the Indian Nation, in the uprising of a spirit of pride of country, of independence, of self-reliance, of dignity of self-respect. The War has quickened the rate of evolution of the world, and no country has experienced the quickening more than our Motherland.

In a conversation I had with Lord Minto, soon after his arrival as Viceroy, he discussed the so-called "unrest in India", and recognized it was the inevitable result of English Ideals of Democracy, of the Japanese victory over Russia, and of the changing conditions in the outer world. I was therefore not surprised to read his remark that he recognized, "frankly and publicly, that new aspirations were stirring in the hearts of the people, that they were part of a larger movement common to the whole East, and that it was necessary to satisfy them to a reasonable extent by giving them a large share in the administration".

But the present movement in India will be very poorly understood, if it be regarded only in connection with the movement in the East. The awakening of Asia is part of a world movement, which has been quickened into marvelous rapidity by the World War. The world movement is towards Democracy, and for the West dates from the breaking away of the American Colonies from Great Britain, consummated in 1776, and its sequel in the French Revolution of 1789. Needless to say that its root was in the growth of modern science, undermining the fabric of intellectual servitude, in the work of the Encyclopaedists, and in that of Jean-Jacques Rousseau and of Thomas Paine. In the East, the swift changes in Japan, the success of the Japanese Empire against Russia, the downfall of the Manchu dynasty in China and the establishment of a Chinese Republic, the efforts at improvement in Persia, hindered by the interference of Russia and Great Britain with her growing ambition, and the creatin of British and Russian "spheres of influence", depriving her of her just liberty, and now the Russian Revolution and the probable rise of a "Russian Republic in Europe and Asia, have all entirely changed the conditions before existing in India,. Across Asia, beyond the Himalayas, stretch free and self-ruling Nations. India no longer sees as her Asian neighbours the huge domains of a Tsar and a Chinese despot, and compares her condition under British rule with those of their subject populations. British rule profited by the comparison, at least until 1905, when the great period of repression set in. But in future, unless India wins Self-Government, she will look enviously at her Self-Governing neighbours, and the contrast will intensify her unrest.

But even if she gains Home Rule, as I believe she will, her position in the Empire will imperatively demand that she shall be strong as well as free. She becomes not only a vulnerable point in the Empire, as the Asian Nations evolve their own ambitions and rivalries, but also a possession to be battled for. Mr Laing once said: "India is a milch-cow of England", a Kamadhenu, in fact, a cow of plenty; and if that view should arise in Asia, the ownership of the milch-cow would become a matter of dispute, as of old between Vashishtha and Vishvamitra. Hence India must be capable of self-defence both by land and sea. There may be a struggle for the primacy of Asia, for supremacy in the Pacific for the mastery of Australasia, to say nothing of the inevitable trade-struggle, in which Japan is already endangering Indian industry and Indian trade, while India is unable to protect herself.

In order to face these large issues with equanimity, the Empire requires a contented, strong, self-dependent and armed India, able to hold her own and to aid the Dominions, especially Australia, with her small population and immense unoccupied and undefended area. India alone has the man-power which can effectively maintain the Empire in Asia, and it is a short-sighted, a criminally short-sighted, policy not to build up her strength as a

Self-Governing State within the Commonwealth of Free Nations under the British Crown. The Englishmen in India talk loudly of their interest; what can this merc handful do to protect their interests against attack in the coming years? Only in a free and powerful India will they be safe. Those who read Japanese papers known how strongly, even during the War, they parade unchecked their pro-German sympathies, and how likely after the War is an alliance between these two ambitious and warlike Nations. Japan will come out of the War with her army and navy un-weakened, and her trade immensely strengthened. Every consideration of sane statesmanship should lead Great Britain to trust India more than Japan, so that the British Empire in Asia may rest on the sure foundation of Indian loyalty, the loyalty of a free and contented people, rather than be dependent on the continued friendship of a possible future rival. For international friendships are governed by National interests, and are built on quicksands, not on rock.

Englishmen in India must give up the idea that English dominance is necessary for the protection of their interests, amounting, in 1915, to £ 3,65,399,000 sterling. They do not claim to dominate the United States of America, because they have invested there £ 6,88,078,000. They do not claim to dominate the Argentine Republic, because they have invested there £ 2,69,808,000. Why then should they claim to dominate India on the ground of their investment? Britons must give up the idea that India is a possession to be exploited for their own benefit, and must see her as a friend, an equal, a Self-Governing Dominion within the Empire, a Nation like themselves, a willing partner in the Empire, and not a dependent. The democratic movement in Japan, China and Russia in Asia has sympathetically affected India, and it is idle to pretend that it will cease to affect her.

But there are other causes which have been working in India, consequent on the British attitude against autocracy and in defence of freedom in Europe, while her attitude to India has, until lately, been left in doubt. Therefore I spoke of a splendid opportunity lost. India at first believed whole-heartedly that Great Britain was fighting for the freedom of all Nationalities. Even now, Mr Asquith declared—in his speech in the House of Commons, reported her last October, on the peace resolution of Mr. Ramsay MacDonald—that "the Allies are fighting for nothing but freedom and (an important addition) for nothing short of freedom", In his speech declaring that Britain would stand by France in her claim for the restoration of Alsace-Lorraine, he spoke of "the intolerable degradation of a foreign yoke". Is such as yoke less intolerable, less wounding to self-respect, here than in Alsace-Lorraine, where the rulers and the ruled are both of European blood, similar in religion and habits? As the War went on, India slowly and unwillingly came to realize that the hatred of autocracy was confined to autocracy in the West, and that the degradation was only regarded as intolerable for men of white races; that freedom was lavishly promised to all except to India; that new powers were to be given to the Dominions, but not to India. India was markedly left out of the speeches of statesmen dealing with the future of the Empire, and at last there was plain talk of the White Empire, the Empire of the Five Nations, and the "coloured races" were lumped together as the wards of the White Empire, doomed to an indefinite minority.

The peril was pressing; the menace unmistakable. The Reconstruction of the Empire was on the anvil; what was to be India's place therein? The Dominions were proclaimed as partners; was India to remain a Dependency? Mr Bonar Law bade the Dominions strike while the iron was hot; was India to wait till it was cold? India saw her soldiers fighting for freedom in Flanders, in France, in Gallipoli, in Asia Minor, in China, in Africa; was she to have no share of the freedom for which she fought? At last she sprang to her feet and cried, in the words of one of her noblest sons: "Freedom is my birthright; and I want it." The words "Home Rule" became her Mantram. She claimed her place in the Empire.

Thus, while she contained to support, and even to increase, her army abroad fighting for the Empire, and poured out her treasures as water for Hospital Ships, War Funds, Red Cross

Organisations, and the gigantic War Loan, a dawning fear oppressed her, least, if she did not take order with her own household, success in the War for the Empire might mean decreased liberty for herself.

The recognition of the right of the Indian Government to make its voice heard in Imperial matters, when they were under discussion in an Imperial Conference, was a step in the right direction. But disappointment was felt that while other countries were represented by responsible Ministers, the representation in India's case was of the Government, of a Government irresponsible to her, and not the representative of herself. No fault was found with the choice, but only with the non-representative character of the chosen, for they were selected by the Government and not by the elected members of the Supreme Council.

It was said to be an epoch-making event that "Indian Representatives" took part in the Conference. Representatives they were, but, as said, of the British Government in India, not of India, whereas their colleagues represented their Nations. They did good work, none the less, for they were able and experienced men, though they failed us in the Imperial Preference Conference and, partially, on the Indentured Labour question. Yet we hope that the presence in the Conference of men of Indian birth may prove to be the proverbial "thin end of the wedge", and may have convinced their colleagues that, while India was still a Dependency, India's sons were fully their equals.

The Report of the Public Services Commission, though now too obviously obsolete to be discussed, caused both disappointment and resentment; for it showed that, in the eyes of the majority of the Commissioners, English domination in Indian administration was to be perpetual, and that 30 years hence she would only hold a pitiful 25 per cent of the higher appointments in the I.C.S. and the Police. I cannot, however, mention that Commission, even in passing, without voicing India's thanks to the Hon. Mr. Justice Rahim, for his rare courage in writing a solitary Minute of Dissent, in which he totally rejected the Report; and laid down the right principles which should govern recruitment for the Indian Civil Services.

India had but three representatives on the Commission; G.K. Gokhale died ere it made its Report, his end quickened by his sufferings during its work, by the humiliation of the way in which his countrymen were treated. Of Mr Abdur Rahim I have already spoken. The Hon. Mr M.B. Chaubal signed the Report, but dissented from some of its most important recommendations. The whole Report was written "before the flood", and it is now merely an antiquarian curiosity.

India, for all these reasons, was forced to see before here a future of perpetual subordination: the Briton rules in Great Britain, the Frenchman in France, the American in America, each Dominion in its own area, but the Indian was to rule nowhere; alone among the peoples of the world, he was not to feel his own country as his own. "Britain for the British" was right and natural; "India for the Indians" was wrong, even seditious. It must be "India for the Empire", or not even for the Empire but "for the rest of the Empire", careless of herself. "British support for British Trade" was patriotic and proper in Britain. "Swadeshi goods for Indians" showed a petty and anti-Imperial spirit in India. The Indian was to continue to live perpetually, and even thankfully, was Gopal Krishna Gokhale said he lived now, in "an atmosphere of inferiority", and to be proud to be a citizen (without rights) of the Empire, while its other component Nations were to be citizens (with rights) in their own countries first, and citizens of the Empire secondarily. Just as his trust in Great Britain was strained nearly to breaking point came the glad news of Mr Montagu's appointment as Secretary of State for India, of the Viceroy's invitation to him and of his coming to hear for himself what India wanted. It was a ray of sunshine breaking through the gloom, confidence in Great Britain revived, and glad preparation was made to welcome the coming of a friend.

The attitude of India has changed to meet the changed attitude of the Governments of India and Great Britain. But let none imagine that that consequential change of attitude connotes any change in her determination to win Home Rule. She is ready to consider terms of peace, but it must be "peace with honour", and honour in this connection means Freedom. If this be not granted, an even more vigorous agitation will begin.

The undermining of belief in the superiority of the white races dates from the spreading of the Arya Samaj and the Theosophical Society. Both bodies sought to lead the Indian people to a sense of the value of their own civilization, to pride in their past, creating self-respect in the present, and self-confidence in the future. They destroyed the unhealthy inclination to imitate the West in all things, and taught discrimination, the using only of what was valuable in Western thought and culture, instead of a mere slavish copying of everything. Another great force was that of Swami Vivekananda, alike in his passionate love and admiration for India, and his exposure of the evils resulting from Materialism in the West.

The process was continued by the admiration of Sanskrit literature expressed by European scholars and philosophers. But the effect of these was confined to the few and did not reach the many. The first great shock to their belief in white superiority came from the triumph of Japan over Russia, the facing of a huge European Power by a comparatively small eastern Nation, the exposure of the weakness and rottenness of the Russian leaders, and the contrast with their hardy, virile opponents, ready to sacrifice everything for their country.

The second great shock has come from the frank brutality of German theories of the State, and their practical carrying out in the treatment of conquered districts and the laying waste of evacuated areas in retreat. The teachings of Bismerck and their practical application in France, Flanders, Belgium, Poland and Serbia have destroyed all the glamour of the superiority of Christendom over Asia. Its vaunted civilization is seen to be but a thin veneer, and its religion a matter of form rather than of life. Gazing from afar at the ghastly heaps of dead and the hosts of the mutilated, at science turned into devilry and ever inventing new tortures for rending and slaying, Asia may be forgiven for thinking that, on the whole, she prefers her own religions and her own civilizations.

But even deeper than the outer tumult of war has pierced the doubt as to the reality of the Ideals of Liberty and Nationality so loudly proclaimed by the foremost Western Nations, the doubt of the honesty of their champions. Sir James Meston said truly, a short time ago, that he had never, in his long experience, known Indians in so distrustful and suspicious a mood as that which he met in them today. And that is so. For long years Indians have been chafing over the many breaches of promises and pledges to them that remain unredeemed. The maintenance here of a system of political repression, of coercive measures increased in number and more harshly applied since 1905, the carrying of the system to a wider extent since the War for the sanctity of treaties and for the protection of Nationalities has been going on, have deepened the mistrust. A frank and courageous statesmanship applied to the honest carrying out of large reforms too long delayed, can alone remove it. The time for political tinkering is past; the time for wise and definite changes is here.

To these deep causes must be added the comparison between the progressive policy of some of the Indian States in matters which most affect the happiness of the people, and the slow advance made under British administration. The Indian notes that this advance is made under the guidance of rulers and ministers of his own race. When he sees that the suggestions, made in the People's Assembly in Mysore are fully considered and, when possible, given effect to he realizes that without the forms of power, the members exercise more real power than those in our Legislative Councils. He sees education spreading, new industries fostered, villagers encouraged to manage their own affairs and take the burden of their own responsibility, and he wonders why Indian incapacity is so much more efficient than British capacity.

Perhaps, after all, for Indians, Indian rule may be the best.

THE AWAKENING OF THE MERCHANTS

Of the many forces that have created New India, the awakening of the Merchants into political life is perhaps the most potent, and the most pregnant with happy possibilities. Sir Dorab Tata, in the Industrial Conference in Bombay in 1915, advocated the yoking together of Politics and Industry. It is now coming about. Hitherto the merchants had remained immersed in their own occupations, but they were awakened by the War to the necessity of taking part in politics by finding that those very occupations were threatened with disaster by the attitude of the Government; as for instance, the refusal to lend a helping hand to industries which had been connected closely with Germany trade and were menaced with ruin by the War; by the refusal to aid the efforts made to replace necessaries, hitherto supplied by Germany, by the founding or financing of factories for their production at home; by the restrictions put on trade under pretext of the War, that prevented the legitimate expansion of promising branches of industry; by the absence of effort to relieve the stringency of the money market, wealthy merchants being unable to obtain cash to meet their liabilities here because their English debtors could not transmit the money they owed; some were even obliged to sell the depreciated Government paper at heavy losing order to maintain their credit; in other cases War Bonds were offered to them in lieu of cash for goods supplied. The details have varied in different centres, and the wealthy and independent merchants of Bombay have suffered less than the merchants of Madras, with whose difficulties I am naturally more familiar.

There, added difficulties constantly arise from the favouritism shown by the Presidency Bank to English, as compared with Indian, clients, and the absence of Indians from its Directorate, complained of for years. The anxiety felt by the merchants was largely increased by the depreciation of Government paper, and apart from the heavy losses of capital incurred when necessity forced holders to sell for cash, an uneasy feeling arose as to the stability of the Government, when its securities fell so low....

The War has turned the attention of Government to the wisdom of utilizing India's immense natural resources, and the Viceroy speaks of organising these resources with "a view to making India more self-contained, and less dependent on the outer world for the supplies of manufactured goods". We heartily endorse this view. This has long been the cry from Indians, for India, with her varieties of soil and climate, can produce all the materials she needs, and with her surplus goods she can, as Phillimore said of her in the 17th century, "with the droppings of her solid feed distant nations". But the East India Company first, the British 'Government next, and lately exploiting bodies of imperialist traders, have vehemently insisted that India should supply raw materials, export them for manufacture abroad, and purchase, preferably within the Empire, the goods manufactured out of them. As Macaulay pointed out, the marvelous expansion of English industry was contemporaneous with the impoverishment of India. The reversal of this policy by the present Viceroy will earn India's undying gratitude, if he fosters Indian industries had not English industries in India. A witness before the Industries Commission stated that India should raise products for use outside, that is, as the East India Company put it, become a plantation for the supply of raw materials. The Viceroy must pardon us, if previous experience has made us anxious on this point. We can not forget that a century ago the traces of iron were found in the Central Provinces, and that nothing was done to extract the metal—England then being the world's shop for iron to her own huge profit, and not desiring a rival. It was left for Tata to seize the opportunity; and his shares of Rs. 30 are now sold at Rs. 1,180. He started a great industry. And Tata's steel is sought so largely that he cannot meet the demand. Had the iron been raised and worked here during these long years, we should not now be dependent on Britain for our machinery the want of which cripples the efforts to found new industries and to expand old ones, in order to supply the demand caused by the necessary absorption of factories in Great Britain for War work....

However, the War has done for India, in awakening the interest of the Government in her industries that which the attempts of Indian patriots have failed to do. The War brought about the Industries Commission and the need for munitions has forced industrial organization for their production. It is for Indian merchants to see, by seizing and utilizing the political weapon, that the organization and encouragement of industries by Government does not reduce Indians to a more subordinate position than they now hold. It is this danger which is playing a great part in the fear which has caused the Awakening of the Merchants. The tea industry, for instance, is in the hands of English planters, and while incomes drawn from other agricultural profits have been taxed incomes derived from tea—which is certainly an agricultural profit—have wholly escaped till lately. If this policy be pursued, and the fostering of industries with Indian money places the industries in foreign hands, Indians will, even more than now, be *dubashes,* and clerks, and other employees of English-captained firms, and will depend ever more and more on wages, drive lower and lower by increasing competition.

Indian merchants have seen the swift expansion of Japanese trade, and know that it is fostered by the Japanese Government both by protection and with bounties. They have to compete with it in their own land. Is it any wonder that they desire an Indian Government? They see Japanese goods underselling them and flooding their own markets. Is it any wonder that they desire a Home Government, that will put duties on these foreign goods and protect their own products?

THE AWAKENING OF THE WOMEN

The position of women in the ancient Aryan civilization was a very noble one. The great majority married, becoming, as Manu said, the light of the Home; some took up the ascetic life, remained unmarried, and sought the knowledge of Brahman. The story of the Rani Damayanti, to whom here husband's ministers came, when they were troubled by the Raja's gambling; that of Gandhari, in the council of kings and warrior chiefs, remonstrating with her headstrong son; in later days, those of Padmavati of Chittoor; of Mirabai of Marwar, the sweet poetess; of Tarabai of Thoda, the warrior; of Chand Bibi, the defender of Ahmednagar; of Ahalya Bai of Indore, the great ruler—all these and countless others are well known.

Only in the last five or six generations has the Indian women slipped away from her place at her husband's side, and left him unhelped in his public life. Even now, they wield great influence over husband and son, but lack through knowledge to aid. Culture has never forsaken them but the English education of their husbands and sons, with the neglect of Sanskrit and the vernacular, has made a barrier between the culture of the husband and that of the wife, and has shut the woman out from her old sympathy with the larger life of men. While the interests of the husband have widened, those of the wife have narrowed. The materializing of the husband has tended also by reaction to render the wife's religion less broad and wise and also, by throwing her on the family priest for guidance in religion instead of on her husband, has made her religion entirely one of devotion; and lacking the strong stimulus of knowledge, it more easily slides down into superstition, into dependcence on forms not understood.

The wish to save their sons from the materializing results of English education awoke keen sympathy among Indian mothers with the movement to make Hinduism an integral part of education. It was, perhaps, the first movement in modern days which aroused among them in all parts of India keen and living interest.

Then the troubles of Indian outside India roused the ever-quick sympathy of Indian women, and the attack in South Africa on the sacredness of Indian marriage drew large numbers of them out of their homes to protest against the wrong.

The partition of Bengal was bitterly resented by Bengali women, and was another factor in the outward-turning change. When the editor of an extremist newspaper was prosecuted for sedition, convicted and sentenced, 500 Bengali women went to his mother to show their sympathy, not by condolences, but by congratulations. Such was the feeling of the well-born women of Bengal.

The Indentured Labour question, involving the dishonour of women, again moved them deeply, and even sent a deputation to the Viceroy composed of women.

These were, perhaps, the chief outer causes; but deep in the heart of India's daughters arose the Mother's voice, calling on them to help her to arise, and to be once more mistress in her own household. Indian women, nursed on her old literature, with its wonderful ideals of womanly perfection, could not remain indifferent to the great movement for India's liberty. And during the last few years the hidden fire long burning in their hearts, fire of love for Bharatmata, fire of resentment against the lessened influence of the religion which they passionately love, instinctive dislike of the foreigner as ruling in their land, have caused a marvelous awakening. The strength of the Home Rule movement is rendered tenfold greater by the adhesion to it of large numbers of women, who bring to its helping the uncalculating heroism, the endurance, the self-sacrifice, of the feminine nature. Our League's best recruits and recruiters are among the women of India, and the women of Madras boast that they marched in procession when the men were stopped, and that their prayers in the temples set the interned captives free. Home Rule has become so intertwined with religion by the prayers offered up in the great Southern Temples—sacred places of pilgrimage—and spreading from them to village temples, and also by its being preached, up and down the country, by Sadhus and Sannyasins, that it has become in the minds of the women and of the over-religious masses, inextricably intertwine with religion. That is, in this country, the surest way of winning alike the women of the higher classes and the men and women villagers. And that is why I have said that the two words, "Home Rule", have become a Mantram.

AWAKENING OF THE MASSES

The awakening of the masses is another startling phenomenon of our times, due of late to the teaching of Sadhus and Sannyasins and the campaign of prayer, just mentioned, but much more to the steady influence of the educated classes permeating the masses for very many years, the classes which, as we shall see, have their roots struck deep in the villages. It must be remembered that the raiyat, though innocent of English, has a culture of his own made up of old tradition and legends and folklore, coming down from time immemorial. He is religious, knows the great laws of Karma and Reincarnation, is industrious and shrewd. He cares very little for who is the "Sirkar", and very much for the agents who come to collect his tax, or to meddle with his fields. In the old days, which for him still live, the Panchayat managed the village affairs, and he was prosperous and contented, save when the King's tax-gatherer came, or soldiers harried his village. These were inevitable, natural evils, like drought or flood; and if a raid came or an invasion, they felt they were suffering with their King, whereas they are crushed now in an iron machinery, without the human nexus that used to exist.

Home Rule has touched the raiyat through his village life, where the present order presses hard upon him in ways that I shall refer to when dealing with agricultural conditions. He resents the rigid payment of tax in money instead of the variable tax in kind, the King's share of the produce. He resents the frequent resettlements, which force him to borrow from the money-lender to meet the higher claim. He wants the old Panchayat back again; he wants that his village should be managed by himself and his fellows, and he wants to get rid of the tyranny of petty officials who have replaced the old useful communal servants.

We cannot leave out of the causes which have helped to awaken the masses, the influence of the Co-operative Movement, and the visits paid to villages by educated men for lectures on sanitation, hygiene, and other subjects. In many parts of the country, where conferences are carried on in the vernacular, the raiyats attend in large numbers, and often take part in the practical discussions on local affairs. They have begun to hope, and to feel that they are a part of the great National Movement, and that for them also a better day is dawning.

The submerged classes have also felt the touch of a ray of hope, and are lifting up their bowed heads, and claiming, with more and more definiteness, their place in the Household of the Mother.

Movements, created by themselves, or originating in the higher castes, have been stirring in them a sense of self-respect. The Brahmanas, awakening to a sense of their long-neglected duty, have done much to help them and the prospect of their future brightens year by year.

By a just Karma the higher castes are finding that attempts are being made by official and non-official Europeans to stir the submerged classes into opposition to Home Rule. They play upon the contempt with which they had been treated, and threaten them with a return of it if "Brahmana Rule", as they call it, is gained. Twenty years ago and more, I ventured to urge the danger to Hindu Society that was hidden within the neglect of the submerged, and the folly of making it profitable for them to embrace Islam or Christianity, which offered them a higher social status. Much has been done since then but it is only a drop in the ocean needed. They know very well, of course, that all the castes, not the highest alone, are equally guilty, but that is a sorry comfort. Large numbers of them are, happily, willing to forget the past, and to work with their Indian fellow-countrymen for the future. It is the urgent duty of every lover of the Motherland to draw these, her neglected children, into the common home.

WHY INDIA DEMANDS HOME RULE

Mr Gandhi's capital idea of a monster petition for the Congress-League scheme, for which signatures were only to be taken after careful explanation of its scope and meaning, has proved to be an admirable method of political propaganda. The soil in the Madras Presidency had been well prepared by a wide distribution of popular literature, and the Propaganda Committee had scattered over the land in the vernaculars a simple explanation of Home Rule. The result of active work in the villages during the last year showed itself in the gathering in less than a month of nearly a million signatures. They have been taken in duplicate, to that we have a record of a huge number of people, interested in Home Rule, and the hosts will increase in ever-widening circles, preparing for the coming Freedom.

India demands Home Rule for two reasons, one essential and vital, the other less important but weighty: First, because Freedom is the birthright of every Nation; secondly, because her most important interest are now made subservient to the interests of the British empire without her consent, and her resources are not utilized for her greatest needs. It is enough only to mention the money spent on her Army, not for local defence but for Imperial purposes, as compared with that spent on Primary education.

Self-Government is necessary to the self-respect and dignity of a People; other-Government emasculates a Nation, lowers its character, and lessens its capacity. The wrong done by the Army Act, which Raja Rampal Singh voiced in the Second Congress as a wrong which outweighed all the benefits of British Rule, was its weakening and debasing effect on Indian manhood. "We cannot", he declared, "be grateful to it for degrading our natures, for systematically crushing out all martial spirit, for converting a race of soldiers and heroes into a timid flock of quill-driving sheep." This was done not by the fact that a man did not carry arms—few carry them in England—but that men were deprived of the right to carry them. A Nation, and individual, cannot develop his capacities to the utmost, without Liberty. And this is recognized everywhere except in India. As Mazzini truly said, "God has written a line of His thought over the cradle of every people. That is its special mission. It cannot be cancelled; it must be freely developed."

For, what is a nation? It is a spark of the Divine Fire, a fragment of the Divine Life, outbreathed into the world, and gathering round itself a mass of individuals, men, women and children, whom it binds together into one. Its qualities, its powers, in a word, its type, depend on the fragment of the Divine Life embodied in it, the Life which shapes it, evolves it, colours it, and makes it One. The magic of Nationality is the feeling of oneness, and the use of Nationality is to serve the world in the particular way for which its type fits it. This is what Mazzini called "its special mission", the duty given to it by God in its birth-hour. Thus

India had the duty of spreading the idea of Dharma, Persia that of Purity, Egypt that of Science, Greece that of beauty, Rome that of Law. But to render its full service to Humanity it must develop along its own lines, and be self-determined in its evolution. It must be itself, and not another. The whole world suffers where a Nationality is distorted or suppressed before its mission to the world is accomplished.

Hence the cry of a Nation for Freedom, for Self-Rule, is not a cry of mere selfishness demanding more Rights that it may enjoy more happiness. Even in that there is nothing wrong, for happiness means fullness of life, and to enjoy such fullness is a righteous claim. But the demand for Self-Rule is a demand for the evolution of its own nature for the Service of Humanity. It is a demand of the deepest Spirituality, an expression of the longing to give its very best to the world. Hence dangers cannot check it, nor threats appeal, nor offerings of greater pleasures lure it to give up its demand for Freedom. Better hardship and freedom, than luxury and thralldom. This is the spirit of the Home Rule movement, and therefore it cannot be crushed, it cannot be destroyed, it is eternal and ever young. Nor can it be persuaded to exchange its birthright for any mess of efficiency-pottage at the hands of the bureaucracy.

Coming closer to the daily life of the people as individuals, we see that the character of each man, woman and child is degraded and weakened by a foreign administration, and this is most keenly felt by the best Indians.

This stunting of the race begins with the education of the child. The schools differentiate between British and Indian teachers; the colleges do the same. The students see first-class Indians superseded by young and third-rate foreigners; the Principal of a college should be a foreigner: foreign history is more important than Indian; to have written on English villages is a qualification for teaching economics in India; the whole atmosphere of the school and college emphasises the superiority of the foreigner even when the professors abstain from open assertion thereof. The Education department controls the education given, and it is planned on foreign models, and its object is to serve foreign rather than native ends, to make docile Government servants rather than patriotic citizens; high spirits, courage, self-respect, are not encouraged, and docility is regarded as the most precious quality in the student; pride in country, patriotism, ambition, are looked on as dangerous, and English, instead of Indian, ideals are exalted; the blessings of a foreign rule and the incapacity of Indians to manage their own affairs are constantly inculcated. What wonder that boys thus trained often turn out, as men, time-servers and sycophants, and, finding their legitimate ambitions frustrated, become selfish and care little for the public weal? Their own inferiority has been so driven into them during their most impressionable years that they do not even feel what Mr Asquith called the "intolerable degradation of a foreign yoke".

It is not a question whether the rule is good or bad. German efficiency in Germany is far greater than English efficiency in England; the Germans were better fed, had more amusements and leisure, less crushing poverty than the English. But would any Englishman therefore desire to see Germans occupying all the highest positions in England? Why not? Because the righteous self-respect and dignity of the free man revolt against foreign domination, however superior. As Mr Asquith said at the beginning of the War, such a condition was "inconceivable and would be intolerable" Why then is it the one conceivable system here in India? Why is it not felt by all Indians to be intolerable? It is because it has become a habit, bred in us from childhood, to regard the "sahab-log" as our natural superiors, and the greatest injury British rule has done to Indians is to deprive them of the natural instinct born in all free peoples, the feeling of an inherent right to self-determination, to be themselves. Indian dress, Indian food, Indian ways, Indian customs, are all looked on as second-rate; the Indian mother-tongue and Indian literature cannot make an educated man. Indians as well as Englishmen take it for granted that the natural rights of every Nation do not belong to them; they claim "a larger share in the government of the country", instead of claiming the government of their own country, and they are expected to feel grateful for "boons", for concessions. Britain is to say what she will give. The whole thing is wrong, topsy-turvy, irrational. Thank God that India's eyes are opening; that myriads of her people realize that they are men, with a man's right to freedom in his own country, a man's right to manage his own affairs. India is no longer on her knees for boons; she is on her feet for Rights. It is because I have taught this, that the English in India misunderstand me, call me seditious; it is because I have taught this, that I am President of this Congress today.

This may seem strong language, because the plain truth is not usually put in India. But this is what every Briton feels in Britain for his own country, and what every Indian should feel in India for his. This is the Freedom for which the Allies are fighting; this is Democracy, the Spirit of the Age. And this is what every true Briton will feel is India's Right, the moment India claims it for herself, as she is claiming it now. When this right is gained, then will the tie between India and Great Britain become a golden link of mutual love and service, and the iron chain of a foreign yoke will fall away. We shall live and work side by side with no sense of distrust and dislike, working as brothers for common ends. And from that union shall arise the mightiest Empire, or rather Commonwealth, that the world has ever known, a Commonwealth that, in God's good time, shall put an end to War...

Many observers of Indian public life have noted the fissiparous tendency in our political associations, and reactionaries make this a reason for denying to us constitutional liberty. Rightly considered, it is a reason for granting it, though to some this statement may seem paradoxical. But what is the position?

We have a Nation, composed of many communities and opinions, trying to obtain liberty. We have above it, a Government, holding all power and all patronage, and able to crush by executive orders those whom it considers to be advocates of excessive changes. It tends to ally itself with any party or community which will help it to stave of legislation that diminishes its power. Its natural tendency is to watch for any sign of fission, and to ally itself with the weaker party to crush the stronger, as did the East India Company in its so-called "conquest of India". If there be no sign of fission, it may be possible to initiate one, on the lines of the dispatch to Lord Lytton when Viceroy of India with regard to a desired War: "If there be no pretext, you must invent one." A similar policy was followed when Dadabhai Naoroji was sent to the British Parliament; Mr Bhowngari was set up against him, and succeeded in ousting a strong reformer and replacing him by reactionary. No political situation could be more unhealthy.

First, take the two great communities of Hindus and Musalmans. They form two natural parties in the Nation, with the Christian Government above them as the third party for whose favour they compete. Hence Hindu-Musalman divisions, riots, and the rest—which do not exist in Indian States, wherein the Ruler belongs to one of the two great religions, and has to rule men of both—and the constant efforts to dissolve the *Entente Cordiale* arrived at after long discussions at Calcutta and at Lucknow last year.

There will always be a number in each community who do not feel themselves bound by any agreement come to by the organized political bodies, containing the more reasonable and far-seeing of each community; and these again, motived by bribe or threat, unofficial but made by officials, an unorganized and irresponsible crowd, will always lend recruits to support the Government, in the hope of obtaining special concessions for their sectional interests.

Hence, also, the anti-Brahmana movement in the Madras Presidency, with its Association of a few hundred members and its three organs in the Press.... The anti-Brahmana movement aims chiefly at places in the administration, and hopes to gain them more easily by praising the Government had opposing Home Rulers.

Hence, also, various similar movements in other Provinces, any stick being good enough for beating the Home Rule dog.

There is not need for anxiety about these divisions, which must always present kaleidoscopic changes so long as India is under the rule of an irresponsible Government.

When the third, non-national, party no longer governs, the National parties will become grouped into healthy constituents of the body politic, distinguished by differences of principle. The use of power will create a sense of responsibility and responsibility will bring about reasonable discipline.

We make too much of these transitory difficulties and quarrels, and given them an importance far beyond their real mischief-making power. They will assume their proper proportions when we have won Home Rule.

I do not propose to dwell on the isolated Reforms for which the Congress has asked during the whole period of its existence. The majority of Congressmen are tired of asking for the same thing over and over again, and feel that it is better to concentrate on Home Rule, since, once the people have power, they can get rid of bad laws and make good ones for themselves.

Indian Legislatures will take up the Congress Resolutions and carry into law all that are applicable to the changed conditions. Free India will separate Executive from Judicial functions, and also separate Revenue officers Judiciary and Police, place the lower Judiciary under the High Court instead of the Executive, pass Education Acts, make trial by Jury general, protect her Emigrants and Indians settled abroad, deal with Land Settlement equitably, organize and develop Indian Industries, examine for her Services within her own borders, reorganize her administration so as to abolish racial inequalities, and establish Military Colleges to fit her youth for the Emperor's Commissions.

The whole of the special legislation against constitutional agitation—as understood in Great Britain—penalizing writing and speech which do not incite to crime nor transgress the law of libel, will be swept away as unworthy of civilized country. The Executive will be deprived of the power to punish without trial, to imprison, incarcerate, impoverish, deport, intern and extern, on secret police accusations and suspicions, and confidential reports of magistrates. No man self thus suffer without knowing his offence, nor be deprived of liberty without open trial and full opportunity of defence. Peaceful political propaganda, processions, flags and meetings will not be interfered with by Magistrates and Police Officers. In fact, India will once more enjoy the ordinary elementary human rights secured by Magna Carta and the Bill of Rights.

Think of the joy of being a free man in a free country, the equal of other civilized men; of breathing in an India at last purged of the poisonous atmosphere of coercion; of knowing that liberty of person and safety of property cannot be touched save by open trial; that one cannot become a criminal unconsciously, and at the whim of an Executive, shrouded in darkness; that one enjoys the ordinary liberty of a civilized human being in a country ruled by law alone, uninterfered with by arbitrary Executive Orders. That security can only come to us with Home Rule.

Fellow-delegates, pardon me that I have kept you so long. Only once in my life can I take this Congress Chair, and speak my heart out to you on this country that we love so well. Who can tell in the present keen strife, if I shall be left free to speak to you again, to work with you as your leader, during this coming year of office? If I am allowed to carry on my work, than I crave your help during the coming year. You have trusted me enough to elect me as your President; trust me enough to work with me as your President, until I prove false to your trust. You cannot always agree with me, and I do not shrink from your criticism. I only ask you not to take for granted the truth of everything said against me by my enemies, for I cannot spare time to answer them. I cannot promise to please you always, but I can promise to strive my best to serve the Nation, as I judge of service. I cannot promise to agree with and to follow you always; the duty of a leader is to lead. While he should always consult his colleagues and listen to their advice, the final responsibility before the public must be his, and his, therefore, the final decision. A general should see further than his officers and his army, and cannot explain, while battles are going on, every move in a campaign; he is to be justified or condemned by his results. Up till now, knowing myself to be of this Nation only by love and service, not by birth, I have claimed no authority of leadership, but have only fought in the front of the battle and served as best I might. Now, by your election, I take the place which you have given and will fill it worthily. Enough of myself. Let us think of the Mother.

To see India free, to see her hold up her head among the Nations to see her sons and daughters respected everywhere, to see her worthy of her mighty past, engaged in building a yet mightier future—is not this worth working for, worth suffering for worth living and worth dying for? Is there any other land which evokes such love for her spiritually, such admiration for her literature, such homage for her valour, as this glorious Mother of Nations, from whose womb went forth the races that now, in Europe and America, are leading the world? And has any land suffered as our India has suffered, since her sword was broken on Kurukshetra, and the peoples of Europe and of Asia swept across her borders, laid waste her cities, and discrowned her Kings? They came to conquer, but they remained to be absorbed. At last, out of those mingled peoples, the Divine Artificer has welded a Nation, compact not only of her own virtues, but also of those her foes had brought to her, and gradually eliminating the vices which they had also brought.

After a history of millennia, stretching far back out of the ken of mortal eyes; having lived with, but not died with, the mighty civilizations of the Past; having seen them rise and flourish and decay, until only their sepulchers remained, deep buried in earth's crust; having wrought, and triumphed, and suffered, and having survived all changes unbroken, India, who has been verily the Crucified among Nations, now stands on this her Resurrection morning, the Immortal the Glorious, the Ever-young and India shall soon be seen, proud and self-reliant, strong and free, the radiant Splendour of Asia, the Light and the Blessing of the World.